NOLO *Your Legal Companion*

"In Nolo you can trust." —**THE NEW YORK TIMES**

OUR MISSION

Make the law as simple as possible, saving you time, money and headaches.

Whether you have a simple question or a complex problem, turn to us at:

NOLO.COM

Your all-in-one legal resource

Need quick information about wills, patents, adoptions, starting a business—or anything else that's affected by the law? **Nolo.com** features free articles in our Nolopedia, legal updates, resources and all of our books, software, forrms and online applications.

NOLO NOW

Make your legal documents online

Creating a legal document has never been easier or more cost-effective! Create an online will or trust, form an LLC, or file a Provisional Patent Application!
Check it out at **http://nolonow.nolo.com**.

NOLO'S LAWYER DIRECTORY

Meet your new attorney

If you want advice from a qualified attorney, turn to Nolo's Lawyer Directory—the only directory that lets you see hundreds of in-depth attorney profiles so you can pick the one that's right for you. Find it at **http://lawyers.nolo.com**.

ALWAYS UP TO DATE

Sign up for NOLO'S **LEGAL UPDATER**

Old law is bad law. We'll email you when we publish an updated edition of this book—sign up for this free service at **nolo.com/ legalupdater**.

Find the latest updates at NOLO.COM

Recognizing that the law can change, we post legal updates during the life of this edition at **nolo.com/updates**.

Is this edition the newest? **ASK US!**

To make sure that this is the most recent edition available, just give us a call at **800-728-3555**.

(Please note that we cannot offer legal advice.)

Please note

We believe accurate, plain-English legal information should help
you solve many of your own legal problems. But this text is not a
substitute for personalized advice from a knowledgeable lawyer.
If you want the help of a trained professional—and we'll always
point out situations in which we think that's a good idea—
consult an attorney licensed to practice in your state.

9th edition

Credit Repair

by Robin Leonard and Attorney John Lamb

NINTH EDITION   APRIL 2009

Editor   LISA GUERIN

Updated by   MARGARET REITER

Cover Design   SUSAN PUTNEY

Production   MARGARET LIVINGSTON

CD-ROM Preparation   ELLEN BITTER

Proofreading   ELAINE MERRILL

Index   THÉRÈSE SHERE

Printing   DELTA PRINTING SOLUTIONS, INC.

Leonard, Robin.

 Credit repair / by Robin Leonard and John Lamb. -- 9th ed.

   p. cm.

 ISBN-13: 978-1-4133-1019-1 (pbk.)

 ISBN-10: 1-4133-1019-2 (pbk.)

 1. Consumer credit--United States--Handbooks, manuals, etc. 2. Finance, Personal--United States--Handbooks, manuals, etc. 3. Consumer credit--Law and legislation--United States. I. Lamb, John. II. Title.

 HG3756.U54L46 2009

 332.7'43--dc22

                        2009004833

Quantity sales: For information on bulk purchases or corporate premium sales, please contact the Special Sales department. For academic sales or textbook adoptions, ask for Academic Sales. 800-955-4775, Nolo, 950 Parker Street, Berkeley, CA 94710.

About the Authors

Robin Leonard graduated from Cornell Law School in 1985. She is the author or co-author of numerous Nolo books, including *Solve Your Money Troubles: Debt, Credit & Bankruptcy*, *How to File for Chapter 7 Bankruptcy*, and *Chapter 13 Bankruptcy: Keep Your Property & Repay Debts Over Time*.

John Lamb has been a consumer lawyer for most of his career (now measured in decades), emphasizing credit, credit reporting, privacy, automobile, and landlord-tenant issues. John has advocated consumer reforms in court and the Legislature and speaks and writes frequently on consumer issues. He is co-author of the eighth edition of *Credit Repair* and the eleventh edition of *Solve Your Money Troubles*, and has updated several other Nolo publications.

Table of Contents

Your Credit Repair Companion..1

1 Assess Your Debt Situation...3

Take Care of Financial Emergencies 4

Face Your Debt Problems 6

Understand Your Options for Dealing With Your Debts...6

2 Avoid Overspending...23

Keep Track of Your Daily Expenditures...24

Total Up Your Income 26

Make a Budget or Spending Plan..29

Prevent Future Financial Problems...34

3 Handling Existing Debts..37

Deal With Current (or Not Seriously Overdue) Debts..40

Use the Form Negotiation Letters Provided in This Book 59

Deal With Creditors on Past Due Accounts...60

Deal With Collection Agencies..65

Tax Consequences of Forgiven Loans 72

4 Clean Up Your Credit Report..75

What Is in a Credit Report?..76

Get a Copy of Your Credit Report...80

Review Your Credit Report 84

Dispute Incomplete and Inaccurate Information...88

Add Information to Your Report..92

Information Showing Stability 93

Explanatory Statements 94

Avoid Identity Theft 95

5 How Creditors and Employers Use Your Credit Report.........................107

Who Can Look at Your Credit Report 108

How Credit Applications Are Evaluated...110

6 Building and Maintaining Good Credit 115

Build Credit in Your Own Name 117

Ask Creditors to Consider Your Spouse's Credit History 117

Get Credit Cards and Use Them Wisely 118

Open Deposit Accounts 130

Work With Local Merchants 132

Obtain a Bank Loan 132

Avoid Credit Repair Clinics 133

Avoid Credit Discrimination 144

Appendixes

A Resources 151

Credit and Debt Counseling Agencies 152

Debtors Anonymous 155

Nolo Publications 155

Other Publications 155

Online Resources 156

State Consumer Protection Agencies 157

Where to Complain About Credit Discrimination 164

B Forms and Letters 165

C How to Use the CD-ROM 247

Installing the Form Files Onto Your Computer 248

Using the Word Processing Files to Create Documents 249

Using the Federal Trade Commission Files 251

Files on the CD-ROM 252

Index

Your Credit Repair Companion

As our country falls on tough economic times, more and more of us are falling into debt—and finding it hard to pay that money back. Unfortunately, the consequences of mounting debt, such as missed payments, defaults, repossessions, and even foreclosures and bankruptcy, eventually find their way into our credit reports.

If you have bad credit, it can be tough to take out a loan, get a new credit card, or open a checking account. Sometimes, bad credit might even prevent you from renting a home or getting a job offer. This can lead to a repetitive cycle in which bad credit prevents you from doing the very things that will help you get back on your feet financially. But it's a cycle you can break by taking action to repair your credit.

Whether you've fallen behind on your bills, been sued, faced a repossession or foreclosure, or even declared bankruptcy, this book will help you take simple and effective steps to repair your credit. You'll learn how make a budget, negotiate with creditors, clean up your credit report, and build and maintain good credit going forward. As you read this information and decide how to handle your situation, keep these important facts in mind:

You're not alone. Economic ups and downs have affected many people. Layoffs and personal bankruptcy filings are on the rise, disposable incomes are falling, and savings are evaporating. Millions of honest, hardworking people—the same ones who receive credit offers almost daily—are having trouble paying their bills.

You have legal rights. Knowing and asserting your rights will help you get bill collectors off your back and give yourself a fresh financial start. Debtors who stand up for themselves often get more time to pay, have late fees dropped, settle debts for less than the full amount they owe, and get negative marks removed from their credit reports.

You can do it yourself. The information and forms in the book are good in all 50 states and the District of Columbia. You can follow the instructions on your own, without having to pay fees to a lawyer or credit repair clinic. (Chapter 6 explains why you should avoid using credit repair clinics.)

Nobody's credit is beyond repair. If you've been through devastating financial times, you may think you'll never get credit again. That's simply not true. As long as your financial troubles are behind you, you'll probably qualify for limited types of credit relatively quickly. Within about two years, you should be able to repair your credit enough to get a major credit card or loan. Many creditors are willing to extend credit to people who have turned their financial situations around, even if their credit records are less than stellar.

This book provides in-depth information on credit repair. Easy-to-use forms in Appendix B and on the enclosed CD-ROM help you with the sometimes daunting tasks of assessing your debts, planning a budget, negotiating with your creditors or bill collectors, and dealing with credit reporting agencies. Using this information, you'll be able to repair your credit and pave the way for a better financial future. ●

Assess Your Debt Situation

Take Care of Financial Emergencies...4

Face Your Debt Problems..6

Understand Your Options for Dealing With Your Debts 6

    Do Nothing...6

    Find Money to Pay Your Debts..7

    Negotiate With Your Creditors... 18

    Get Outside Help to Design a Repayment Plan.. 18

    File for Chapter 7 Bankruptcy 19

    Pay Over Time With Chapter 13 Bankruptcy 21

If you're facing a financial emergency, you should take care of that before rebuilding your credit. Once any immediate concerns are out of the way, you can take a step back, tally up your debts, and assess your options for dealing with them.

SKIP AHEAD

If your debt problems are behind you and you're only concerned with cleaning up your credit report, skip ahead to Chapter 4, "Clean Up Your Credit File." Also read Chapter 2, "Avoid Overspending."

Take Care of Financial Emergencies

A financial emergency is any situation that may leave you homeless or without some very important property or service. A pending eviction, a letter threatening foreclosure, an IRS seizure of your house, a utility cut-off, and a car repossession are financial emergencies. A nasty letter or threatening phone call from a bill collector, while unpleasant, is not an emergency. (If you are being hassled by a collection agency, see Chapter 3.)

If you face an emergency, you'll need to act on it right away. Begin by contacting the creditor and finding out exactly what you'll need to do to keep your wheels, your home, or other valuable property. Before you agree to anything, however, you may want to talk to a lawyer to make sure you aren't getting yourself deeper into trouble. For example, a new agreement for reduced or delayed payments may make your life easier right now, but it may also eliminate rights you currently have, add significantly to the interest you'll owe, or give a creditor more rights to collect a debt. If a creditor wants you to agree to make a payment on a very old debt or to make any changes to an existing loan or agreement (other than to reduce or delay your payments), an attorney can help you figure out whether the agreement will solve your problems or make them worse.

CAUTION

If you know you will need a lawyer, start looking for one right away. Waiting will only make your problems more difficult to resolve. If your income is low, you may qualify for free legal assistance from a government or nonprofit legal aid organization. If not, your friends or family members may be able to recommend a lawyer. Even if that lawyer doesn't practice consumer law, he or she may know someone who does. Another option is to contact your state bar association; many maintain lists of attorneys who specialize in particular fields, such as consumer law. Or, you could use an online directory, such as Nolo's lawyer directory, at http://lawyers.nolo.com.

When to Get Help Beyond This Book

This book can help you assess your finances and repair your credit. If you need to take immediate action, however, you'll have to consult other resources. In some situations, you'll want to see a lawyer right away. You may also be able to find the answers you need in another Nolo resource.

When to Get Help Beyond This Book

Seek additional help if...	Explanation	Where to get help
You're behind on your house payments.	Your lender has the option of foreclosing—declaring the entire balance due, selling the house at an auction and kicking you out.	General information on foreclosures is in Chapter 1. You can get more specific help from your lender, a lawyer, or *The Foreclosure Survival Guide*, by Stephen Elias (Nolo).
You owe child support or alimony.	If you can't afford to pay your child support or alimony, you need a court order reducing your obligation. Don't hesitate; child support and alimony are virtually never modified retroactively.	Contact your local child support enforcement agency. Although these agencies focus on enforcing support orders, many also assist with reviewing existing orders. Or visit DivorceNet (www.divorcenet.com) for links to state self-help services. Many states have online legal forms to request child support modification. Or, see a lawyer.
You owe income taxes.	The IRS can seize virtually all of your assets of value and close to 100% of your wages without first suing you. You have several options in dealing with the IRS. You may be able to negotiate an installment agreement for repayment or drastically reduce what you have to pay.	See *Stand Up to the IRS*, by Frederick W. Daily (Nolo) or see a tax attorney.
You face eviction.	In some states, an eviction can take place in just three days. Rather than risk being homeless, take steps to get immediate help.	In California, see *California Tenants' Rights*, by Janet Portman and David Brown (Nolo). Outside of California, you can get an overview of eviction and eviction defense issues in *Every Tenant's Legal Guide*, by Janet Portman and Marcia Stewart (Nolo). Or, contact a local tenants' rights group or a tenants' rights lawyer.
You've been sued.	If you just received court papers, you need to file a response with the court within a tight time limit. If the creditor already has a judgment, it can try to attach your wages, take money from bank accounts and place a lien on your real estate (and in some states, personal property). You may be able to prevent certain collection tactics, particularly if you don't own much.	See *Money Troubles: Debt, Credit & Bankruptcy*, by Robin Leonard and John Lamb (Nolo). Or, see a lawyer.
You are considering bankruptcy.	Many people overwhelmed by their debts conclude that bankruptcy is the best option. There are two types, called "chapters" of bankruptcy for consumers. In Chapter 7, you ask that your debts be wiped out. In Chapter 13, you set up a repayment plan whereby your creditors receive some—or all—of what you owe.	Forms and instructions for filing a Chapter 7 bankruptcy are in *How to File for Chapter 7 Bankruptcy*, by Stephen Elias, Albin Renauer, and Robin Leonard. Forms and instructions for filing a Chapter 13 bankruptcy are in *Chapter 13 Bankruptcy: Keep Your Property & Repay Debts Over Time*, by Stephen Elias and Robin Leonard. For information on figuring out if either Chapter 7 or Chapter 13 bankruptcy is right for you, see *The New Bankruptcy: Will It Work for You?*, by Stephen Elias. (All are published by Nolo.)

Face Your Debt Problems

Some people with debt problems believe that the less they know, the less it hurts. They think, "I'm already having trouble paying my bills. I can't stand the thought of knowing just how much I can't pay." But you must come to terms with your total debt burden. You cannot take steps to rebuild your credit without knowing exactly where your money goes (and where it needs to go instead).

Figuring out what you owe may result in a pleasant surprise. Most debt counselors find that people tend to overestimate—not underestimate—their debt burden. This may bring little comfort to those of you who find out that you owe more than you thought, but there is always a benefit: Knowing what you really owe is the only way to make wise choices about how you spend your money.

Use Form F-1, Outstanding Debts (in Appendix B and on the CD-ROM), to tally up your total debt burden. You can get the amount from the most recent bills you've received. If you've thrown out your bills without opening them, you can probably find out the balance by calling the customer service department of the creditor or checking your account information online.

Many creditors have automated telephone systems that provide balance and payment information automatically, without requiring you to speak to a person. Some creditors may also provide account information on their websites. You may have to register—by providing your name and account information and choosing a password—to access your data.

If you must speak with a person and you are concerned about being hassled by creditors you've been avoiding, ask for balance information only. If the customer service representative turns into a bill collector, explain that you are exploring your options and need to know how much you owe before you proceed. Let the representative know that you will contact the company as soon as possible, but for now you need to know only how much you owe. If the representative still hassles you, hang up. You'll just have to estimate how much you owe that creditor or wait for your next bill.

Total up your past due installment bills, such as credit cards and loans, plus any regular monthly obligations that are overdue, such as your utility bill.

Understand Your Options for Dealing With Your Debts

Your options for handling your debts will depend on your situation, including the type of debts you have, how much you owe, how much you earn, and your financial goals. This section discusses some common strategies for dealing with debt.

Do Nothing

Surprisingly, the best approach for some people deeply in debt is to take no action at all. If you have very little income and property and don't expect this to change any time soon, you may be what's known as "judgment proof." This means that anyone who sues you and obtains a court judgment won't be able to collect, simply because you don't have anything they can legally take. You can't be thrown in jail for not paying your debts. And state and federal laws prohibit a creditor—even the IRS—from taking away such essentials as basic clothing, ordinary household furnishings, personal effects, food, most Social Security benefits, disability benefits, unemployment, or public assistance.

So, if you don't anticipate having a steady income or property a creditor could grab, sitting tight could be a viable strategy. Your creditors may decide not to sue you because they know they can't collect. Many will simply write off your debt and treat it as a deductible business loss on their income tax returns. In several years, the debt will become legally uncollectible under state law. (See Chapter 3 for information on how to stop communications from collection agencies.)

 RESOURCE

Keeping exempt property. You can find a complete list of exempt property—property you get to keep even if creditors sue you or you file for bankruptcy—at www.legalconsumer .com. Just enter your zip code to find out what property is exempt in your state; this free site also provides loads of information for those considering bankruptcy.

Find Money to Pay Your Debts

If you can come up with a chunk of cash to pay off some of your debts, your financial woes may lessen. Even if you feel desperate, however, you shouldn't jump at every opportunity to get cash fast. If you make a bad choice, you'll get yourself deeper into debt. This section discusses some options you might consider to raise money, as well as some you should avoid. It's not a complete list. Unfortunately, new scams and bad deals crop up every day. Keep in mind that if an offer or deal seems too good to be true, it probably is. So, proceed cautiously, whatever you are considering.

Get Some Of Your Tax Refund Early

Many people have much more money withheld from their paychecks than they will need to pay their income tax for the year. By adjusting the withholding to better match your income, you can get more money in each paycheck to help you keep current or catch up on bills each month, instead of having to wait until the end of the year to get a refund. Ask your employer for a new IRS W-4 form and complete it following the instructions or with help from a tax advisor. The goal is to adjust your withholding so you can keep more of your income but still won't owe any taxes at the end of the year. Once you return the form to your employer, you should start seeing more money with your next paycheck. (If your income increases, don't forget to readjust your W-4 withholding to match.)

If your income is low enough to qualify for an Earned Income Tax Credit (EITC), you may be eligible to get an advance EITC. This allows you to get some of your EITC with each paycheck and the rest at the end of the year. Without the advance, you have to wait a whole year to get any of your EITC money. To get an advance EITC, you need to get an IRS W-5 form from your employer or the IRS, complete it following the instructions or with help from a tax advisor, and return it to your employer. (If your income increases, or you start supporting fewer dependents, don't forget to readjust your W-5.)

Sell a Major Asset

One way you can raise cash and keep associated costs to a minimum is to sell a major asset, such as a house or car. This may be a good idea if you can no longer afford your house or car payments. You will almost always do better selling the property yourself rather than waiting to get cash back from a foreclosure or repossession.

With the proceeds of the sale, you'll have to pay off anything still owed on the asset and any secured creditor to whom you pledged the asset as collateral. Then you'll have to pay off any liens placed on the property by your creditors. You can use anything that's left to help pay your other debts. But, before you take this step, be sure you have affordable alternative housing or transportation available. If not, you'll be in worse shape than before—without a roof over your head or a car to get to work.

If you own a house, consider all the pros and cons carefully before you sell it. In today's housing market, your house may be worth more in a year or two than it is today. Selling it will deprive you of an asset that can make you money over time and may result in your being locked out of the housing market once you are back on your feet. At the very least, consider whether you may get more for your house if you sell it later on, giving you more money to pay your creditors.

Cut Your Expenses

Another excellent way to raise cash is to cut your expenses. This will also help you in negotiating with your creditors, who will want to know why you can't pay your bills and what steps you've taken to live more frugally. Here are some suggestions:

- Shrink food costs by clipping coupons, buying on sale, purchasing generic brands, buying in bulk, and shopping at discount outlets.
- Improve your gas mileage by tuning up your car, checking the air in the tires, and driving less—carpool, work at home (telecommute), ride your bicycle, take the bus or train, and combine trips.
- Conserve gas, water, and electricity.
- Discontinue cable (or at least the premium channels) and subscriptions to magazines and papers. Most cable companies offer a low-rate basic service that they don't advertise. Be sure to ask.

- Instead of buying books and CDs, borrow them from the public library. Read magazines and newspapers there, too.
- Make long distance calls only when necessary and at off-peak hours. Also, compare programs offered by the various long distance carriers to make sure you are getting the best deal. If you need a cell phone and reception is good at your home, consider getting rid of your land line.
- If you have a cell phone that you don't absolutely need, contact your carrier and find out whether you'll have to pay a penalty to cancel your contract. If not, go ahead and cancel it. If you must have a cell phone for emergencies, negotiate for a less expensive plan with your company or with another. Make sure that changing the plan won't require you to buy a new phone or bind you to a new one- or two-year contract with a large early termination penalty.
- Carefully review your regular monthly bills for any charges you don't recognize. Your telephone or cell phone service, cable, or credit card accounts may impose fees for services you don't need, such as voice mail or call waiting, credit card protection plans, or a variety of so-called membership services. Call and find out what the services are and cancel any you don't need; confirm the cancellation in writing.

- Put off major purchases unless they're absolutely necessary. If you must buy a vehicle, an appliance, or furniture, try to get it second-hand.
- Carry your lunch to work; eat dinner at home, not at restaurants.
- Stop buying gifts and taking vacations until you're back on your feet.
- Stop spending money on luxuries that can add up, such as expensive coffee drinks.
- Don't charge anything that you can't pay off, or that won't exist (like groceries or meals) when the bill comes.

TIP

Service members can cut expenses and more. Service members, reservists, and their dependents can use the Servicemembers Civil Relief Act to reduce payments on credit obtained before entering active duty and stop collection efforts while they are on active duty. For example, any interest on a debt owed by the service member or jointly by the service member and his or her spouse must be reduced to 6% (and the payments based on the interest must also be reduced) if the service member makes a written request to the creditor. You can also stop eviction or collection proceedings on contracts to purchase real or personal property that you entered into before beginning active service. Contact your base legal assistance office for information.

Withdraw or Borrow Money From a Tax-Deferred Account

If you have an IRA, 401(k), or other tax-deferred retirement account, you can get cash to pay off debts by withdrawing money from it before retirement—but in most cases, you'll pay a penalty and taxes. Or, with a 401(k) plan, you may be able to borrow money from it (instead of withdrawing it). There are serious disadvantages to both options—you should only consider doing either to pay off debts if you have other substantial retirement funds or you are truly desperate. And, even then, this should be a last resort. Always look to raise money from nonretirement resources first.

Different plans have different requirements for borrowing and withdrawing money. Withdrawing money early from a tax-deferred account is expensive. Generally, any money that you take out of your 401(k) plan before you reach age 59½ is treated as an early distribution on which you'll owe penalties and income taxes.

Instead of withdrawing money, you can usually borrow up to half of your vested account balance, but not more than $50,000. Then you pay the money back, with interest, over five years. If you can't pay the money back within five years (or immediately, if you leave your job), your "loan" will be treated like an early withdrawal and you'll pay both an early distribution tax and income tax.

RESOURCE

For more on tapping into a retirement plan. If you're seriously considering using the money in your retirement plan or IRA to pay off your debts, get a copy of *IRAs, 401(k)s & Other Retirement Plans: Taking Your Money Out*, by Twila Slesnick and John C. Suttle (Nolo).

Refinance Your Home Loan

A new federal law may help you reduce and refinance your home loan, despite the downturn in the housing market. The law sets up a temporary program called Hope for Homeowners (H4H) for those who refinance before September 30, 2011. The new loan must not be for more than 90% of the current value of your home. If your home's value has declined, your monthly payments on the new loan could be a lot less than your current loan payments. You can get the new loan only if your current lender agrees to accept it as payment in full and to waive all late payment and prepayment fees. If the lender thinks you probably won't be able to repay the existing loan, it may consider this program to avoid having to take over another foreclosed home. See "Mortgage Payments" in Chapter 3 for more details on this program.

Obtain a Home Equity Loan or Credit Line

When property values are declining and credit is scarce, it can be hard to find home equity loans or lines of credit. However, some banks, savings and loans, credit unions, and other lenders are still offering home equity loans (also called "second mortgages") and home equity lines of credit (also called "HELOCs"). Lenders who make these loans will loan only a percentage of your equity in the market or appraised value of the house—typically between 50% and 80%. For example, if the current value of your house is $200,000 and you owe $100,000 on it, you might qualify for an equity loan of $60,000, which would increase your total housing debt to $160,000, or 80% of the house's value. The lender will also consider your credit history, income, and other expenses when deciding whether, and how much, to loan to you.

Obtaining a home equity loan has advantages and disadvantages. If all of your debts are unsecured and your house is exempt from collection, it's almost never a good idea to put your home into jeopardy by getting a second mortgage or home equity line of credit. If you're behind on your house payment, you'll be better off negotiating a mortgage workout with your lender. (For more on mortgage workouts, see *Solve Your Money Troubles: Debt, Credit & Bankruptcy*, by Robin Leonard and Margaret Reiter (Nolo).)

If you decide that you do want a home equity loan because you aren't able to negotiate a mortgage workout or for some other reason, be sure you understand all the terms before you sign on the dotted line. It is extremely important that you find out how much the loan will cost you each month and determine whether you can afford it. *If you can't afford it, you will likely lose your home.*

Consider the following pros and cons of home equity loans and credit lines.

Advantages of Home Equity Loans and Credit Lines

- You can borrow a fixed amount of money and repay it in equal monthly installments for a set period of time (home equity loan). Or, you can borrow as you need the money, drawing against the amount granted when you opened the account; you'll pay off this type of loan as you would a credit card bill (home equity line of credit or HELOC).
- The interest you pay may be fully deductible on your income tax return.

Disadvantages of Home Equity Loans

- Some home equity loans are sold by predatory lenders at very high rates. Predatory lenders target people in financial trouble or with past credit problems. Often, predatory lenders count on the borrower not being able to make the loan payments and expect to foreclose on the house (force the sale of the house) when the borrower fails to make payments. The Federal Trade Commission (FTC) recommends avoiding any lender who tells you to falsify a loan application, pressures you to apply for a loan, or for more money than you need, or pressures you to take on monthly payments you can't afford.
- Teaser rates might make a home equity loan look more attractive than it is. Equity loans often have a variable interest rate that rises or falls with a particular interest rate index (sometimes referred to as

adjustable rate mortgages or ARMs). But often, the rate for the first six months to three years is much lower. Once the initial period ends, the rate automatically jumps up to the regular variable rate, which can make your loan payments much higher. Many people have recently been caught in this trap, when loans they took out in the past couple of years suddenly cost a lot more every month, and they were unable to refinance to lower their payments. If you're considering an equity loan, make sure you know the teaser rate, the regular rate, when the regular rate kicks in, and how much your payments will likely be then.

- You are obligating yourself to make another monthly or periodic payment. If you are unable to pay, you may have to sell your house or, even worse, face the possibility of foreclosure. *Before you take out a home equity loan, be sure you can afford the monthly payment.*

- While interest may be deductible, it can be high. Your tax deduction doesn't save you the full amount of interest you pay; instead, it allows you to subtract that interest from your income when you calculate your income tax. So your true savings from taking an interest deduction is only a fraction of the interest you pay out in the first place.

- Some loans are "interest only" loans— your monthly payments pay only the interest on the loan and do not reduce the principal amount. You could make payments for years and still owe the full amount you borrowed.

- You may have to pay an assortment of up-front fees for an appraisal, credit report, title insurance, and points. These fees can cost thousands of dollars. In addition, for giving you an equity line of credit, many lenders charge a yearly fee of $50 or so.

- You must pay off the equity loan, plus what you still owe on your original mortgage, when you sell your house.

Use the Equity in Your Home If You Are 62 or Older

A variety of plans help older homeowners make use of the equity in their homes without having to move, give up title to the property, or make payments on a loan. The most common types of plans are reverse mortgages.

Reverse mortgages are loans against the equity in the home that provide cash advances to a homeowner and require no repayment until the loan term ends or the home is sold. The borrower can receive the cash in several ways: a lump sum, regular monthly payments, a line of credit, or a combination. Because the borrower does not make payments, the amount of money owed increases over the life of the loan. The borrower retains title to the home and must pay the property taxes, insurance, and the costs of keeping up the property.

There are pros and cons to reverse mortgages. In general, a reverse mortgage works best for people who are at least 62 years old and have a lot of equity in their homes. In most cases, the reverse mortgage lender will consider your age, the amount of equity you have in your home, and current interest rates to determine how much it will lend you. You'll have to pay fees like closing costs (title insurance, escrow fees, and appraisal fees), loan origination fees, accrued interest, and, in most cases, an additional charge to offset the lender's risk that you won't repay. (A reverse mortgage is usually paid back from the proceeds of selling the house after the owner's death.) Almost every state allows lenders to offer reverse mortgages.

There are some drawbacks to reverse mortgages. Your heirs cannot inherit the house from you unless they pay off the loan after your death. A reverse mortgage may also affect your continued eligibility for need-based government benefits programs like Supplemental Social Security (SSI) and Medicaid.

A reverse mortgage may also restrict your freedom. Often, the entire reverse mortgage comes due if you are no longer living in your home. Some lenders treat an extended stay away from your home, such as a long trip, visit to your children, or stay in an assisted living facility, as evidence that you are no longer living in the home or haven't properly secured it in your absence—and, therefore, that you entire loan must be paid off immediately.

The most widely available reverse mortgage plans are the FHA's Home Equity Conversion Mortgage Program and Fannie Mae's Home Keeper Mortgage Program.

Additional Resources on Reverse Mortgages

You can get free information on reverse mortgages from the following organizations:

- The federal Department of Housing and Urban Development (HUD). Call them at 800-569-4287 or visit their website, www.hud.gov and select "Information for Seniors" for facts about reverse mortgages, referrals to lenders, and lists of HUD-approved housing counselors.
- AARP (formerly the American Association of Retired Persons). Call them at 800-209-8085 or visit their website, www.aarp.org/money/revmort, for tips on evaluating reverse mortgages, eligibility and repayment requirements for federally insured reverse mortgages, and a reverse mortgage calculator.
- Fannie Mae. Call them at 800-732-6643 or visit their website, www.fanniemae.com, for consumer information on reverse mortgages.
- The National Center for Home Equity Conversion. Visit their website, www.reverse.org, for answers to frequently asked questions about reverse mortgages.

The lender or another party may suggest that you purchase an annuity in conjunction with a reverse mortgage. An annuity is an insurance product, financed out of the home's equity, that provides monthly payments to the borrower beginning immediately or some years later.

Think carefully about whether an annuity is right for you. Many consumer experts recommend against purchasing an annuity because it ties up the money from the reverse mortgage for an extended period, imposes additional transaction costs, imposes substantial penalties for early withdrawal, and may not benefit elderly homeowners (who may not live to see their first annuity payment, if there is a delay of several years or more). Indeed, California now prohibits lenders from requiring homeowners to purchase an annuity as a condition of obtaining a reverse mortgage.

Borrow From Family or Friends

In times of financial crisis, some people are lucky enough to have friends or relatives who can and will help out. Before asking your college roommate, mom and dad, uncle Paul, or someone similar, consider the following:

- Can the lender really afford to help you? If the person is on a fixed income and needs the money to get by, you should look elsewhere for a loan.
- Do you want to owe this person money? If the loan comes with emotional strings attached, be sure you can handle the situation before taking the money.
- Will the loan help you out, or will it just delay the inevitable (most likely, filing for bankruptcy)? Don't borrow money to make payments on debts

you will eventually discharge in bankruptcy.

- Will you have to repay the loan now, or will the lender let you wait until you're back on your feet? If you have to make payments now, you're just adding another monthly payment to your already unmanageable pile of debts.
- If the loan is from your parents, can you treat it as part of your eventual inheritance? If so, you won't ever have to repay it. If your siblings get angry that you're getting some of Mom and Dad's money, be sure they understand that your inheritance will be reduced accordingly.

Borrow Against Your Life Insurance Policy

If you've had a life insurance policy for some time, you have probably accumulated "cash value" in the policy, which you may be able to borrow. The insurance company will expect you to repay the amount borrowed (typically, in installment payments), and if you don't repay it before you die, the proceeds received by your beneficiaries will be reduced by the unpaid amount. Your insurance broker or the insurance company can explain more about borrowing against your insurance policy.

Options to Avoid

Borrowing From a Finance Company

A few finance companies lend money to consumers. These companies make secured consolidation loans for which you must pledge your house, car, or other personal property as collateral. The loans are just like second mortgages or secured personal loans: You'll usually be charged interest of 10% to 15%, and if you default on the loan, the finance company can foreclose on your home or take your property.

Finance companies and similar lenders also make unsecured consolidation loans—that is, they may lend you some money without requiring that you pledge any property as a guarantee that you'll pay. But the interest rate on these loans can be astronomical, often reaching 25% or more. Lenders also charge all kinds of fees—many undisclosed—bringing the effective interest rate closer to 50%.

If you want to take out a consolidation loan, you are better off borrowing from a bank or credit union than a finance company. Many finance companies engage in illegal or borderline collection practices if you default and are not as willing as banks and credit unions to negotiate if you have trouble paying. Furthermore, loans from finance companies may be viewed negatively by potential creditors who see them in your credit file. They often imply prior debt problems.

Tax Refund Anticipation Loans

Although getting a tax refund fast is often a good way to get quick cash, you should probably avoid a refund anticipation loan (RAL). An RAL is a loan offered by a private company for the short period between the date when the taxpayer receives it and the date when the IRS repays it by depositing

the taxpayer's refund into the lender's account (usually only a week or two). The amount of the loan is the amount of your anticipated refund minus the loan fees (which are often quite high) and the tax preparation fee. According to the National Consumer Law Center, for example, if your refund is $2,600 (the recent average), the cost of the loan would range from about $58 to $110. That results in an effective annual percentage rate (APR) of 83% to 161% for the loan! If you also paid a typical tax preparation fee of $163 to $178, your total costs could be as much as $288.

It is usually better to be patient and wait for your refund, rather than pay the high fee for an RAL. In most cases, you can file your return electronically and get the money quickly (by having the refund deposited directly into your account, for example).

In addition to being extremely expensive, RALs also pose some risks. You must repay the loan even if your refund is denied, is less than expected, or is frozen. If you can't repay the loan, the lender may assign the debt to a collection agency. The unpaid debt will appear on your credit report. And, if you apply for an RAL again next year, the lender may take that refund to pay this year's unpaid RAL debt, even if you use a different lender or tax preparer.

TIP

Get free or low-cost help with your tax filing. Some people get an RAL because they can't afford the tax preparation fee. If your adjusted gross income is no more than about

$56,000, however, you probably qualify for a free service to help you prepare and file your taxes online. (To find out more, go to www.irs.gov and search for "Freefile.") If you don't qualify for free tax preparation, some tax preparers will let you pay over time or will charge you less than you'd pay for an RAL in exchange for your agreement to have the refund deposited in a bank account of the tax preparer's choosing and to allow him or her to deduct the fee before paying you the rest. If your refund is denied or is less than expected, however, this could pose some of the same risks as an RAL.

The military has classified an RAL as a kind of predatory loan and limits the annual percentage rate on refund anticipation loans to 36% for active duty service members or their dependents. Military personnel can avoid even that expense by getting assistance from a base legal assistance office to file electronically and have the refund deposited within a week or two in their own bank account.

For more information on how to get a refund sooner and for answers to other tax questions, contact the IRS at 800-829-1040 (voice) or 800-829-4059 (TDD), or visit its website at www.irs.gov.

Payday Loans

The payday loan industry is growing fast. In many states, these loans are illegal. In others, lenders may offer a similar type of loan, but call it something else. Either way, think twice before you get one of these loans.

A payday loan works like this: You give the lender a check and get back an amount of money less than the face value of the check. For example, if you give the lender a postdated check for $300, it may give you $250 in cash and keep the remaining $50 as its fee. The lender holds the check for a few weeks (often until your payday). At this time, you must pay the lender the face value of the check ($300), usually by allowing it to cash the check. If you can't make the check good, the lender requires you to pay another fee ($50 in this example). At this point, you owe the lender $350 (the $250 borrowed plus the first $50 fee, plus a new fee of $50). Many people who can't make the original check good get into a "treadmill of debt" because they must keep writing new checks to cover the fees that have accumulated, in addition to paying off the amount borrowed. The annual percentage rate on payday loans is astronomical, ranging from 200% to 600% or more.

Payday loans have been a particular problem for members of the military in recent years. Federal rules limit to 36% the annual percentage rate that lenders can charge active duty service members or their dependents in extensions of consumer credit, including payday loans. This means, for example, that now a payday lender cannot charge a service member more than $1.38 in interest on a $100 loan for two weeks. Payday lenders are not permitted to roll over loans to military personnel or their dependents either, unless the new loan has more favorable terms, such as a lower interest rate.

A payday loan is a very expensive way to borrow money. To find out more about the payday loan laws in your state, visit the National Consumer Law Center's website at www.consumerlaw.org.

Pawnshops

Visiting a pawnshop should be one of the last ways you consider raising cash. At a pawnshop, you leave your property, such as jewelry, a television, or a musical instrument. In return, the pawnbroker lends you approximately 50% to 60% of the item's resale value; the average amount of a pawnshop loan is $75 or so.

You are given a few months to repay the loan, and are charged interest, often at an exorbitant rate. If you default on your loan to a pawnshop, the property you left at the shop becomes the property of the pawnbroker.

Auto Title Pawn

In an auto title pawn (a "title loan" in some states), you borrow money against the value of your paid-for motor vehicle. You keep and drive the vehicle after receiving the loan, but the lender keeps the vehicle's title as security for repayment and also keeps a copy of your keys. If you cannot make the loan payments, the lender repossesses the vehicle, sells it, and keeps the proceeds. Some lenders might try to come after you for any deficiency—the difference between what you owe and what the lender was able to get for your car. The lender may repossess the vehicle even if you miss only one payment. The monthly cost of these loans can be as high as $63 to $181 for a one-month, $500 title loan. Monthly finance

charges of 25% (300% annual interest) are common. Online title lenders quote annual percentage rates of up to 651%.

Auto title loan businesses often target members of the military. Under federal law and regulations, creditors cannot charge active members of the military or their dependents more than a 36% annual percentage rate on a loan for 181 days or fewer on a vehicle if the creditor takes the vehicle's title as security. (This limit does not apply to loans used to purchase the vehicle in the first place.)

Heavily Advertised Easy Solutions to Debt Problems

Watch out for television, radio, or Internet ads that claim easy solutions to debt problems. Sometimes, you can't tell exactly what these companies are offering. Some may turn out to be ads for expensive consolidation loans you should avoid, often with high interest rates, hidden fees, and security clauses that put property you already own at risk. Others may be unlicensed people claiming they can eliminate your debts through bankruptcy; often, these services file incorrectly or don't follow through, which makes it harder for you to get bankruptcy relief if you need it. But most are companies that offer services called debt management, negotiation, pooling, settlement, or prorating. They claim to be able to get creditors to accept must less than what you owe, but what they really do is charge high fees to take your money and distribute it to your creditors—something you can do on your own.

No matter what they call their services, these companies generally produce poor results and charge very high fees and interest rates. They siphon off your limited resources in debt consolidation charges, pay only a few (if any) creditors, and jeopardize much of your property.

These companies claim that they can negotiate with creditors on your behalf, promising substantially reduced payments and an end to collection calls from creditors. They charge hefty fees for this service, which most consumers can do on their own. Instead of helping you obtain relief and work your way out of debt, the debt negotiator may leave you with even more negative information in your credit report and being sued by collectors. In extreme cases, companies reportedly have used consumers' money to pay the company's operating expenses instead of paying the consumers' creditors. Even if the company provides the services promised, you're better off using the money you would spend on the fee to make payments to your creditors. If you cannot negotiate with your creditors or make payments on your own, see "Get Outside Help to Design a Repayment Plan," below.

These debt practices are either regulated or prohibited in most states. These laws usually don't apply to nonprofit organizations, lawyers, and merchant-owned associations claiming to help debtors.

Negotiate With Your Creditors

If you can get some money, consider negotiating with your creditors. Negotiation can buy you time to get your finances in order. You can also negotiate to get your creditors to agree to accept considerably less than you owe as a complete settlement of your debts.

You can find suggestions and forms for negotiating with your creditors in Chapter 3.

Get Outside Help to Design a Repayment Plan

Many people dread negotiating with their creditors. They may feel guilty for not paying their bills or unsure of their negotiating skills. Or, their creditors may be so adamant that the process is too unpleasant to stomach.

If you don't want to negotiate with your creditors, there are people and organizations available to help you. Creditors are often more than happy to work with respected organizations that work with debtors who are serious about repaying their debts. Reputable nonprofit credit and debt counseling agencies (see Appendix A), the United Way, and a church or synagogue are all excellent prospects. These organizations will help you figure out how much you owe, how much you can afford to pay each month, and what your various options are, including bankruptcy. A credit or debt counseling agency will also talk to your creditors for you.

Before signing up with any credit counseling service, talk to others who have used the service and check it out with your local Better Business Bureau. If there are complaints, that's a warning. But that doesn't necessarily mean you can trust a business that hasn't received any complaints: A business can change names or defraud a lot of people before the complaints catch up to it.

> **CAUTION**
>
> **Use caution with lawyers, credit repair clinics, and for-profit organizations.** A lawyer can help, but lawyers charge high fees that may not be justified, especially when you're heavily in debt. Whatever you do, don't use a credit repair clinic. (For more information on this, see Chapter 6.) You should also avoid companies that advertise a lot on TV, radio, or the Internet that they can solve your debt problems; they often charge high fees and may not deliver what they promise. For information on choosing reliable credit counselors or negotiators, see Appendix A.

File for Chapter 7 Bankruptcy

Chapter 7 bankruptcy is the type of bankruptcy most people have heard about. It allows you to wipe out most consumer debts: credit cards, medical bills, and the like. In exchange, however, you might have to surrender some of your property, such as a second car, valuable electronic equipment, or a vacation home. To file for Chapter 7 bankruptcy, you fill out a packet of forms that describe your property, income, expenses, debts, and any recent purchases and gifts. Then you file the forms with the federal bankruptcy court in your area.

Filing for bankruptcy puts into effect an "automatic stay" that immediately stops most of your creditors from trying to collect what you owe them. So, at least temporarily, creditors cannot legally "garnish" (take) your wages; empty your bank account; go after your car, house, or other property; or cut off your utility service.

> **CAUTION**
>
> **The automatic stay may not protect you from eviction.** Filing for bankruptcy used to prohibit landlords from proceeding with an eviction, unless they got a court order allowing them to move forward. Now, the law is different: If the landlord already has a judgment for possession, he or she may be able to evict you despite the automatic stay. Even if the landlord doesn't yet have a judgment, you may be evicted—despite your bankruptcy filing—for endangering the property or for illegal use of controlled substances on the premises.

Until your bankruptcy case ends, your past financial problems are in the hands of the bankruptcy court. Nothing can be sold or paid without the court's consent. Most property and income you acquire after you file for bankruptcy is yours to use as you wish, however.

At the end of the bankruptcy process, most of your debts are "discharged" (wiped out) by the court. You no longer legally owe the debts you owed when you filed for bankruptcy. If you incur debts after filing, however, you are still obligated to pay them.

And you can't file for Chapter 7 bankruptcy again for another eight years from the date of your first filing.

Before the bankruptcy process ends, a creditor might try to convince you to "reaffirm" (commit to paying off) a debt after your bankruptcy discharge. Think twice before you reaffirm a debt. You do not have to reaffirm any debt; if you do, you must pay it off even though your other debts have been discharged. Any agreement to reaffirm a debt must be written and filed with the bankruptcy court. You can cancel a reaffirmation agreement before your debts are discharged or within 60 days after the agreement is filed with the court. If an attorney did not help you negotiate the reaffirmation agreement, it must be approved by the court.

Of course, bankruptcy isn't for everyone. One reason is that some debts *cannot* be erased in Chapter 7 bankruptcy, including:

- child support or alimony obligations
- student loans, unless repaying would cause you undue hardship (which is very tough to prove)
- court-ordered restitution—payments you're ordered to make after a criminal conviction
- most federal, state, and local income taxes less than three years past due, and any money borrowed or charged to pay those tax debts
- debts for death or injury caused by your intoxicated driving
- debts from a marital settlement agreement or divorce decree, and
- debts that a bankruptcy judge rules were incurred as a result of

a wrongful act on your part—for example, debts incurred from fraud (such as lying on a credit application or writing a bad check); intentional injury (such as assault, battery, false imprisonment, libel, or slander); larceny (theft); or breach of trust or embezzlement.

Not everyone can use Chapter 7 bankruptcy. You won't be eligible if:

- You received a discharge of your debts in a Chapter 7 case you filed within eight years of filing your current Chapter 7 case.
- You received a discharge of your debts in a Chapter 13 case you filed within six years of filing your current Chapter 7 case (unless you paid 100% of your unsecured debts in your prior Chapter 7 case, or paid at least 70% of those debts and got an order saying you filed the Chapter 13 case in good faith and made your best effort to pay).
- You defrauded your creditors.
- A previous bankruptcy case you filed was dismissed within the last 180 days because you violated a court order, the court found that your filing was fraudulent or constituted an abuse of the bankruptcy system, or you requested a dismissal after a creditor asked the court to lift the automatic stay.
- Your average income in the six months before you file is higher than the median income in your state for a family of your size, and you would have sufficient money left—after subtracting certain allowed

expenses—to pay certain debts over a five-year period. This requirement is referred to as "the means test," and those who flunk it can be required to use Chapter 13 rather than Chapter 7.

RESOURCE

For more information on Chapter 7 bankruptcy, see *How to File for Chapter 7 Bankruptcy*, by Stephen Elias, Albin Renauer, and Robin Leonard, or *The New Bankruptcy: Will It Work for You?*, by Stephen Elias, both published by Nolo.

Pay Over Time With Chapter 13 Bankruptcy

If you have steady income and think you could squeeze out regular monthly payments, Chapter 13 bankruptcy may be a good option. Chapter 13 allows you to keep your property and use your disposable income (net income less reasonable expenses) to pay all or a portion of your debts over three to five years. You can use wages, benefits, investment income, business earnings, or any other income to make your payments.

CAUTION

Your "income" may be higher than you think. The new bankruptcy law requires filers to use some odd (and possibly inaccurate) figures when calculating how much they will have left over each month to repay their debts. For example, your "income" is not the actual amount you bring home each month; it is your average gross income during the six months before you filed for bankruptcy, which could well be higher than your current income. And, filers who earn more than the median income for their state cannot deduct all of their actual expenses when figuring out their disposable income. For certain expenses, they must use figures set by the IRS, which might be lower than actual expenses, especially in metropolitan areas. For more information, see *Chapter 13 Bankruptcy*, by Stephen Elias and Robin Leonard (Nolo).

Most people file for Chapter 13 bankruptcy to make up missed mortgage or car payments and get back on track with their original loan, or to pay off a tax debt or student loan. These are not the only reasons people file for Chapter 13 bankruptcy, however.

If you cannot complete a Chapter 13 repayment plan—for example, you lose your job six months into the plan and can't make the payments—the bankruptcy court has the authority to change your plan. If the problem looks temporary, you may be given a grace period, an extended repayment period, or a reduction of the total owed. If it's clear that you can't possibly complete the plan because of circumstances beyond your control, the bankruptcy court might even let you discharge (cancel) your debts on the basis of hardship.

If the bankruptcy court won't let you modify your plan or give you a hardship discharge, you have the right to:

- convert to a Chapter 7 bankruptcy, or
- dismiss your Chapter 13 case. A dismissal of your case would leave

you in the same position as you were in before you filed, except that you'll owe less because of the payments you made. Your creditors will add to the debt the interest that was suspended from the time you filed your Chapter 13 petition until it was dismissed.

RESOURCE

For more information on Chapter 13 bankruptcy, see *Chapter 13 Bankruptcy*, by Stephen Elias and Robin Leonard, or *The New Bankruptcy: Will It Work for You?* by Stephen Elias, both published by Nolo. ●

Avoid Overspending

Keep Track of Your Daily Expenditures 24

Total Up Your Income.. 26

Make a Budget or Spending Plan 29

Prevent Future Financial Problems 34

SKIP AHEAD

If you skip this section, come back later. If you'd rather clean up your credit report or pay off your debts before doing a budget, skip ahead, but be sure to return to this chapter later. If you don't make a budget, you'll have a very tough time maintaining your improved credit.

To get out of debt and improve your credit, you must understand where your money goes. With that information in hand, you can make intelligent choices about how to spend your money. If you'd rather not create a budget yourself, you can contact a nonprofit credit or debt counseling organization. Information on credit and debt counseling agencies is located in Appendix A.

RESOURCE

Budgeting help. Several excellent computer programs, such as Quicken, can help you keep track of your expenses, particularly those paid by check or credit card. Many of these programs have budget features as well. Be sure you have an opportunity to record your cash outlays, however, before relying on these budgeting features: Many commercial budgeting programs analyze expenses you pay by check but overlook the most obvious source of payment—cash.

Keep Track of Your Daily Expenditures

Your goal in this chapter is to create a monthly budget comparing your average monthly expenses to your total monthly income. You can get started by completing Form F-2, Daily Expenditures (copies are below, in Appendix B, and on the CD-ROM), which gives you space to record everything you spend over the course of a week. Here's how to use the form:

1. Make eight copies of the form so you can record your expenditures for two months. (You'll want to track expenses for a couple of months to make sure your budget isn't based on a week or two of unusually high or low expenses.) If you are married or live with someone with whom you share expenses, you should each can record your own expenditures.

2. Select a Sunday to begin recording your expenses.

3. Record that Sunday's date in the blank at the top of one copy of the form.

4. Carry that week's form with you at all times.

5. Record every expense you pay by cash or cash equivalent. "Cash equivalent" means check, ATM or debit card, or automatic bank withdrawal. Be sure to include bank fees. Also, don't forget savings and investments, such as deposits into savings accounts, certificates of deposit, or money market accounts, or purchases of investments such as stocks or bonds.

Daily Expenditures for Week of _____

Sunday's Expenditures	Cost	Monday's Expenditures	Cost	Tuesday's Expenditures	Cost	Wednesday's Expenditures	Cost
Daily Total:		Daily Total:		Daily Total:		Daily Total:	

Thursday's Expenditures	Cost	Friday's Expenditures	Cost	Saturday's Expenditures	Cost	Other Expenditures	Cost
Daily Total:		Daily Total:		Daily Total:		Weekly Total:	

F-2

Don't record expenses you charge on a credit card. Your goal is to get a picture of where your cash goes, and you won't actually pay off a credit card purchase right away. When you make a payment on a credit card bill, that's when you should list the items your payment covered as an expense on your sheet. If you don't pay the entire bill each month, list older items you charged that total a little less than the amount of your payment, and attribute the rest of your payment to interest.

EXAMPLE: On Sunday night, you pay your bills for the week and make a $450 payment toward your $1,000 credit card bill. The $1,000 includes a $500 balance from the previous month, a $350 airline ticket, a few restaurant meals, and accrued interest. On your Daily Expenditures form for Sunday, list $450 in the second column. In the first column, identify corresponding expenses—for example, the plane ticket and one restaurant meal—and attribute some of it to interest. In this example, you have to look at your credit card statements from previous months.

6. At the end of the week, put away the form and take out another copy. Go back to Step 3.
7. Once you've tracked expenses for eight weeks, list on any form under the category "Other Expenditures" seasonal, annual, semiannual, or

quarterly expenses you incur but did not pay during your two-month recording period. The most common are property taxes, car registration fees, magazine subscriptions, tax preparation fees, and insurance payments. But there are others. For example, if you do your recording in the winter months, don't forget summer expenses such as camp fees for your children, or pool maintenance. Similarly, in the summer or spring you probably won't account for your annual holiday gift expenses. Think broadly and be thorough.

Total Up Your Income

Of courses, what you spend accounts for only half of the picture. You also need to add up what you earn. Use Form F-3, Monthly Income From All Sources (copies are below, in Appendix B, and on the CD-ROM).

If you are married or live with someone with whom you share expenses, include income information for both of you.

Column 1: Source of income. In Part A, list the jobs for which you receive a salary or wages. In Part B, list all self-employment for which you receive income, including farm income and sales commissions. In Part C, list any other sources of income. Here are some examples of other kinds of income:

- **Bonus pay.** List all regular bonuses you receive, such as an annual $1,000 end-of-year bonus.
- **Dividends and interest.** List all sources of dividends or interest—for example,

Monthly Income From All Sources

1 Source of income		2 Amount of each payment	3 Period covered by each payment	4 Amount per month
A. Wages or Salary				
Job 1: _____ _____	Gross pay, including overtime:	$ _____	_____	
	Subtract:			
	Federal taxes	_____		
	State taxes	_____		
	Social Security (FICA)	_____		
	Union dues	_____		
	Insurance payments	_____		
	Child support wage withholding	_____		
	Other mandatory deductions (specify): _____ _____	_____		
	Subtotal:	$ _____	_____	_____
Job 2: _____ _____	Gross pay, including overtime:	$ _____	_____	
	Subtract:			
	Federal taxes	_____		
	State taxes	_____		
	Social Security (FICA)	_____		
	Union dues	_____		
	Insurance payments	_____		
	Child support wage withholding	_____		
	Other mandatory deductions (specify): _____ _____	_____		
	Subtotal:	$ _____	_____	_____
Job 3: _____ _____	Gross pay, including overtime:	$ _____	_____	
	Subtract:			
	Federal taxes	_____		
	State taxes	_____		
	Social Security (FICA)	_____		
	Union dues	_____		
	Insurance payments	_____		
	Child support wage withholding	_____		
	Other mandatory deductions (specify): _____ _____	_____		
	Subtotal:	$ _____	_____	_____

F-3

Monthly Income From All Sources (cont'd)

1 Source of income		2 Amount of each payment	3 Period covered by each payment	4 Amount per month
B. Self-Employment Income				
Job 1: _____	Gross pay, including overtime:	$ _____	_____	
_____	Subtract:			
	Federal taxes	_____		
	State taxes	_____		
	Self-employment taxes	_____		
	Other mandatory deductions (specify): _____			
	_____	_____		
	Subtotal:	$ _____	_____	_____
Job 2: _____	Gross pay, including overtime:	$ _____	_____	
_____	Subtract:			
	Federal taxes	_____		
	State taxes	_____		
	Self-employment taxes	_____		
	Other mandatory deductions (specify): _____			
	_____	_____		
	Subtotal:	$ _____	_____	_____
C. Other Sources				
Bonuses _____		_____		_____
Commissions _____		_____		_____
Dividends and interest _____		_____		_____
Rent, lease, or license income _____		_____		_____
Royalties _____		_____		_____
Note or trust income _____		_____		_____
Alimony or child support you receive _____		_____		_____
Pension or retirement income _____		_____		_____
Social Security _____		_____		_____
Other public assistance _____		_____		_____
Other (specify): _____		_____		_____
_____		_____		_____
_____		_____		_____
_____		_____		_____
_____		_____		_____
	Total monthly income			$ _____

F-3

bank accounts, security deposits, or stocks.

- **Alimony or child support.** Enter the type of support you receive for yourself (alimony, spousal support, or maintenance) or on behalf of your children (child support).

- **Pension or retirement income.** List the source of any pension, annuity, IRA, Keogh, or other retirement payments you receive.

- **Other public assistance.** Enter any public benefits you receive, such as SSI, public assistance, disability payments, veterans benefits, unemployment compensation, workers' compensation, or other government benefits.

- **Other.** Identify any other sources of income, such as a tax refund or payments you receive from friends or relatives. If, within the past 12 months, you received any one-time lump sum payment (such as the proceeds from an insurance policy or from the sale of a valuable asset), do not list it as income.

Column 2: Amount of each payment. For each source of income you listed in Parts A and B of Column 1, enter the amount you receive each pay period. If you don't receive the same amount each period, average the last 12. Then enter your deductions for each pay period. Again, if these amounts vary, enter an average of the last 12 months. For the income you listed in Part A, you probably need to look at a pay stub to see how much is deducted from your paycheck. Subtract the deductions and enter your net income in the "Subtotal" blank in Column 2.

In Part C, enter the amount of each payment for each source of income. If these amounts vary, enter an average of the last 12 months.

Column 3: Period covered by each payment. For each source of income, enter the period covered by each payment—such as weekly, twice monthly (24 times a year), every other week (26 times a year), monthly, quarterly (common for royalties), or annually (common for farm income).

Column 4: Amount per month. Multiply or divide the subtotals (or amounts in Part C) in Column 2 to determine the monthly amount. For example, if you are paid twice a month, multiply the Column 2 amount by two. If you are paid every other week, multiply the amount by 26 (for the annual amount) and divide by 12. (The shortcut is to multiply by 2.167.)

When you are done, total up Column 4. This is your total monthly income.

Make a Budget or Spending Plan

Once you've tracked your expenses and income for a couple of months, you're ready to create a budget or spending plan. Use Form F-4, Monthly Budget (copies are below, in Appendix B, and on the CD-ROM).

You have two goals in making a budget: to control any impulse you may have to overspend and to start saving money (an essential part of repairing your credit). The figures you entered on Forms F-2 and F-3 will form the basis for your budget.

To make and use a monthly budget, follow these steps:

1. Make several copies of Form F-4. Making a budget you can live with is a process of trial and error, and you may have to draft a few plans before you get it right.

2. Get out Forms F-2 and F-3, which list your income and expense figures.

3. Review the expenses listed on Form F-4. As you'll see, they are divided into common categories, such as home expenses, food, and transportation. If you don't have any expenses in a particular category, you can cross it out, delete it on your computer, or simply leave it blank. If you have a type of expense that isn't listed on the form, add that category to a blank line.

4. In the first column (labeled "Projected"), list your average actual monthly expenses in each category. Calculate these amounts by adding together your actual expenses for the two months you tracked, then dividing the total by two. If you have seasonal, annual, or quarterly expenses, include a monthly amount for those as well. For example, if you pay $3,600 in property taxes each year, you should list a projected expense of $300 a month ($3,600 divided by 12) in this category.

5. Add up all of your projected monthly expenses and enter the total on the line marked "Total Expenses" at the bottom of the "Projected" column.

6. Enter your projected monthly income (from Form F-3) below your projected total expenses.

7. Compare your projected income to your projected expenses. If you are spending more than you earn, you'll either have to earn more or spend less to make ends meet. Unless you're anticipating a big raise, planning to take on a second job, or selling valuable assets, you'll probably have to lower your expenses. Review each category to look for ways to cut costs. Rather than trying to cut out an entire expense, look for expenses you can reduce slightly without depriving yourself of items or services you really need. For example, you might be willing to forego one trip to a restaurant per month, subscribe to a less expensive cable package, or spend less on clothing.

8. Return to your budget and enter the adjustments you came up with. When you're finished, add up these new figures and come up with a new total expense amount. If it's less than your income, your budget is complete. If not, go back and try to find other places to cut back.

9. Label the remaining columns with the months of the year. Unless you wrote your budget on the first of the month, start with next month. During the month, write down and update your expenses in each category.

10. At the end of the month, total up how much you spent. How did you do? Are you close to your projected figures? If not, go back and try to make some changes to keep the numbers in balance.

Monthly Budget

Expense Category	Projected												
Home													
Rent/mortgage													
Property tax													
Insurance													
Homeowners assn. dues													
Telephone													
Gas/electric													
Water/sewer													
Cable													
Garbage/recycling													
Household supplies													
Housewares													
Furniture/appliances													
Cleaning													
Yard/pool care													
Repairs/maintenance													
Food													
Groceries													
Breakfast out													
Lunch out													
Dinner out													
Coffee/tea													
Snacks													
Clothing													
Clothes, shoes/ accessories													
Laundry, dry cleaning													
Mending													

Monthly Budget (cont'd)

Self Care													
Toiletries/cosmetics													
Haircuts													
Massage													
Gym membership													
Donations													

Health Care													
Insurance													
Medications													
Vitamins													
Doctor													
Dentist													
Eye care													
Therapy													

Transportation													
Car payments (buy or lease)													
Insurance													
Registration													
Gas													
Maintenance/repairs													
Parking													
Tolls													
Public transit													
Parking tickets													
Road service (such as AAA)													

Entertainment													
Music													
Movies/rentals													
Concerts, theater, ballet, etc.													
Museums													

Monthly Budget (cont'd)

Sporting events												
Hobbies/lessons												
Club dues or membership												
Film/developing costs												
Books, magazines/ newspapers												
Software/games												
Dependent Care												
Child care												
Clothing												
Allowance												
School expenses												
Toys/entertainment												
Pets												
Food/supplies												
Veterinarian												
Grooming												
Education												
Tuition												
Loan payments												
Books/supplies												
Travel												
Gifts/Cards												
Personal Business												
Supplies												
Copying												
Postage												
Bank/credit card fees												
Legal fees												
Accountant												

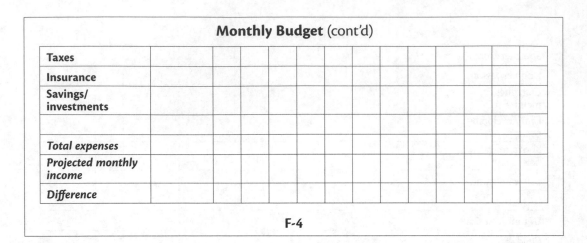

Monthly Budget (cont'd)

Taxes											
Insurance											
Savings/ investments											
Total expenses											
Projected monthly income											
Difference											

F-4

Check your figures periodically to keep track of how you're doing. Don't think of your budget as etched in stone. If you do, and you spend more on an item than you've budgeted, you'll only find yourself frustrated. Use your budget as a guide. If you constantly overspend in one area, don't berate yourself: Instead, change the projected amount for that category and find another place to cut. Keep in mind that a budget is just a tool to help you recognize what you can afford and where your money is going.

Prevent Future Financial Problems

There are no magic rules that will solve everyone's financial troubles. But the following suggestions should help you stay out of trouble. If you have a family, everyone will have to participate—one person cannot do all the work alone. So make sure your spouse or partner, and the kids, understand that the family is having financial difficulties, and agree together to take the steps that will lead to financial recovery.

1. **Create a realistic budget and stick to it.** This means periodically checking in and readjusting your figures and spending habits.

2. **Don't impulse buy.** When you see something you hadn't planned to buy, don't purchase it on the spot. Go home and think it over. It's unlikely you'll return to the store and buy it.

3. **Avoid sales.** Buying a $500 item on sale for $400 isn't a $100 savings if you didn't need the item to begin with. It's a $400 expense that was unnecessary.

4. **Get medical insurance if at all possible.** Even a stopgap policy with a large deductible can help if a medical crisis comes up. You can't avoid medical emergencies, but living without medical insurance is an invitation to financial ruin.

5. **Charge items only if you can afford to pay for them now.** If you don't currently have the cash, don't charge based on future income—sometimes future income doesn't materialize. An alternative is to toss all of your credit cards in a drawer and commit to living without credit for a while. Or, even better, cancel the cards that you really don't need. (To learn the correct way to cancel a credit card, see Chapter 6.) If you must charge, here's a good rule of thumb: Don't charge anything that won't exist when the statement arrives (such as meals, groceries, or movie tickets).

6. **Avoid large rent or house payments.** Obligate yourself to only what you can now afford and increase your mortgage or rent payments only as your income increases. Consider refinancing your house if your payments are unwieldy.

7. **Avoid joint loan obligations.** If you incur a joint debt, you're probably liable for all of it if the other person defaults. If you cosign or guarantee a loan, your signature obligates you as if you were the primary borrower. You can't be sure that the other person will pay.

8. **Don't try to save or invest until you have paid off high-cost debt.** It doesn't make sense to save or invest money at a low rate of interest while you still owe debt on which you are paying a high rate of interest; you'll get further behind every day. Instead, put any extra money you have toward the credit card debt so you can pay it off sooner. Once you've retired your high-interest debts, you can start saving for the next rainy day.

9. **Don't make high-risk investments.** Invest conservatively, opting for certificates of deposit, money market funds, and government bonds over riskier investments such as speculative real estate, penny stocks, and junk bonds.

10. **Use common sense.** People today use credit and debit cards for everything —dry cleaning, sandwiches, frappuccinos, groceries, movies, cocktails, postage, gum, and so on—and feel that their finances are in good shape because they have cash in their wallets or purses. These little expenses are hard to keep track of and add up quickly by the end of the month, often becoming budget busters. If you're in tough financial times, leave the credit and debit cards at home and pay cash for these things (or forgo them). If you find that you really love expensive coffee drinks, pay cash for them or, better yet, enjoy one as a treat when your finances are back on track.

Handle Existing Debts

Deal With Current (or Not Seriously Overdue) Debts 40

    Rent Payments 41

    Mortgage Payments.. 43

    Utility and Telephone Bills... 47

    Car Payments.. 48

    Loans for Which You Pledged Collateral Other Than a
       Motor Vehicle.. 49

    Student Loans... 50

    Insurance Policies 54

    Doctor, Dentist, Lawyer, and Accountant Bills 55

    Credit Card Bills... 55

Use the Form Negotiation Letters Provided in This Book 59

Deal With Creditors on Past Due Accounts 60

Deal With Collection Agencies 65

    Getting a Collection Agency Off Your Back 67

    Negotiating With a Collection Agency 67

    Offering a Lump Sum Settlement 68

    Offering to Make Payments... 68

    When the Collection Agency Gives Up 69

    Illegal Debt Collection Practices 69

    If a Collection Agency Violates the Law 71

Tax Consequences of Forgiven Loans 72

To repair your credit, you must pay attention to two different kinds of debts: debts that aren't overdue (such as current charges on your utility bill) and your past due accounts (such as an unpaid phone bill from last month or a doctor's bill from last year). You cannot repair your credit if you ignore your past due debts—those default notations will stand out in your credit report. In addition, if you repair your credit and later default on debts that are now current, you will have wasted the time and effort you spent on repairing your credit in the first place.

Stabilize your financial situation before you worry about repairing your credit. Focus your energy on finding a job or other income source and paying accounts in order to keep your home, car, and other necessities. There are some things you can do to improve your credit even when your financial situation is still shaky (see Chapter 4 on how to clean up your credit report), but for the most part, your credit record will improve only after you demonstrate to creditors that you are back on your feet financially.

RESOURCE

More on past due bills. For more detail on paying your past due bills and contacting your creditors about accounts on which you are current, see *Solve Your Money Troubles: Debt, Credit & Bankruptcy*, by Robin Leonard and Margaret Reiter (Nolo).

Tips for Sending Letters

Throughout this chapter, we advise you to send various letters to your creditors, depending on your situation. When you send a letter, follow these guidelines:

- Type your letters or neatly fill in the blanks of the letters in Appendix 3 or on the CD-ROM.
- Keep a copy of all correspondence for yourself.
- *Never* send originals of documents that support your claim (such as a note marked "paid" or a canceled check); send only copies and keep the originals.
- Send by certified mail, with a return receipt requested.
- If you are enclosing money, use a cashier's check or money order if you have any debts in collection—not a check. Otherwise, the recipient of the check could pass your checking account number on to any debt collector, which will make it easier for the collector to grab your assets to collect the debt.
- Follow up telephone calls with a letter confirming the details of the discussion and any agreements you reached.
- If you communicate with a creditor or debt collector by email, print and keep copies of all message and replies. Always keep copies of all communications— and don't handle important discussions by phone or some other medium that won't give you a written record of the conversation.

Secured and Unsecured Debts

To successfully negotiate with your creditors, you must understand your options, which often depend on whether your debts are secured or unsecured. Understanding this distinction will also help you decide which debts to pay first.

A **secured debt** is one for which a specific item of property (called "collateral") guarantees payment of the debt. One way for a debt to be secured is for you to sign an agreement to create a secured debt and specify the collateral. If you don't pay, the creditor has the legal right to take the collateral. Because of this, these debts will usually be your highest priority (unless you don't care if you lose the collateral). The other way a debt becomes secured is for a creditor to record a lien (a notice that you owe the creditor money) against the property.

Common examples of secured debts include:

- mortgages and home equity loans (also called "second mortgages")—loans to buy, refinance, or fix up a house or other real estate
- loans for cars, boats, tractors, motorcycles, planes, or RVs
- personal loans from finance companies for which you pledge real estate or personal property, such as a paid-off motor vehicle
- charges on a department store charge account for which the store requires you to sign a security agreement pledging the item purchased as collateral for your repayment (most store charges are not secured), and

- tax liens, judgment liens, mechanics liens, and child support liens.

Unsecured debts have no collateral. For example, when you charge a television set on your Visa card, the creditor can't take the television back if you don't pay your Visa bill. If the credit card company wants to be paid, it must sue you, get a judgment for the money you owe, and try to collect. A creditor who wins a lawsuit typically can go after your wages, bank accounts, and valuable property.

The majority of debts are unsecured. Some common unsecured debts include:

- credit and charge card purchases and cash advances (such as Visa, MasterCard, American Express, or Discover Card)
- gasoline charges
- most department store charges
- student loans
- bills from doctors, dentists, hospitals, accountants, and lawyers
- alimony and child support
- loans from friends or relatives, unless you gave the person a note secured by some property you own
- rent, and
- utility bills.

Usually, paying unsecured debts should be a lower priority than paying secured debts. However, because collectors of some unsecured debts—such as student loans and unpaid child support—are allowed to use more aggressive collection tactics than the typical unsecured creditor, those debts deserve more attention.

Deal With Current (or Not Seriously Overdue) Debts

 SKIP AHEAD

If you've already fallen behind on all your debts, jump ahead. Go to "Deal With Creditors on Past Due Accounts," below.

To repair and maintain your credit, you need to stay current—or to not get too far behind—on your existing debts. If it looks like you won't be able to, your best bet is to contact your creditors before you miss a payment.

Negotiating with your creditors to get more time to pay or to change the terms of your agreement isn't particularly difficult. Creditors generally like to hear from people who anticipate having problems paying their bills. If you simply skip your payment, the creditor assumes the worst—that you're a deadbeat trying to get away with not paying. If you call or write in advance, however, your creditor will often help you through your difficulties. Merchants, lenders, and other creditors are aware of unemployment rates, underemployment trends, income reductions, corporate mergers and downsizing, and other sour economic realities. And, when times turn good again, they're going to want—and need—your business. So they may be willing to accommodate you now.

As soon as you realize that you're going to have trouble paying your bills, contact your creditors. Your goals are twofold: You want time to pay and you don't want the creditor to report your bill as past due to credit bureaus. Calling your creditors is faster than writing, but if you find it easier to express yourself on paper than over the phone, go ahead and write. If you call, follow up your call with a confirming letter so that you and the creditor have some evidence of what you agreed to. If you write, make sure your letter will get there before your payment is due.

Your success with your creditors will depend on the type of debt, the creditor's policies, and your ability to negotiate. Follow these tips when dealing with your creditors:

- **Explain the problem clearly.** Tell the creditor why you're struggling, whether it's a job loss, emergency expenses for your child's health, costs of caring for an aged family member, or a large back tax assessment.
- **Mention any development that points to an improving financial condition.** Creditors like to hear about disability or unemployment benefits beginning, job prospects, an expense about to end (such as a child finishing school), the end of a strike, a job recall, or a small inheritance on the way.
- **If you can afford it, send a token payment.** This shows the creditor that you are serious about paying but just can't pay the full amount now. Of course, the creditor might also take your money and refuse to negotiate with you.

Negotiation is often a good strategy, but it doesn't always work. Some creditors simply will not negotiate with debtors. Despite the fact that creditors get at least something when they negotiate settlements with debtors, many ignore debtors' pleas for help and continue to call demanding payment. But there's certainly no harm in trying. Even if you have a creditor or two who won't negotiate, at least you'll know that you gave it your best shot.

 SKIP AHEAD

Skip ahead if you don't have a particular kind of debt discussed below. This section gives advice for dealing with specific types of debts: rent and mortgage payments, utility and telephone bills, car payments, secured loans, student loans, insurance policies, bills from professionals, and credit card payments. Read only the sections that apply to you.

Rent Payments

Many landlords will let their tenants pay rent late for a month or two, especially if the tenant has been reliable in the past. You will have the best chance of working out a payment plan if you contact the landlord promptly.

If your rent is too steep for your budget, you could try asking for a reduction. Many landlords won't agree, but it might work it you live in an area where property values have declined or the vacancy rate has increased. The landlord may agree to accept a partial payment now and the rest later. The landlord may even temporarily lower your rent, rather than have to evict you or rerent the place if you move out.

If your landlord agrees to a rent reduction or late payments, send by certified mail, or hand deliver, a letter confirming the arrangement. (See the sample, below.) Be sure to keep a copy for yourself. If you hand deliver the letter, ask the landlord or manager to initial and date your copy of the letter to confirm that it was received. Once the understanding is written down, the landlord will have a hard time evicting you as long as you live up to your new agreement.

> ### Sample Letter to Landlord
>
> May 5, 2009
>
> Frank O'Neill
> 1556 North Lakefront
> Minneapolis, MN 67890
>
> Dear Frank:
>
> Thanks for being so understanding. This letter is to confirm the telephone conversation we had yesterday.
>
> My lease requires that I pay rent of $1,000 per month. You agreed to reduce my rent to $850 per month, beginning June 1, 2009 and lasting until I find another job, but not to exceed six months. That is, even if I haven't found a new job, my rent will go back to $1,000 per month on December 1, 2009.
>
> You also agreed that I can pay my rent this month on the 15th, and on the 5th of each month after that until December 2009, when my rent will once again be due on the 1st.
>
> Thank you again for your understanding and help. As I mentioned on the phone, I am following all leads in order to secure another job shortly.
>
> Sincerely,
>
> *Abigail Landsberg*
> Abigail Landsberg

If your landlord refuses to help out, your options are limited. If you don't pay the amount of rent you obligated yourself to pay, your landlord can—and no doubt will—evict you. You are usually better off trying to get a roommate (with the landlord's permission, if it's required) or moving out before any eviction takes place.

If you have a month-to-month lease, you merely have to give your landlord the amount of notice required under your rental agreement before you move out (often 30 days). Of course, if moving out means living on the streets, you might as well stay and see what action the landlord takes. This is especially true in areas where evictions can take several weeks.

If you have a written lease, you will violate it by moving out and stopping your rent payments before the lease term expires. If you know of someone who can take over your lease, recommend that person to your landlord. The landlord should accept the person unless the landlord has another tenant in mind, the person's rental history is poor, or the person's credit is bad and the landlord is convinced that he or she couldn't pay the rent. Even if you don't find someone to take over the lease, in most states the landlord has a duty to "mitigate" damages, which means that the landlord must use reasonable efforts to rerent the home to replace the rent you didn't pay. If the landlord rerents the property, you'll have to pay only for the period during which the property is vacant, plus the landlord's reasonable costs to find a new tenant (advertising expenses, for example). If you advanced one or two months' rent or paid a security deposit when you moved in, the landlord should put that money toward any amount you owe.

If you end up owing your landlord some money and don't pay it, your landlord might report the amount due to the credit reporting agencies or to tenant-screening services (which are similar to credit reporting agencies but gather information specifically for property owners and managers). Not all landlords report this information. But any time the landlord takes court action—files an eviction lawsuit or sues you for a balance owed—you can be sure it will show up in your credit report and tenant history.

> **RESOURCE**
>
> **Tenant information.** You can find complete information on your rights as a tenant in *Every Tenant's Legal Guide*, by Janet Portman and Marcia Stewart (Nolo).

Mortgage Payments

Your options for dealing with your house payments depend on your financial situation and your lender. If you need a break for only a month or two, you may be able to negotiate a short-term solution. If your house payments are going to be too high for the foreseeable future, refinancing may be an option. If you can't afford the mortgage or refinance, you'll have to consider ways of getting out of your house.

Negotiate a Short-Term Deal

If you're facing a temporary financial crunch but you think you should be back on track soon, contact your lender. Some lenders are willing to negotiate short-term arrangements to ease your burden, such as deferring or waiving late charges, accepting interest-only payments, applying prior prepayments to what you owe, or temporarily reducing or suspending payments.

Refinance

If you're facing long-term financial problems and can no longer afford your mortgage payments, refinancing might be an option. By refinancing, you might be able to lower your monthly payments by getting a lower interest rate and/or taking more time to repay what you owe. Be realistic when considering a refinance, however. If you can't afford your new payments, refinancing won't be much help—in fact, it could make your financial situation even worse.

A new federal program, Hope for Homeowners (H4H), may help you get refinancing. This program, for homeowners who refinance before September 30, 2011, was intended to help the many people who've found themselves with mortgages they can't afford as a result of the recent decline in house prices.

Under the H4H program, the new loan you get can be for no more than 96.5% of the current value of your home; the exact amount depends on how much of your income will go to pay the mortgage. If your home's value has declined, your new loan might be quite a bit smaller than your existing one—and your monthly payments will be a lot less, too. What's the catch? You can only get the new loan if your current lender agrees to accept the new loan amount as payment in full for your existing mortgage and to waive all late payment and prepayment fees. In exchange for these concessions, the government insures that you will repay the loan.

To qualify for this program, you must meet all of these requirements:

- You must have taken out a loan on your primary residence before January 1, 2008.
- You must have made at least six full payments on your mortgage.
- As of March 1, 2008, your mortgage payments must have been at least 31% of your gross monthly income.
- You can't have any ownership interest in any other residences.
- You can't have deliberately defaulted or engaged in fraud.

Loans under the Home for Homeowners program are fixed interest rate loans for 30 to 40 years, for a total loan amount of up to $550,440. You must pay an insurance premium of 3% of the loan amount up front (you can include this in the amount you borrow) and an additional annual 1.5% premium with your monthly payments. You will also have to pay standard closing costs allowed by the Federal Housing Administration (FHA), which can also be folded into the loan. If you have a second (or any additional) mortgage on your home, that lender will be paid when you get the new loan.

The FHA also gets a piece of the action when you sell your home: It receives a sliding share of your initial equity in the home for the first five years, and a 50% share in any increase in your home's value. If you sell your home at a profit after five years have passed, you get half of the increased value, and the FHA shares the other half with any second (or additional) mortgage lender that gave up its right to payment when you refinanced. You cannot put any additional loans on your home for the first five years of the new loan, except in certain circumstances for emergency repairs.

To find out more about the H4H program or to start the process, ask your lender or contact a housing counselor approved by the Department of Housing and Urban Development (HUD) by calling 800-569-4287 or 800-877-8339 (TDD), or by going to www.hud.gov.

If You Can't Pay or Refinance

If you can no longer afford your mortgage and refinancing isn't available, you have three options:

Sell your house. Selling a house in a down market isn't easy. But if you can't get your payments reduced to an amount you can afford, selling may be your best option. Many investors and savvy buyers look to buy "distressed" houses—houses in or near foreclosure. You won't get top dollar, but you should be able to at least save some of the equity you have built up and avoid doing serious damage to your credit. But do not get taken by an unscrupulous "equity skimmer" or "foreclosure consultant." Equity skimmers try to buy houses for a small fraction of their market value, often through misrepresentation, deceit, or intimidation. Foreclosure consultants promise to help homeowners in foreclosure, charge high fees for little or no service, and then purchase the home at a fraction of its value.

Watch Out for Foreclosure Scams

Foreclosure scams rely on the homeowner's desperation and ignorance for their success. They also often rely on the homeowner's faith in humanity ("no one would kick me when I'm down") or shared heritage or national origin ("someone of my culture wouldn't trick me"). The more you know about these scams, the less likely you are to fall victim to one of them. Here are three to watch out for:

- **Phantom rescue:** The scammer charges excessive fees for some phone calls or paperwork that the homeowner could have done and for a promise of representation that never happens. The scammer abandons the homeowner when the time for reinstatement—which should have been used to get current on the loan, negotiate with the lender, or find effective assistance—runs out. The foreclosure then proceeds.

- **Bailout:** The scammer tells the homeowner to surrender title to the house, with the promise that he or she can rent it and buy it back from the scammer later. The homeowner may be told that surrendering the title is necessary so that someone with better credit can get new financing to save the house. The terms of the buyback are so onerous that the homeowner can't buy the house back, and the rescuer pockets the equity.

- **Bait and switch:** Here, the homeowner doesn't realize that he or she is surrendering title to the house in exchange for the promised rescue. The scammer may trick the homeowner into surrendering title (perhaps when signing new loan documents), or may simply forge the homeowner's signature on the deed. The scammer then keeps the house or sells it and keeps the profit.

Walk away from your house. Depending on your state laws, whether the loan is for the purchase of the home, and whether the loan was made available through particular government programs, you may not owe any more money to the lender if you simply give up your home. This may be worth considering if you cannot afford the payments, the house is worth less than you owe, and you can find another place to rent at much less per month. This is a drastic step, however, and you should consult an attorney who specializes in these kinds of transactions before making a decision.

To give up your home, you transfer your ownership interest in your home to the lender—called a "deed in lieu of foreclosure." Lenders don't have to accept your deed in lieu, but many will. Keep in mind that with a deed in lieu, you won't get any cash back, even if you have lots of equity in your home. And it may have negative tax consequences. (See "Tax Consequences of Forgiven Loans," below.") The deed in lieu will also appear on your credit report as a negative mark. If you opt for a deed in lieu, try to get concessions from the lender—after all, you are saving it the expense and hassle of foreclosing on your home. For example, ask the lender to eliminate negative references on your credit report or give you more time to stay in the house.

Let the lender foreclose. If the lender forces a sale of your house, you may still owe money. In most states, if the sale price doesn't cover what you owe, the lender is entitled to a "deficiency balance"—the difference between the amount you owe the foreclosing lender and the amount for which the foreclosing lender sells the house.

How a Foreclosure Works

If you haven't been able to sell your house and you don't just walk away, your lender will probably foreclose. Here's a general description of what to expect (the exact process and timelines vary from state to state). After you miss a few payments, the lender will send you a letter reminding you that your payments are late and imposing a late fee. If you don't respond, the lender will wait another 60 days or so and then send you a notice telling you that your loan is in default and that it will begin foreclosure proceedings unless it receives payment.

After getting this notice, you have about 90 days to "cure" the default and reinstate the loan—pay all your missed payments, late fees, and other charges. If you can't bring the loan current, the only way to avoid foreclosure is to sell the house during this period. If you were being picky before, now is the time to accept any offer.

If you don't cure the default, the lender applies to a court for an order allowing it to sell your house at an auction. (Obtaining court approval is not necessary when the lender issues a deed of trust instead of a mortgage. The two documents are virtually the same, except that the holder of a deed of trust can forgo court involvement, which, in some circumstances and in some states, may eliminate the lender's right to collect a deficiency balance from you.) Then the lender publishes a notice of the sale in a newspaper. Between the dates when the notice is published and the sale takes place, most lenders let you reinstate the loan by making up the back payments and penalties.

If you don't reinstate the loan or sell the house, the lender will "accelerate" the loan. This means you no longer can reinstate the loan. The only way you can keep your house is by paying the entire mortgage balance immediately.

If you don't pay the balance, your house will be sold at a foreclosure sale. Anyone with a financial interest in your house will attend. The house is sold to the highest bidder, often for a price well below its market value.

When the Federal Government Owns Your Loan

Millions of American homeowners' loans are owned by Fannie Mae or Freddie Mac. These are private corporations created by the U.S. government.

Both companies' default programs emphasize foreclosure prevention whenever feasible. They offer rate reductions, term extensions, and other changes for people in financial distress, especially for people experiencing involuntary money problems due to things such as an illness, death of a spouse, or job loss. One possible option would allow you to make partially reduced payments for up to 18 months.

If you can't get help from your loan servicer, contact Fannie Mae or Freddie Mac directly at:

- Fannie Mae, 800-732-6643, www.fanniemae.com
- Freddie Mac, 800-373-3343, www.freddiemac.com

RESOURCE

Want more information on fore-closure? Check out *The Foreclosure Survival Guide*, by Stephen Elias (Nolo). It will help you sort through your options, including negotiating a mortgage workout with your lender, declaring bankruptcy, fighting the foreclosure in court, or simply staying in your house for as long as possible while the foreclosure proceeds.

Even if your problem looks long term, the lender may try to work with you to avoid foreclosure. In the past, lenders were quick to start foreclosure proceedings. In recent years, however, they have looked at new ways to work out mortgage delinquencies short of foreclosure.

If you want to try to work something out with your lender, begin negotiating as early as possible. Also, it's often a good idea to get help from a nonprofit debt counselor or lawyer with experience in mortgage workouts. For information on HUD-approved mortgage counseling agencies in your area, call 800-569-4287.

Utility and Telephone Bills

Most electric, gas, water, and telephone companies will let you get two or three months behind before turning off your service or taking other steps to collect what you owe. Some utility companies have programs that allow delinquent customers to pay the overdue amount in installments over several months. Call the company's billing department to see if it offers this type of program.

Many utility companies offer reduced rates to elderly and low-income people and have emergency funds to help pay the bills of low-income people. If you face high heating bills in the winter or air conditioning bills in the summer, you may want to see if your utility company offers "level payments." This means that the annual bill is averaged and paid in equal payments over 12 months. During a designated month of the year, the actual bills are calculated against your level payments and you are either billed for the balance owed or given a refund for any overpayment.

To find out if you qualify for reduced rates, level payments, "lifeline" programs, or other assistance offered by the utility company, call and ask. In addition, in many areas, charitable groups—especially religious organizations—offer assistance to low-income people who need help with their utility bills. Take advantage of any assistance available to you. It can be a real hassle, and expensive, to get your utility service back after it's been shut off for nonpayment of your bill.

Keep in mind that most northern states prohibit termination of heat-related utilities during the winter months. Other states also have a limited prohibition against shutoffs for households with elderly or disabled residents and occasionally for households with infants. Usually, you must show financial hardship to qualify. But, even if you qualify for a prohibition against utility shutoff, you'll still owe the bill.

Car Payments

Your options for handling car payments depend on whether you buy or lease your vehicle.

Purchase Payments

If you suspect you'll have trouble making your car payments for several months, your best bet is to sell the car, pay off the lender, and use whatever is left to pay your other debts or buy a more affordable used car.

Selling the car is not a good strategy if you're "upside down" (that is, you owe more on the car than you can sell it for). If you can pay the difference between the loan amount and the car's market value, then selling the car will at least free up the amount of your car payment each month. Don't even consider transferring the car to someone who promises to make the monthly payments for you. Such a transfer almost certainly will violate your purchase contract and probably is illegal. Also, the business or person who takes the car may not make the payments. Then you'll be responsible for the default on the loan, which will become part of your credit record.

If you want to hold onto your car and you miss a payment, call the lender *immediately* and speak to someone in the customer service or collections department. Don't delay. Cars can be, and often are, repossessed within hours of the time payment was due. There are several reasons for this: The creditor doesn't have to get a court judgment before seizing the car; cars lose value fast, so a creditor who has to auction it off will want to do so quickly to get the largest possible return; and cars are mobile and have been known to disappear before they can be repossessed.

If you can convince the lender that your situation is temporary, the lender may grant you an extension, which means that you can make the delinquent payment at the end of your loan period. However, the lender probably won't grant an extension unless you've made at least six payments on time. Also, most lenders charge a fee for granting an extension and don't grant more than one a year.

Instead of granting an extension, the lender may rewrite the loan to reduce the monthly payments. This means, however, that you'll make payments for a longer period of time and pay more total interest.

In deciding whether to hold onto the car, don't forget to consider your monthly insurance payment. You will have to maintain your insurance coverage if you decide to keep the car. Lenders usually consider failure to maintain insurance to be a default, which can lead to repossession. Also, the lender can obtain insurance to protect its interest in the car, which usually is very expensive, and hold you responsible for the premiums.

Lease Payments

Nearly 30% of new cars are leased, rather than purchased. The reasons are many, but most people who lease like the lower monthly payments that accompany vehicle lease contracts.

If you can't afford your lease payments, your first step is to review your lease agreement. If your total obligation under the lease is less than $25,000 and the lease term exceeds four months (many leases meet these two requirements), the federal Consumer Leasing Act (15 U.S.C. §§ 1667-1667e) requires that your lease disclose the cost and terms of ending your lease agreement early.

If you want to cancel your lease, look carefully at the provisions of your lease agreement describing what happens if you terminate the lease early. You can count on incurring an early termination penalty.

If you can't figure out how much you'll owe, inform the dealer in writing that you want to end the lease early and ask how much you'll owe. The dealer will contact you with the amount. If the dealer has already assigned (sold) the lease, then contact the leasing company.

Some consumers have successfully challenged the amount owed or persuaded the leasing company to drop large penalties for early termination where the formula used to calculate the amount owed was not defined clearly or not included in the lease agreement. If you want to pursue this option, you'll need to contact a lawyer. Not all courts agree about what "confusing" means in this context—the best way to find out how your local court has dealt with the issue is to speak to a lawyer who has experience with auto leases.

Loans for Which You Pledged Collateral Other Than a Motor Vehicle

If a personal loan or store agreement is secured—for example, you pledged a refrigerator or couch as collateral for your repayment on that item—the lender probably won't agree to reduce what you owe. Instead, it may threaten to send a truck over and take the property. Rarely do lenders repossess personal property other than motor vehicles, however, because appliances and furniture bring in little money at auctions. Thus, if you simply stop paying, the lender will probably sue you before grabbing your new couch.

If you propose something reasonable, the lender may extend your loan or rewrite it to reduce the monthly payments. This will keep the property from being repossessed and keep you from being sued.

Student Loans

Under certain circumstances, you may be able to cancel your obligation to repay your federally guaranteed student loans, defer your payments, or enter into a payment schedule that better fits your income. If you're in default, you may be able to get out of default and avoid a lawsuit, wage garnishment, or loss of your tax refund.

The student loan scheme is quite complex, depending on the type of loan you have and when you obtained it. Before taking action on your loan, you must understand what kind of loan it is. Your ability to negotiate with your lender, defer your payments, or possibly cancel your loan may depend on the type of loan you have.

There are three primary kinds of federally guaranteed student loans: campus-based loans, bank loans, and Department of Education–issued loans. Campus-based loans are called Perkins Loans or the older National Direct/Defense Student Loans (NDSLs). Bank loans are called Federal Family Education Loan Program (FFELP) loans and include Stafford Loans (previously called Guaranteed Student Loans (GSLs) or Federal Insured Student Loans (FISLs)), PLUS Loans (loans for parents), SLS Loans, and consolidation loans. Loans issued directly by the Department of Education are called

Direct Loans and include Stafford, PLUS, and consolidation loans.

If you can use any of the options covered in this section, you should: Don't just put off paying your loan. Agencies attempting to collect student loans are allowed to use extraordinary measures that aren't available for other types of collections, such as intercepting your tax refund.

How to Get More Information About Your Student Loans

You can find information about your student loans (including help figuring out what type of loans you have) through the National Student Loan Data System, at www.nslds.ed.gov (or call 800-433-3243). It will provide you with loan and grant amounts, outstanding balances, loan status, and disbursements.

If you've tried the above and still have trouble getting information, call the Student Loan Ombudsman toll-free, at 877-557-2575.

RESOURCE

Student loan information. You can find further information on student loans in *Funding Education Beyond High School: The Guide to Federal Financial Aid*, published by the U.S. Department of Education. You can obtain a copy from the Department of Education's Federal Student Aid Information Center (800-433-3243) or the Department of Education's website, http://studentaid.ed.gov. Also, check out the website of the Student Loan Borrower Assistance Program, www.studentloanborrowerassistance.org. This valuable site is packed with free information about types of student loans, repayment options, cancelling a loan, default, collections, and much more.

Canceling a Student Loan

Depending on the type of loan you have and when you obtained it, you may be able to cancel all or a portion of your loan—or even get a refund of money you already paid—under one of the following circumstances:

- The former student for whom the loan was taken has died.
- You become totally and permanently disabled.
- You received the loan after January 1, 1986, and your school closed before you could complete your program of study or you withdrew from school no more than 90 days before the school closed.
- The school falsely certified you as eligible for an FFELP loan you received after January 1, 1986, because you did not have a high school diploma when you enrolled, and the school did not properly test you to determine if you had the ability to benefit from the course (for example, the school did not properly time its entrance exam, did not properly score it, did not use an exam relevant to the course, did not use an approved exam, or improperly assisted you to pass the exam).
- The school falsely certified you as eligible for a loan received after January 1, 1986, because the student loan was the result of identity theft.
- The school falsely certified you as eligible for an FFELP loan received after January 1, 1986, because the school signed your loan application without your authorization.
- You left school and were entitled to a refund but never received the money.
- You teach in a Department of Education–approved school serving low-income students or in a designated teacher shortage area (other types of teacher cancellations are available for Perkins loans).
- You serve in the U.S. military in an area of hostility or imminent danger (partial cancellation for Perkins loans only).
- You're a full-time employee of a public or nonprofit agency providing services to low-income, high-risk children and their families (Perkins loans only).
- You're a full-time nurse or medical technician (Perkins loans only).
- You're a full-time law enforcement or corrections officer (Perkins loans only).
- You're a full-time staff member in a Head Start program (Perkins loans only).
- You're a Peace Corps or VISTA volunteer (Perkins loans only).

To discharge or cancel a student loan—or to determine whether you qualify to do so—call the holder of your loan or the Department of Education's FSA Collection Office at 800-621-3115. Be aware that your loan holder may not inform you of all the options available to you. For this reason, it pays to first learn about your options by reading *Funding Education Beyond High School* (see above). For more information on ways to cancel your loan, go to www.ed.gov/offices/OSFAP/DCS/loan. cancellation.discharge.html.

Obtaining a Deferment of Your Student Loan Payments

You may be able to defer (postpone) repayment of a federal student loan even if you are behind on your payments, as long as you aren't more than 270 days behind when you apply for a deferment (or more than six months behind when you apply for an unemployment deferment).

This section lists deferments only for loans disbursed after July 1, 1993. If you have loans disbursed at an earlier date, you can get more information from the Department of Education's website at www.ed.gov or by calling your loan holder.

You can request a deferment on any federal loan disbursed after July 1, 1993, if any of the following are true:

- You are enrolled in school at least half-time.
- You are enrolled in an approved graduate fellowship program or a rehabilitation program for the disabled.
- You are unable to find full-time employment.
- You are suffering from economic hardship.

For loans made after July 1, 2001, you can also get a deferment while you are on active military duty.

In addition, you can defer a Perkins loan for most of the reasons listed in "Canceling a Student Loan," above.

To obtain a deferment of a federal student loan, contact the current holder of your loan. If you don't know who currently holds your loan, contact the financial or educational institution you initially borrowed from. If that institution has sold your loan or sent it elsewhere, it will tell you.

Ask the holder of your loan to send you a deferment application form. The holder of your loan may require you to submit supporting documentation, such as periodic verifications of your job search if you obtain an unemployment deferment. Be sure to comply. Deferment forms are available on the Department of Education's website, www.ed.gov.

Obtaining a Forbearance of Your Student Loan Payments

If you don't qualify for a deferment but are facing hard times financially, your lender may still allow you to postpone payments or temporarily reduce them. An arrangement of this sort, called a "forbearance," also temporarily stops collection efforts Although forbearances are easier to obtain than deferments—you may be able to obtain a forbearance even if your loan is in default—they are less attractive because interest continues to accrue while you are not making payments, no matter what type of loan you have.

Lenders typically have the authority to grant forbearances in six-month increments for up to two years. There is no stated condition for qualifying—it's usually just up to the lender. Call your lender and ask.

Consolidating Your Student Loans

If you want to repay your loans but can't afford the payments and don't qualify for cancellation, deferment, or forbearance, you may be able to consolidate your loans.

When you consolidate, you lower your monthly payments by combining multiple loans into one packaged loan and extending your current repayment period. You may also be able to refinance several loans, or just one loan, at a lower interest rate. But be aware that if you extend your repayment period, you will increase the amount of money you pay in interest over the life of your loan—sometimes dramatically. Even so, consolidation is one way to keep your head above water and avoid default. And if you've already defaulted, consolidation can help you get back on track.

Requesting a Flexible Payment Option

If you have a Direct or FFELP Stafford loan, you can pay it back in any of the four ways listed below. If you have a Direct PLUS loan, you can pay it back in the first three ways listed below:
- the standard ten-year repayment schedule
- an extended repayment schedule—the length of your payback period depends on the amount of your loan,

from 12 years for loans under $10,000 to 30 years for loans over $60,000
- a graduated repayment schedule—you can pay off your loan in as many as 30 years by making lower payments in the early years of the loan and higher payments later, and
- an income-contingent repayment plan (for Direct loans) or an income-sensitive repayment plan (for FFELP loans)—your payments change each year based on the amount of your income, the amount of your student loan, and your family size.

Financial institutions are not obligated to offer extended, graduated, or income-contingent repayment plans, but many do so in order to remain competitive with the government direct lending program. While these payment options can offer much relief, using them can cost you a lot. For example, if you stretch your payments out for 20 or 30 years, you will wind up paying thousands—possibly tens of thousands—of dollars more in interest than you would have if you paid your loans off in ten years.

Many websites have calculators to help you figure out your monthly payments under different payment plans. Check out the calculators on the Department of Education's website at www.ed.gov. Many loan servicers also have online payment calculators.

Getting Out of Default

You can get out of default on any government loan if you make a certain number of payments under a "reasonable and affordable" payment plan and then rehabilitate the loan. This is how it works: You have the right to a payment plan that is reasonable and affordable based on your financial circumstances. If you make six consecutive timely payments under this plan, you will become eligible for new student loans and grants. Only enter into this payment arrangement if you can truly afford it. If you default, you won't get another chance to get out of default this way.

If you make nine payments on time within ten consecutive months, you will be able to "rehabilitate" your loan—meaning you'll no longer be in default.

Once you're out of default, you will have to repay the loan within ten years (unless you qualify for deferment or roll the loan into a consolidation loan). So, if you've been paying very small amounts under the reasonable and affordable payment plan, when you get out of default, your monthly payment amount may rise dramatically. If you can't afford the new amount, you should request one of the flexible repayment options described above.

You can find more information on handling defaulted loans at the Department of Education's student aid website, http://federalstudentaid.ed.gov. Select "Locate/Repay Your Federal Student Loans," then select the link for defaulted loans.

Insurance Policies

Most insurance policies have 30-day grace periods—that is, if your payment is due on the tenth of the month and you don't pay until the ninth of the following month, you won't lose your coverage. A few companies won't terminate your policy as long as you pay your premium within 60 days after it's due. If you don't pay within 60 days, your policy will surely be canceled.

If you want to keep your insurance coverage, contact your insurance agent. You can reduce the amount of your coverage or increase your deductible, thereby reducing your premiums. This can usually be done easily for auto, medical, dental, renters', life, and disability insurance. It will be harder for homeowners' insurance, because you'll probably have to get authorization from your mortgage lender, who won't want your house to be underinsured.

If you have a life insurance policy with a cash value—an amount of money building up that you'll receive if you cancel the policy before it pays out—you can usually apply the cash value toward your premiums. The company will treat the use of the cash value as a loan. Your policy's cash value won't decrease, but you are theoretically required to repay the money. (If you don't repay it, the proceeds your beneficiaries receive when you die will be reduced by the amount you borrowed.) Or, you can simply ask that the cash reserves be used to pay the premiums. This will reduce your cash value, but you won't have to repay anything.

Perhaps the best way to keep life insurance coverage while reducing the payments is to convert a whole or universal policy (with relatively high premiums and a cash value build-up) into a term policy (with low premiums and no cash value.) You may lose a little of the existing cash value as a conversion fee, but it may be worthwhile if you get a policy that costs far less to maintain.

Doctor, Dentist, Lawyer, and Accountant Bills

Many doctors, dentists, lawyers, and accountants are accommodating if you communicate how difficult your financial problems are and try to get their sympathy. They may accept partial payments, reduce the total bill, drop interest or late fees, and delay sending bills to collection agencies.

> **CAUTION**
>
> **Don't sign up for a "health finance" plan.** Some credit card companies give doctors and dentists "scripts" to use when talking to patients about paying for health care. Patients are asked to either pay cash up front for treatment or to sign up for the credit card company's high interest health finance plan. Avoid this credit trap by trying to arrange a payment plan directly with your health care provider, not with a credit card company or other third party.

Credit Card Bills

If you can't pay your credit card bill (including a department store or gasoline card bill), contact the credit card company. Most will insist that you make the minimum monthly payment, usually 1% to 4% of the outstanding bill, but in no event less than $15 to $20. If you convince the company that your financial situation is bleak, it may reduce your payments to a smaller percentage of the outstanding balance. And, if you have an excellent payment history, the company may let you skip a month or two altogether.

> **CAUTION**
>
> **Pay your credit card bills on time.** Paying late can result in a hefty late fee (sometimes $39 or more), an increase in the interest rate on your account (the new rate can be as high as 32% or more), and a negative entry on your credit report. All of these actions can cause other creditors to increase their interest rates as well. If you pay less than the full amount owed, you incur more interest charges. This is a strategy you should employ only temporarily. Otherwise, your balance will increase faster than you will be able to pay it off. You may even wind up with a balance that's higher than your credit limit, resulting in even more fees.

While you are paying off your balance, some credit card companies will help by waiving late fees. It's almost impossible to get a credit card company to reduce interest that has already accumulated. Some will stop adding future interest charges, however, if you get assistance from a reputable credit or debt counseling agency. (See Appendix A.) The company may also freeze your credit line—that is, not let you incur any more charges—if you pay less than the minimum.

Ask the company to report your payments to a credit reporting agency as on time while you pay off your balance. If you keep to the new schedule, the credit card company shouldn't report the debt as past due.

If you can't pay a charge card bill—such as an American Express Green Card—you must approach the creditor differently. Charge cards are much less common than credit cards. Normally, you are required to pay off your entire charge card balance when your bill arrives. If you don't, you'll get one month in which no interest is charged. After that, you'll be charged interest in the neighborhood of 20%. Call the charge card company and ask that you be given a monthly repayment plan for paying off the bill. Offer to pay only what you can afford. But remember, if you pay only a very small amount, interest will accumulate and your balance will go up faster than you can pay it off. The company usually doesn't report this arrangement to credit reporting agencies if you pay the monthly amount you agreed to.

If You Dispute a Credit Card Bill

There are several reasons you might dispute a credit card bill. There might be a simple math error on the bill, such as a charge for $550 rather than $55. There might be changes that you made but don't think you should have to pay—for example, because the item you bought didn't work properly. Or, if your credit card information was stolen, unauthorized charges might appear on your bill.

Credit Card Billing Errors

If you find an error in your credit card statement, immediately write to the company that issued the card. Send a separate letter; don't just scribble a note on the bill. The credit card company must receive your letter within 60 days after it mailed the bill to you. You can use Form F-5, Error on Credit Card Bill, in Appendix B or on the CD-ROM. Give your name, your account number, an explanation of the error, and the amount involved. Also enclose copies of supporting documents, such as receipts showing the correct amount of the charge. Send the letter to the particular address designated by the creditor for this purpose. Check the back of your statement for this address or call the company to get it. You can withhold the portion of the required payment that you dispute, including finance charges, but you must pay the portion that you do not dispute.

The credit card company must acknowledge receipt of your letter within 30 days, unless it corrects the error within that time. The card issuer must, within two billing cycles (but in no event more than 90 days after it receives your letter), correct the error or explain why it believes the amount to be correct. If your bank issued the card and you have authorized automatic payments from your deposit account, the bank cannot deduct the disputed amount or related finance charges from your account while the dispute is pending if it receives your billing error notice at least three business days before the automatic payment date.

What Is a Billing Error?

"Billing errors" include:

- an extension of credit not clearly identified on your bill
- a math error
- a charge on your bill for which you need more information
- failure to mail you a periodic statement
- an extension of credit to someone who was not authorized to use your card
- an extension of credit for property or services that were never delivered to you
- the company's failure to credit your account properly, and
- an extension of credit for items that you returned because they were defective or different from what you ordered.

During the two-billing-cycle/90-day period, the card issuer cannot report the disputed amount as delinquent to credit reporting agencies or other creditors. Likewise, the card issuer cannot threaten or actually take any collection action against you for the disputed amount. But it can include the disputed amount on your monthly billing statements. And it can apply the amount in dispute to your credit limit, thereby lowering the total credit available to you. The card issuer can also add interest to your bill on the amount you dispute, but if the issuer later agrees you were correct, it must drop the interest accrued.

If the card issuer sends you an explanation but doesn't correct the error and you are not satisfied with its reason, you have ten days to respond. Send a second letter explaining why you still refuse to pay. If the card company then reports your account as delinquent to a credit bureau or anyone else, it must also state that you dispute that you owe the money. At the same time, the issuer must send you the name and address of each credit bureau and anyone else to whom it reports the delinquency. When the dispute is resolved, the issuer must send a notice to everyone to whom it has reported the delinquency. If the card issuer doesn't comply with any of these error resolution procedures, it must credit you the amount you disputed, plus the interest on that charge, up to a total of $50, even if the bill was correct.

Disputes About Credit Card Purchases

If you believe you shouldn't have to pay a charge on your bill—for example, because the item you bought was defective or you didn't order the item listed—you can often withhold payment if the seller refuses to replace, repair, or otherwise correct the problem. (15 U.S.C. § 1661i.) If you dispute a charge because an item wasn't delivered as ordered or you refused to accept it because it was defective, you could also dispute the charge as a billing error, following the rules described in "Credit Card Billing Errors," above, if you haven't missed the 60-day deadline.

You can withhold only the balance on the disputed item or service that is still unpaid when you first notify the seller or card issuer of the problem. If you already paid part of the bill, the amount you paid is applied first to late charges, then finance charges, then your purchases, starting with the oldest. So, if you owe a lot of fees and charges, you may not have paid off much—if any—of the disputed amount.

There are some conditions you must meet in order to use this law. First, you must make a good-faith effort to resolve the dispute with the seller. Second, you must explain to the credit card company, in writing, why you are withholding payment. Third, if you used a Visa, MasterCard, or other card not issued by the seller, you can refuse to pay only if (1) the purchase cost more than $50, and (2) you made the purchase in the state where you live or, if you live in a different state, within 100 miles of your home. (Your state's law determines whether a purchase you made from home by telephone or on the Internet is considered a purchase made in your state or in the state where the merchant is located.)

These distance and amount limitations don't apply if the credit card was issued by the seller (such as a department store card issued by the store), the seller controls the card issuer or vice versa, or the seller obtained your order by mailing you an advertisement in which the card issuer participated, urging you to use the card to make the purchase.

If you conclude that you are entitled to withhold payment, write a letter to the credit card company explaining why you aren't going to pay. Describe the steps you took to resolve the problem with the merchant. Before you mail the letter, look at the fine print on the back of your bill or call the credit card company to find out where to send it. Credit card companies have special addresses they use for this type of correspondence. If you don't send it to the correct address, the company can disregard your letter. Use Form F-6, Dispute Credit Card Bill, in Appendix B or on the CD-ROM. And don't forget to keep a copy of the letter for your records.

CAUTION

Check your credit report following a billing dispute or error. Despite laws designed to protect consumers, a credit card issuer may negligently report an outstanding balance it removed from your card, fail to report that you dispute a charge, or fail to report that the dispute is resolved. Be sure to check your credit file. (See Chapter 4.)

If Someone Uses Your Credit Card Without Your Permission

Unauthorized credit card use—when someone steals your credit card number or otherwise uses it without your permission—is a growing problem, due in part to the huge volume of credit card business transacted over the phone and Internet. Fortunately, federal law offers some protection if this happens to you.

Your liability for unauthorized use of your credit card is limited to $50. So, if someone steals your card and uses it, your credit card lender cannot require you to pay more than $50 of those charges. Some credit card issuers waive the $50, especially for Internet transactions.

You may be required to pay up to $50 only if the credit card was actually presented to the merchant. If the purchase was made by telephone or on the Internet—in other words, the card was not actually presented to the merchant, but only a number was provided—you have no liability at all, not even for the first $50 worth of charges.

It is very important to report unauthorized credit card use as soon as you know about it. If you call before any charges are incurred, you are not liable for anything—not even $50. If there is an unauthorized charge on your bill, you can dispute the charge the same way you dispute a billing error.

! CAUTION

Be careful using debit cards. The protections discussed above don't apply to charges made with debit cards. You may be liable for $500 in unauthorized transfers if you don't notify the card issuer within two business days after you realize your card is missing. (If the card wasn't actually presented to a merchant but was instead used by phone or on the Internet, you aren't liable for the first $500.) You may be liable for unlimited loss if (1) you gave your debit card and PIN to someone who drains your account (unless you instructed the card issuer not to honor that person's transactions) or (2) you didn't notify the card issuer that an unauthorized transfer appears on your statement within 60 days after it was mailed, and providing proper notice could have prevented the loss. Some card issuers, and some states, cap your potential loss at $50.

Use the Form Negotiation Letters Provided in This Book

Negotiating with your creditors to request a reduction, extension, or other repayment program can be somewhat intimidating. Fortunately, sending a short letter can simplify the process considerably. Appendix B and the CD-ROM include form letters you can send to creditors. Use these to confirm telephone conversations or to start the negotiation process. Be sure to keep a copy of whatever you send.

At the top of the form you're using, above the "Attn: Collections Department" line, type or write the creditor's name and address. Most items on the forms are self-explanatory. At the bottom, be sure to sign your name and provide the address that appears on your bill. If you are asking the creditor to get in touch with you, include your home phone number.

Usually, before you send any money, it is better to reach an agreement, in writing, with the creditor to accept less that what you owe as payment in full or to change the timing or amount of your payments. You can use Forms F-7 and F-8 for this purpose.

In some situations, you can settle a debt for less than the full amount you owe even if the creditor hasn't already agreed to it. You can use Forms F-15 (for use outside of California) and F-16 and F-17 (for use in California) to send a check with your letter if you dispute the amount owed but haven't reached an agreement with the creditor to pay less. If you don't dispute the amount you owe and you want the creditor to accept less as payment in full but you haven't reached an agreement with the creditor for this arrangement, you can use Form F-18 to send a check for the lesser amount.

Before using Forms F-15, F-16 and F-17, or F-18, however, consider using Form F-7 or F-8 to seek an agreement before you send any payment. Although the law says that you won't owe any more money if the creditor cashes a check you send as payment in full, the creditor might insist that you still owe money anyway. This means you'll still get collection calls, and your credit report won't reflect that you've paid the debt. In this situation, even if you're in the right, you may have to get an attorney to enforce the law.

If you use Forms F-8, F-9, F-10, F-11, or F-12, you will need to state reasons why you can't make full payment. Here are the kinds of things creditors and lenders look for:

- a job layoff, reduction in hours, sporadic employment, or pay cut, coupled with a good-faith effort to find work or increase your income
- a large and unexpected tax assessment
- a divorce or separation resulting in more bills you have to pay or your ex-spouse's failure to pay bills the court ordered him or her to pay
- a permanent or temporary disability— disabilities may include a heart attack, stroke, or cancer, or something less drastic like repetitive motion syndrome, or
- inadequate medical insurance coverage following a major illness or accident.

Deal With Creditors on Past Due Accounts

It's important to know whether the person trying to collect your past due debt works for the business or person who first extended you credit (the creditor) or for a company or lawyer hired by a creditor to collect the debt (a collection agency). A creditor who sets up a separate office (operated under a different name) to collect its own debts also qualifies as a collection agency. Depending on who is trying to collect, you have different legal rights and may want to employ different strategies. If any of your debts are being pursued by a collection agency, read "Deal With Collection Agencies," below.

If you have past due accounts, you may be able to take care of the debts and start repairing your credit. Here are two requests you can make to a creditor using Form F-7, in Appendix B or on the CD-ROM:

- Ask that an unpaid debt and negative information in your credit file associated with the debt be removed from your credit file in exchange for full or partial payment. Creditors rarely withdraw reporting, but you may be able to convince a debt collector to do so. If so, be sure to get written confirmation from the creditor or collector that it will acknowledge the debt as paid in full when you pay the agreed amount, and that it will submit a Universal Data Form (a standard form creditors use to report to credit reporting agencies), deleting the "account/trade" line.

• If the creditor puts you on a new schedule for repaying the debt, consider asking the creditor to "re-age" your account, which makes the current month the first repayment month and stops showing late payments. Sometimes, the creditor won't re-age the account until you make two or three monthly payments first.

Think carefully before asking a creditor to re-age the account, especially if it's been reported as delinquent for some time. Re-aging means that the account will appear on your credit report for seven years after the repayment date, rather than seven years after the earlier delinquency date. Some consumer advocates argue that re-aging an account is a bad idea for this reason. On the other hand, some debt management plans favor re-aging because the account appears as current on the credit report.

Most creditors will not re-age accounts or remove negative marks, but it never hurts to ask. Contact the creditor's collections or customer service department and make an offer. Tell whomever you speak to that you cannot afford to pay more, but that you'd really like to pay a good portion of the bill. Explain your financial problems—be bleak, but never lie. Get the creditor's agreement in writing (send your own confirming letter if need be) before sending any money.

When negotiating, it's helpful to know where you are in the collection process. Collection efforts almost always begin with past due invoices or letters. One day, you open your mail box and find a polite letter from a creditor reminding you that you seemed to have overlooked the company's most recent bill. "Perhaps it's already in the mail. If so, please accept our thanks. If not, we'd appreciate prompt payment," the letter or invoice states.

This "past due" form letter is the kind that almost every creditor sends to a customer with an overdue account. If you ignore it, you'll get a second one, also automatically sent. In this letter, most creditors remain friendly but want to know what the problem is. "If you have some special reason for withholding payment, please let us know. We are here to help." Some creditors also suspend your credit at this point; the only way to get it back is to send a payment.

If you don't answer the second letter, you'll probably receive three to five more form letters. Each will get slightly firmer. By the last letter, expect a threat: "If we do not receive payment within ten days, your credit privileges will be canceled. Your account will be sent to a collection agency and your delinquency will be reported to a credit reporting agency. You could face a lawsuit, wage attachment, or lien on your property."

After you've received a series of collection letters, you may conclude that you no longer have leverage to negotiate. This is not so: You always have leverage, because you have what they want—money.

Appendix B and the CD-ROM include several form letters you can use to send to creditors for your past due accounts. The forms are described in the chart "Forms For Negotiating With Your Creditors," below. Find the form that fits your situation and send it off.

Tips on Negotiating With Creditors

You are most vulnerable at this time. Be sure you truly understand any new loan terms and can afford to make the payments required by a new agreement.

Here are some tips that will help you in your negotiations:

- Get outside help negotiating if you need or want it.
- If your request is turned down, ask to speak to a supervisor.
- Adopt a plan and stick with it. If you owe $1,100 but can't afford to pay more than $600, don't agree to pay more.
- Try to identify the creditor's bottom line. For example, if a bank offers to waive two months' interest if you pay the principal due on your loan, perhaps the bank will actually waive three or four months of interest. If you need to, push it.
- Don't split the difference. If you offer a low amount to settle a debt and the creditor proposes that you split the difference between a higher demand and your offer, don't agree to it. Treat the split-the-difference number as a new top and propose an amount between that and your original offer.
- Don't be intimidated by your creditors. If they think you can pay $100, they will insist that $100 is the lowest amount they can accept. Don't believe them. It's fine to hang up and call back a day later. Some of the best negotiations take weeks.
- Try to settle with a lump sum. Many creditors will settle for less than the total debt if you pay in a lump sum, but will insist on 100% if you pay over time.
- Get a signed release. If you settle for less than the full amount owed, make sure the creditor signs a release stating that your partial payment excuses you from the remaining balance. (See Forms F-7 and F-8.)
- Be careful not to give up more than you get. A creditor may waive interest, reduce your payments, or let you skip a payment and tack it on at the end. But tread cautiously. The creditor is likely to ask for something in exchange, such as getting a cosigner (who will be liable for the debt if you don't pay, even if you erase the debt in bankruptcy), waiving the statute of limitations (the number of years the lender has to sue you if you stop making payments), paying higher interest, paying for a longer period, giving a security interest in your house or car, or waiving your right to sue for illegal conduct by the creditor in the initial transaction. If you're asked to sign anything you don't understand or have concerns about, don't sign it. First, consult with a credit counselor or lawyer.

\multicolumn{3}{c}{**Forms for Negotiating With Creditors**}
No.	Form Name	Use if …
F-7	Offer (Reduced) Lump Sum Payment	You want the creditor to agree to accept a reduced amount, remove negative information from your credit report, or both, if you pay a lump sum.
F-8	Offer Payment Schedule to Pay Off (Reduced) Debt	You want the creditor to accept installment payments to pay off the debt (or to accept a reduced amount paid in installments as payment in full) and to improve the information in your credit report.
F-9	Request Short-Term Lower Payments	You need a few months of reduced payments but then intend to resume full payments.
F-10	Request Long-Term Lower Payments	You need to make reduced payments indefinitely.
F-11	Request to Pay Nothing Short-Term	You can't make any payments for a few months but intend to resume full payments shortly.
F-12	Request to Pay Nothing Long-Term	You've concluded that you won't be able to make any payments for an indefinite period.
F-13	Request Rewrite of Loan Terms	You want the lender to rewrite the loan to permanently reduce the amount of each payment.
F-14	Offer to Give Secured Property Back	You want the lender to take back the collateral and forgive any remaining balance you owe on the debt.
F-15	Cashing Check Constitutes Payment in Full on Disputed Amount (Outside of California)	You dispute the amount you owe and want to send the creditor a check for part of the debt with a conspicuous notation, "Cashing this check constitutes payment in full." Before using this remedy, you should consider using Form-7 or Form-8 instead, to get the creditor to agree to accept less, for the reasons explained in "Use the Form Negotiation Letters Provided in This Book," above.
F-16 & F-17	Cashing Check Constitutes Payment in Full on Disputed Amount (California)	You live in California, you dispute the amount you owe, and you want to send the creditor a check for part of the debt with a conspicuous notation, "Cashing this check constitutes payment in full." Before using this remedy, you should consider using Form-7 or Form-8 instead, to get the creditor to agree to accept less, for the reasons explained in "Use the Form Negotiation Letters Provided in This Book," above.
		If you decide to use this remedy, you must send two letters. The first (Form F-16) tells the creditor that you intend to send a check for a lesser amount in full satisfaction of the claim. To do this, the amount of the claim must be uncertain, you must dispute the amount of the claim in

	Forms for Negotiating With Creditors (cont'd)	
No.	**Form Name**	**Use if ...**
		good faith, and you must offer the check in good faith as full satisfaction of the claim. State all of this in the first letter (Form F-16). Then, send a second letter (Form F-17) along with the check within a reasonable amount of time after the first; two weeks is probably reasonable, depending on the situation. When you send the check, write conspicuously on the front of it and in your cover letter that the check is offered as full satisfaction of the claim.
		If the creditor has designated a particular person, office, or place for communications about disputed debts (often indicated in a billing statement), you must send your letters there or to the proper collection agent working for the creditor if you are no longer dealing with the creditor company itself.
		If the creditor cashes the check and all other conditions have been met, the claim against you is discharged. However, if the creditor did not designate a particular person, office, or place to send letters about disputed debts, and repays you within 90 days after cashing your check, your letters and check do not discharge your debt.
F-18	Cashing Check Constitutes Release of All Claims	You don't dispute the amount you owe but want the creditor to accept less as payment in full and to release you, your spouse, and anyone else liable on the debt from having to pay any more. You should write conspicuously on the check, "Cashing this check constitutes payment in full." Before using this remedy, you should consider using Form F-7 or Form F-8 instead to get the creditor to agree to accept less, for the reasons explained in "Use the Form Negotiation Letters Provided in This Book," above.
F-19	Inform Creditor of Judgment Proof Status	You have no property your creditors can take to pay what you owe, even if they sue you or you file for bankruptcy. You are judgment proof if your only source of income is exempt government benefits or disability payments, you have little or no equity in a house or car, and you have limited personal property. Remember, different rules apply to student loan debts: Even if you are judgment proof, a creditor may still be able to collect. See "Student Loans," above, for more information.

No.	Form Name	Use if ...
F-20	Inform Creditor of Plan to File for Bankruptcy	You intend to file for bankruptcy. Don't incur any more charges on the account after you send this letter. If you do, you won't be able to erase those debts in your bankruptcy case. The creditor will claim that you never intended to pay them because you knew you were going to file for bankruptcy and try to get them wiped out.

Forms for Negotiating With Creditors (cont'd)

If the creditor rejects your proposal or wants more evidence that you are genuinely unable to pay, consider contacting a non-profit credit or debt counseling agency. (See Appendix A for information on finding one.)

If the debt is quite large or one of many, consider hiring a lawyer to write a second letter asking for additional time. The lawyer won't say anything different from what you would, but a lawyer's stationery carries clout. And it may be especially worth the few hundred dollars it will cost if you have many outstanding debts and need substantial help. When a creditor learns that a lawyer is in the picture, the creditor may be willing to compromise, assuming that you'll file for bankruptcy otherwise.

Unless you're judgment proof or plan to file for bankruptcy, the best overall advice is not to ignore the debt or try to hide from the creditor. Usually, the longer you put off resolving the issue, the worse the situation and consequences will become. Whether you negotiate directly with the creditor or obtain a lawyer's assistance, the best strategy almost always is to engage with the creditor.

> **CAUTION**
>
> **Be specific with the lawyer about what you want done.** If you're not clear with the lawyer that you want him or her only to write a letter to your creditors on your behalf, the lawyer may do much more and send you a bill for work you didn't authorize and can't afford. Ask for a written statement showing what the lawyer will charge for each service to be provided.

Deal With Collection Agencies

If you ignored (or didn't receive) the creditor's letters and phone calls, or you failed to make payments as promised on a new repayment schedule, your bill was probably turned over to a collection agency.

In dealing with collection agencies, remember this: A person who works at a collection agency does not have your best interest at heart. *A collection agent wants your money.* To get it, the agent may ask you to confide in him or her regarding your personal problems. The agent may claim to be trying to save you from ruining your credit or pose as your friend and counselor. Don't believe it: A collection agent doesn't really care about your problems or your credit rating. His or her only goal is to get you to send money.

By taking some time to understand how collection agencies operate, you'll know how to respond when they contact you. Consider the following facts about collection agencies.

A collection agency takes its cues from the creditor that hired it. The collection agency can't sue you without the creditor's authorization, although that authorization is routinely granted. Similarly, if the creditor insists that the agency collect 100% of the debt, the agency cannot accept less from you, although it can agree to accept installment payments. To reduce the total amount you pay, the collection agency must get the creditor's okay, or you'll have to contact the creditor yourself.

Contacting the creditor directly can often be to your benefit, because the creditor has broader discretion in negotiating than the collection agency does. Unfortunately, however, some creditors won't deal with you after your debt has been sent to a collection agency unless you raise a legitimate dispute with the creditor or make three consecutive monthly payments to the collection agency first. Even if you don't have a dispute, try negotiating with the creditor before negotiating with a collection agency. Send Form F-21, Request Direct Negotiation With Creditor, in Appendix B or on the CD-ROM, to the collection agency and send a copy to the creditor.

A collection agent will try to contact you very soon after the creditor hires the agency. Professional debt collectors know that the earlier they strike, the higher the chance of collecting. For example, if an account is three months overdue, bill collectors typically have a 75% chance of collecting it. If it's six months late, the chances of collecting drop to 50%. And, if the bill's been owed for more than a year, collectors have only a one in four chance of recovering the debt.

A collection agency usually keeps between 25% and 60% of what it collects. The older the account, the higher the agency's fee. Sometimes, the agency charges per letter it writes or phone call it places—usually about 50¢ per letter or $1 per call. Thus, some collection agencies are very aggressive about contacting debtors.

If you're contacted by a collection agency, you can delay collection efforts if you raise legitimate questions about the debt. For example, if you question the accuracy of the balance owed or the quality of the goods you received, the agency will have to verify the information with the creditor. If you raise a legitimate concern, the collection agency will send the debt back to the creditor—collection agencies don't pursue debtors who have a legitimate beef with creditors. Getting the debt sent back to the creditor should remove any "sent to collection agency" notation in your credit file; ask the creditor to instruct the credit reporting agency to remove this notation.

Use Form F-22, Dispute Amount of Bill or Quality of Goods or Services Received, in Appendix B and on the CD-ROM, to raise a legitimate concern about the amount of a bill or the quality of goods or services received.

Getting a Collection Agency Off Your Back

You have the legal right to tell a collection agency to leave you alone. Simply write to the collection agency and tell it to cease all communications with you. Use Form F-23, Collection Agency: Cease All Contact, in Appendix B and on the CD-ROM. By law, the agency must then stop contacting you, except to tell you that:

- collection efforts against you have ended, or
- the collection agency or creditor will invoke a specific remedy against you, such as suing you.

If a collection agency contacts you to tell you that it intends to invoke a specific remedy, it must truly plan to do so. The agent cannot simply write to you several times saying "We're going to sue you" and then drop the matter.

You also can buy some time by requesting information from the collection agency. The collection agency must send you a so-called "validation notice" within five days of its first contact with you. The validation notice tells you the amount of the debt and the name of the creditor. It also says that you may dispute the validity of the debt or part of it within 30 days after receiving the notice; that if you don't, the agency will assume the debt is valid; that if you do dispute the debt or part of it, the agency will send you a verification of the debt; and that the agency will send you the name and address of the original creditor if you request it.

You can buy some time by sending the agency a written request for any of the following information within 30 days after you receive the validation notice:

- The name and address of the original creditor. Your request can say, "Please send me the name and address of the original creditor who claims that I owe this debt."
- Verification of the existence and amount of the debt. Your request can say, "I dispute the debt," or "I dispute this portion of the debt: _____ ."
- Verification of the existence and amount of the judgment on which the claim is based. Your request can say, "I dispute the debt represented by the judgment and request verification of the debt's existence and amount."

If you request any of this information, the agency must stop efforts to collect the debt, or any part that you dispute, until it mails you the information.

Negotiating With a Collection Agency

Although most creditors initially insist that collection agencies collect 100% of a debt, if you make a sweet enough offer, the collection agency may convince the creditor to accept less. Often, the creditor has all but given up on you and will be thrilled if the collection agency can collect anything. Knowing that, keep in mind the following:

- The collection agency didn't lay out the money initially. It doesn't care if you owe $250 or $2,500. It just wants to maximize its return, which is usually a percentage of what it collects.

- Time is money. Every time the collection agency writes or calls you, it spends money. The agency has a strong interest in getting you to pay as much as you can as fast as possible. It has less interest in collecting 100% of what you owe over five years.

Offering a Lump Sum Settlement

A collection agency has more incentive to settle with you if you can pay all at once. If you owe $500 and offer $300 on the spot to settle the matter, the agency can take its fee, pass the rest on to the creditor (who writes off the difference on its tax return as a business loss), and close its books.

If you decide to offer a lump sum, understand that no two collection agencies accept the same amount to settle a debt. Some want 75%–80%. Others—especially if they are the second or third agency to try to collect your debt—will take 50¢ or less on the dollar. But be careful. Once the agency sees you are willing to pay something, it will assume it can talk you into paying more. Of course, this is a good reason to start by offering less than you know you can pay.

If you can get the debt removed from your credit report in exchange for paying a little more, it may be worth it. But never agree to more than you can afford. And don't let the collection agency know where that money is coming from. If you mention a parent, friend, or distant relative who "may be able to help you out," the collection agent may think you can come up with the entire amount.

Whatever you agree to over the phone, be sure to send a confirming letter and keep a copy for your records. The letter should state that the creditor is accepting the lump sum payment in settlement of the entire amount that you owe. You could use Form F-7 or F-8 by choosing the check boxes that apply and substituting your agreement for the last sentence. For example, "This letter confirms the agreement of October 2, 2008, in which you agreed to accept $565 as payment in full for my outstanding bill and to delete this debt from my credit reports." Or, you could use Form F-15 and add your agreement as a final sentence before you sign the letter.

Pay by cashier's check or money order. Paying by personal check is less desirable, because the agency will know your account number. If you pay in cash, get a signed receipt and keep it for at least four years. Don't pay the *original creditor* unless the agency instructs you to do so in writing.

Offering to Make Payments

If you offer to make monthly payments, the agency has little incentive to compromise for less than the full amount. It still must chase you for payment, and statistics show that many debtors stop paying after a month or two. If you succeed in convincing the creditor (through the collection agency) to remove the "past due" notation in your credit report in exchange for paying off the debt or to re-age your account in agreement for paying under a new schedule (see "Deal With Creditors on Past Due Accounts," above), remember that the past due notation goes back into your file as soon as you miss a payment under your new agreement.

But if you have no choice—you simply can't afford a lump sum—offer installments. If the creditor (through the collection agency) won't remove the negative credit report notation right away, get back in touch after you've made six months of payments and again ask them to remove the notation. State that the negative marks are keeping you from getting good credit, a place to live, a good job, or anything else you've been denied, and that with better credit/place to live/job, you will be more secure and better able to pay off the debt. Be sure to keep a copy of the letter for your records.

> CAUTION
> **Don't offer more than you can afford.** Make sure you can afford any lump sum payment or installment arrangement that you offer. And be sure that making these payments won't keep you from paying higher-priority debts (like your mortgage).

When the Collection Agency Gives Up

If collection efforts by the collection agency fail, the creditor and agency will put their heads together and decide whether or not to pass your debt on to an attorney for collection. They will consider the following:

- the likelihood of winning
- the likelihood of collecting—whether you are currently employed or apt to become employed or have other assets from which the creditor could collect (such as a bank account or a house on which the creditor could record a lien)
- whether the contract requires you to pay lawyer's fees (most loan agreements and credit contracts do)—which means the collection agency can tack its lawyer's fee onto the judgment against you, and
- whether or not you recently filed for bankruptcy (you may have to wait eight years to file again).

Illegal Debt Collection Practices

The federal Fair Debt Collections Practices Act (FDCPA) prohibits a collection agency from engaging in many kinds of activities. (15 U.S.C. §§ 1692 and following.) If a collection agency violates the law, you have the right to sue the agency. If the creditor that hired the agency was involved in the unlawful conduct, you may also be able to sue the creditor. If the behavior is truly outrageous, the creditor may waive the debt and remove the negative marks from your credit report in exchange for your agreement not to sue.

Under the FDCPA, a collection agency cannot legally engage in any of the following activities.

Communications with third parties. With a few exceptions, a collection agent cannot contact other people except to locate you. When contacting other people, the agent must state his or her name and that he or she is confirming or correcting location information about you. The agent cannot:

- give the collection agency's name, unless asked
- state that you owe a debt, or
- contact the person more than once unless the person requests it or the agent believes the person's first response was wrong or incomplete.

There are a few exceptions to this general rule. Collectors are allowed to contact:

- your attorney. If the collector knows you are represented by an attorney, it must talk only to the attorney, not you, unless you give it permission to contact you, or your attorney doesn't respond to the collector's communications.
- a credit reporting agency, and
- the original creditor.

Collectors are also allowed to contact your spouse, your parents (only if you are a minor), and your codebtors. But collectors cannot contact these people if you have already told them (in writing) to stop contacting you.

Communications with you. A collection agent cannot contact you:

- at an unusual or inconvenient time or place—the debt collector must assume that calls before 8 a.m. and after 9 p.m. are inconvenient unless the collector knows otherwise, or
- at work, if the collector knows that your employer prohibits you from

receiving collections calls at work. If you are contacted at work, tell the collector that your boss prohibits such calls.

Harassment or abuse. A collection agent cannot engage in conduct meant to harass, oppress, or abuse you. The agent cannot:

- use or threaten to use violence or harm you, another person, or your or another person's reputation or property
- use obscene, profane, or abusive language
- publish your name as a person who doesn't pay bills, such as in a "deadbeats" list
- list your debt for sale to the public
- call you repeatedly, or
- place telephone calls to you or any other person without identifying him- or herself.

False or misleading representations. A collection agent cannot:

- claim to be a law enforcement officer, suggest that he or she is connected with the government, or send you a document that looks like it's from a court or government agency
- falsely represent the amount you owe, the character or legal status of the debt, or the amount of compensation the agent will receive
- falsely claim to be an attorney or send you a document that looks like it's from a lawyer
- communicate false credit information, including failing to tell someone you dispute a debt
- use a false business name

- claim to be employed by a credit bureau, unless the collection agency and the credit bureau are the same company, or
- threaten to take action that he or she does not intend to take or cannot take.

Unfair practices. A collection agent cannot engage in any unfair or outrageous method to collect a debt. Specifically, the agent cannot:

- add interest, fees, or charges not authorized in the original agreement or by state law
- solicit a postdated check for the purpose of threatening you with criminal prosecution
- accept a check postdated by more than five days unless the agent notifies you between three and ten days in advance of when it will be deposited
- deposit a postdated check prior to the date on the check, or
- call you collect or otherwise cause you to incur communications charges.

If a Collection Agency Violates the Law

More than a few collection agencies engage in illegal practices when attempting to collect debts. Low-income and non-English speaking debtors are especially vulnerable. Some collectors send fake legal papers and visit debtors pretending to be sheriffs. The collectors tell debtors to pay immediately or threaten to take the debtors' personal possessions. Other collectors use vulgarity and profanity to threaten debtors. Another favorite tactic is to harass the debtor's parents or adult children.

If a collection agent violates the law—be it a large or small violation—complain loud and clear. If you're loud enough about the abuse you suffered—and you've got a witness backing you up—you have a chance to get the whole debt canceled in exchange for dropping the matter. Use Form F-24, Complaint About Collection Agency Harassment, in Appendix B and on the CD-ROM, to complain about a collection agency.

Here are some suggestions of where to send your complaint letter:

- **The creditor.** The creditor may be disturbed by the collection agency's tactics and concerned about its own reputation.
- **The Federal Trade Commission.** See Chapter 4 for addresses and phone numbers.
- **Your state consumer protection office.** See Appendix A.

You also have the right to sue a collection agency for harassment and for violation of the FDCPA. You can represent yourself in small claims court or hire an attorney; you can recover attorney's fees and court costs if you win. You're entitled to any actual damages (including pain and suffering) and, even if you didn't suffer damages, up to $1,000 for any FDCPA violation. You might also get punitive damages if the collector's conduct was particularly horrible. To win, you'll probably need to have a witness and to produce documentation of repeated abusive behavior. If the collector calls five times in one day, and then you never hear from him or her again, for example, you probably don't have a case.

Some attorneys specialize in debt collection abuse cases. For a list of consumer-oriented lawyers, see the National Association of Consumer Advocates website, www.naca.net.

Tax Consequences of Forgiven Loans

Some of the strategies in this chapter might result a creditor's agreeing to forgive part of what you owe. Be advised, however, that this could result in a larger tax bill. You might owe money to the IRS if you settle a debt with a creditor or the creditor writes off money you owe (that is, the creditor stops trying to collect, declares the debt uncollectible, and reports it as a tax loss to the IRS). Debts subject to this rule include money you owe after a home foreclosure, property repossession, or default on a credit card bill.

Any bank, credit union, savings and loan, finance company, credit card company, other financial institution, or federal government agency that forgives or writes off $600 or more of the principal of a debt (the amount not attributable to fees or interest) must send you and the IRS a Form 1099-C at the end of the year. These forms are for reporting income, which means you must report that amount on your tax return, and the IRS will consider it part of your income on which you must pay tax.

Even if the financial institution issues a Form 1099-C, however, you may not have to count the forgiven amount as income. Here are some examples of exceptions that may apply:

- A mortgage to buy, build, or substantially improve your principal home, or the part of a refinancing that paid the amount still owed for that debt, was partly or wholly forgiven in 2007 through 2012, through restructuring or foreclosure. This exception applies only to mortgages with a balance of less than $2 million if you file singly or file jointly with your spouse (the limit is $1 million if you are married and file individually).
- A nonbusiness debt was canceled before 2007 as a result of Hurricane Katrina (see IRS Publication 525, *Taxable and Nontaxable Income*, for details).
- A student loan was canceled because you worked in a profession and for an employer as promised when you took out the loan (see IRS Publication 525 for details).
- The canceled debt would have been deductible if you had paid it.
- The cancellation or write-off of the debt is intended as a gift (this would be unusual).
- You discharged the debt in Chapter 11 bankruptcy.

You also don't have to pay tax on the forgiven debt if you were insolvent before the creditor agreed to waive or write off the debt. Insolvency means that your debts (including the one that was forgiven) exceed the value of your assets. You can avoid reporting the debt as income only to the extent of your insolvency. For example, if your debts come to $40,000 and your assets are worth $38,000, you are insolvent by $2,000. If a creditor forgives a debt of $3,000, you can subtract only that $2,000, so you'll still have to pay tax on the remaining $1,000.

If you receive a Form 1099-C, you may need to complete IRS Form 982, *Reduction of Tax Attributes Due to Discharge of Indebtedness,* to show that an exception applies. You can download the form and instructions from the IRS website, www.irs.gov. Unfortunately, using this form can be complicated, especially if you're claiming the insolvency exception; you might need help from an accountant to complete it correctly. ●

Clean Up Your Credit Report

What Is in a Credit Report? 76

    Personal Information 76

    Accounts Reported Monthly 78

    Accounts Reported When in Default 78

    Public Records 79

    Inquiries 79

    Investigative Reports 79

Get a Copy of Your Credit Report 80

    Getting Free Credit Reports 80

    Which Credit Reporting Agencies to Use 82

Review Your Credit Report 84

    Review Sample Credit Reports 84

    Combined Reports 85

    How Long Items Can Stay in a Credit Report 86

    Review Your Report 86

Dispute Incomplete and Inaccurate Information 88

Add Information to Your Report 92

    Positive Account Histories 93

Information Showing Stability 93

Explanatory Statements 94

Avoid Identity Theft 95

    What's in a Stolen Name? 95

    How Can an Identity Be Stolen? 96

    How to Protect Yourself 97

    Protecting Your Social Security Number 99

    If Your Identity Is Stolen 101

    Identity Theft Protection Products and Insurance 105

Credit reporting agencies are for-profit companies that gather and sell information about a person's credit history. They sell credit information on consumers to banks, mortgage lenders, credit unions, credit card companies, department stores, car dealers, insurance companies, landlords, and employers. These companies and individuals use the credit information to supplement applications for credit, insurance, housing, and employment.

Credit reporting agencies may also provide identifying information concerning a consumer—name, address, former address, place of employment, and former place of employment—to government agencies. If a government agency is considering extending credit, reviewing the status of an account, or attempting to collect a debt, granting a license or other benefit, or investigating international terrorism, the agency is entitled to the complete credit report.

There are three major credit reporting agencies: Equifax (www.equifax.com), Experian (www.experian.com), and TransUnion (www.transunion.com). Recently a fourth, Innovis, has joined the scene (www.innovis.com). There are also thousands of smaller credit reporting agencies, known as "affiliates." Open up your yellow pages and look under "Credit Reporting Agencies." You may see none, one, two, or all three of the major credit reporting agencies. You will probably also see dozens of affiliates. The affiliated companies get their information from Equifax, Experian, and TransUnion, so this chapter focuses on the reports issued by those companies.

What Is in a Credit Report?

Information in your credit report can be broken down into five main categories:

- personal information about you
- accounts reported monthly
- accounts reported when in default
- public records, and
- inquiries.

Credit reports may also contain a credit score. (See Chapter 5.) Finally, some special credit reports, called investigative reports, contain even more information.

Credit reports do not contain information about race, religious preference, medical history, personal lifestyle, political preference, friends, or other information not related to credit.

Personal Information

A credit report usually includes your name and any former names, past and present addresses, Social Security number, and employment history (including salary). Credit reporting agencies get this information from creditors, who get it from you every time you fill out a credit application. For this reason, it is very important that your credit applications be accurate, complete, and legible.

Whether you are married, separated, divorced, or single, your credit report should contain information about you only. Information about your spouse should appear in your report only if you are both permitted to use or obligated to pay an account. For example, information about joint accounts should appear on both spouses' credit reports.

Expanding Credit Checks

We expect credit card issuers and other lenders to conduct a credit check before approving an application. But employers? Insurance companies? What could your credit history have to do with job performance or insurability? A lot, say the companies that do the screening. In fact, tens of thousands of employers review credit reports as part of evaluating job candidates. Employers use this information to judge financial honesty and integrity, as well as the risk of bribery of people with a lot of debt. And, once you're hired, employers can use the report for just about anything related to the job, including promotion and reassignment decisions.

Federal law requires that an employer obtain your written approval before conducting a credit check. Deciding whether to authorize an employer to get your credit report leaves many employees and job applicants in a bind. If you say no, you may look like you're hiding something and be turned down for the job. If you say yes, and the employer doesn't like what it sees, you have the right to see your report and dispute any inaccuracies before being rejected for the job. (In some states, you can get a copy of your credit report at the same time the employer does.)

But what if the contents are accurate? The best you can do is claim that your problems are behind you and have little or no bearing on job performance.

Insurance companies, too, routinely check on applicants before issuing a policy. Most health and life insurers request information on your medical history—mostly about major illnesses—from the Medical Information Bureau (MIB) in Boston (www.mib.com). Other insurers are permitted to check reports, although their use is infrequent and questionable. An insurance company cannot obtain a consumer report that contains medical information without your consent.

Other specialized reporting agencies provide information to creditors, employers, landlords, or insurance companies. U.D. Registry, ChoicePoint, and similar companies provide information to landlords about evictions (also called unlawful detainer actions). A few companies, such as TeleCheck, provide check account histories (check bouncing, ATM use, debit card payment) to banks reviewing checking account applications. All of these companies are governed by the federal and state laws regulating credit reporting agencies.

Accounts Reported Monthly

The bulk of information in your credit report is your credit history. Certain creditors (see below) provide monthly reports to credit reporting agencies showing the status of your account with them. Your credit report will contain the following information on these accounts:

- name of the creditor
- type of account
- account number
- when the account was opened
- maximum credit allowed
- your payment history—that is, whether you take 30, 60, 90, or 120 days to pay; whether the account has been turned over to a collection agency; whether the account has been discharged in bankruptcy; or whether you are disputing any charges
- your credit limit or the original amount of a loan, and
- your current balance.

Creditors who provide monthly reports generally include:

- banks, savings and loans, credit unions, finance companies, and other commercial lenders that issue credit cards and make mortgage, personal, car, and student loans
- nonbank credit and charge card issuers (such as American Express, Discover, and Diners Club)
- large department stores
- oil and gas companies, and
- other creditors receiving regular monthly installment payments.

Accounts Reported When in Default

Many businesses provide information to credit reporting agencies only when an account is past due or the creditor has taken collection action against you, including turning the account over to a collection agency. In these situations, your credit report will generally include the following:

- name of the creditor
- type of account
- account number, and
- your delinquency status—whether you're 60, 90, or 120 days late; whether the account has been turned over to a collection agency or you've been sued; or whether the account has been discharged in bankruptcy.

If a creditor has placed an account for collection or charged it off, the creditor must report the month and year of the delinquency—the last payment you missed —that caused the action. The creditor must report the delinquency date within 90 days of reporting the account as charged off or placed for collection.

Creditors who generally report accounts only when they are past due or in collection include:

- landlords and property managers
- utility companies
- local retailers
- insurance companies
- magazines and newspapers
- doctors and hospitals, and
- lawyers and other professionals.

While creditors tend to report these accounts only when they are past due, credit reporting agencies increasingly gather monthly information from utility companies, phone companies, and local retailers to add to credit reports. The goal is to increase the data contained in files of individuals, such as young people and immigrants, who don't have much traditional credit history.

Public Records

Public records are maintained by government agencies and are accessible to anyone. Local, state, and federal court filings are public records. So is the data kept at land records offices. Credit reporting agencies use private companies to search public records for information such as:

- lawsuits (including divorces and evictions)
- court judgments and judgment liens
- foreclosures
- bankruptcies
- tax liens
- mechanic's liens, and
- wage garnishments.

Federal law also requires child support enforcement agencies to report child support delinquencies to credit reporting agencies.

Inquiries

The final items in your credit report are called "inquiries." These are the names of creditors and others (such as a potential employer) who have requested a copy of your report during the previous year or two.

Credit inquiries usually fall into two categories. The first category contains inquiries that show up only on the report that you see, not on the report that creditors

get. There are several types of inquiries in this category, including creditors that request your credit report for promotional purposes (think of all those preapproved credit card applications you get in the mail), current creditors that review your report periodically to check up on you, and notations when you've requested a copy of your own credit report. These are often called "soft" inquiries

The second category of inquiries appears on the report sent to prospective creditors and employers (they also appear on the report you get). These inquiries—often called "hard" inquiries—consist of creditors that have requested your report after you have applied for credit with them.

Creditors don't like to see a credit report with lots of hard inquiries. It makes you look like you're desperately applying for new credit. This is why it's important to be careful when shopping for new credit. Used car dealers, in particular, often try to get you to sign a form allowing them to look at your credit report, even if you're just window-shopping. Don't agree to this until you are serious about entering into a deal. (For more on how this can affect your credit score, see "Tips for Raising Your Credit Score," in Chapter 5.)

Investigative Reports

Some special credit reports, called investigative reports, have even more information than regular credit reports. The big difference is that they include information on your character, general reputation, personal characteristics, or mode of living, gathered from interviews with third parties such as your neighbors or friends. Because this information is personal and invasive, additional rules apply to these reports.

Creditors do not usually request these investigative reports. Insurers and employers are the most likely to ask for them, but they must tell you when they request a report, and must disclose the nature and scope of the investigation upon your written request. They also must have a legitimate reason to request the report and, in some situations, they must get your consent. Businesses that procure employees for prospective employers (such as "headhunters") must get the consumer's consent before conducting the investigation and again before telling the employer the results.

Get a Copy of Your Credit Report

You can't clean up your credit unless you know exactly what's in your credit report. You start by getting a copy. Then you review it and dispute the incorrect items.

Getting Free Credit Reports

You are entitled to a free copy of your credit report once every twelve months from each of the three major nationwide credit reporting agencies, Equifax, Experian, and TransUnion. You can get your free report from any or all of them by contacting the Annual Credit Report Service:
- by phone at 877-322-8228
- by mail at P.O. Box 105281, Atlanta, GA 30348-5281, or
- online at www.annualcreditreport.com.

There are also a number of specialty credit reporting agencies that keep records on particular types of transactions, such as tenant histories, insurance claims, medical records or payment, and check writing. Although you are entitled to a free credit report each year from these agencies, there isn't a centralized service for requesting them. Instead, you have to contact each agency individually to ask for your report—and you may need to call different phone numbers for different types of reports. For example, you can contact ChoicePoint to get your tenant history report (877-448-5732), your insurance claims report (866-312-8076), or your employment history report (866-312-8075). For your medical history report from the Medical Information Bureau, call 866-692-6901. For a check writing report from Telecheck, call 1-800-366-2425.

You must provide your name, address, Social Security number, and date of birth when you order a report. If you have moved in the last two years, you may have to give your previous address. You also may be required to provide information that only you would know, such as the amount of your monthly mortgage payment.

The free credit reports you receive will not include your credit score unless you pay extra. As explained in Chapter 5, it might not be worth the cost.

In addition to your free annual report, you are entitled to another free copy of your credit report if any one of the following is true:
- **You've been denied credit because of information in your credit file.** You are

Tips for Sending Letters

Throughout this chapter, we advise you to send various letters to your creditors, depending on your situation. When you send a letter, follow these guidelines:

- Type your letters or fill in the blanks of the letters in Appendix B or on the CD-ROM.
- Keep a copy of all correspondence for yourself.
- *Never* send originals of documents that support your claim (such as a note marked "paid" or a canceled check); send only copies and keep the originals.
- Send by certified mail, with a return receipt requested.
- If you are enclosing money, use a cashier's check or money order—not a personal check—if you have any debts in collection. Otherwise, the recipient of the check could pass your checking account number on to a debt collector, which will make it easier for the collector to grab your assets to collect the debt.
- Follow up telephone calls with a letter confirming the details of the discussion and any promises made by you or the other party.
- If you communicate with a creditor or debt collector by email, print and keep copies of all your messages and discussion chains.

entitled to a free copy of your file from the credit reporting agency that reported the information. (A creditor that denies you credit in this situation will tell you the name and address of the credit reporting agency reporting the information that led to the denial.) You must request your copy within 60 days of being denied credit.

- **You are unemployed and planning to apply for a job within 60 days** following your request for your credit report. You must enclose a statement swearing that this is true. It might also help to include a copy of a recent unemployment check, layoff notice, or similar document verifying your unemployment. You are entitled to one free report from each agency in any 12-month period.

- **You receive public assistance.** Enclose a statement swearing that this is true and a copy of your most recent public assistance check as verification. You are entitled to one free report from each agency in any 12-month period.

- **You reasonably believe your credit file contains errors due to someone's fraud,** such as using your credit cards, Social Security number, name, or something similar. Here, too, you will need to enclose a statement swearing that this is true. You are entitled to one free report in any 12-month period.

- **You are a victim of identity theft or fraud or think that you may be.** The FCRA gives consumers the right to request free credit reports in connection with fraud alerts.

- If you suspect in good faith that you are, or may be, a victim of identity theft or another fraud, you can instruct the three major agencies to add a "fraud alert" to your file. You can request a free copy of your report from each agency once it places the fraud alert in your file.
- If you are a victim of identity theft, you can send the three major agencies an identity theft report and instruct them to add an extended fraud alert to your file. You can request two free copies of your credit report from each agency during the next 12 months once it places the extended fraud alert in your file. See "Avoid Identity Theft," below, for more on identity theft and fraud alerts.

For additional copies—or if you don't qualify for a free copy—you'll have to pay about $10. Many websites offer a free copy with a 30-day trial membership for one of their services, such as credit monitoring. If you don't want the service, be sure to cancel it within the 30 days to avoid a monthly fee. You should receive your credit report in a week to ten days.

Which Credit Reporting Agencies to Use

If you haven't checked your credit report lately, request a copy from one of the major credit reporting agencies. If you find errors in the first credit report, get copies of your report from the other two agencies. If you think you may be the victim of identity

---

Beware of Imposter Sites

The three major credit bureaus have set up one central website, toll-free number, and mailing address for ordering free credit reports (listed above). The only authorized website is www.annualcreditreport.com.

Other websites have similar names and advertise that they offer free credit reports, but beware. The free report often comes with strings attached, such as a service that you have to pay for when the introductory period ends, and some sites collect personal information. Don't respond to an email or click on a pop-up ad claiming to offer free credit reports. The official annualcreditreport.com website will never send you an email solicitation for your free report, use pop-up ads, or call you to ask for personal information.

Some imposter sites have names confusingly similar to annualcreditreport.com, so make sure you're using the right URL.

Once you have provided the required information to annualcreditreport.com, you will be directed to the three major credit agencies' individual websites. They may offer to sell you additional services (credit monitoring products or credit scores, for example) but you are not required to purchase them to receive your free report.

---

theft, it's best to get a report from all three. (In this era of rampant identity theft, it's very important to make sure your report contains information only about you.)

If you already received your free annual credit reports from the nationwide credit reporting agencies within the last 12 months, use Form F-25, Request Credit File, in Appendix B or on the CD-ROM, to request your credit file. You may have to provide the following information:

Full name. The agency cannot process your request without your name. It's important that you provide your full name, including generations (Jr., Sr., III) and any other versions of your name that you use, such as "Trevor J. (aka T.J.) Williams."

Date of birth. A credit reporting agency may provide your report without your date (or at least year) of birth. But this information helps distinguish you from anyone else with a similar name, so you should include it.

Social Security number. Most agencies require this. They use it to distinguish between people with the same or similar last names. You can instruct the agency not to include the first five digits of your Social Security number (that is, to truncate your Social Security number) on the report it sends you to protect against identity theft.

Spouse's name. It's not absolutely necessary, but, again, it helps distinguish you from anyone else with a similar name.

Telephone number. You may be asked to provide your telephone number. You may hesitate to include it, knowing that bill collectors can get it by getting a copy of your credit file. But, unless it's unlisted, they can also get it from directory assistance, a reverse directory, or an Internet "people finder" service. If you are being hounded by bill collectors, you may not want to give out an unlisted telephone number. On the other hand, if you're trying to repair your credit, you will want to make sure your phone number is in your file. It is one sign of stability your future creditors look for.

Current address. You won't get a copy of your credit report if you don't include your address.

Previous addresses. Agencies ask for this if you've been at your current address fewer than two to five years. Again, it helps distinguish you from other people with similar names.

Your signature. You must sign the letter.

Agencies are trying to move away from paper requests for credit reports by encouraging people to order through their websites. If you prefer not to order over the Internet, the agency may have a toll-free number or may accept written requests. Check each agency's requirements on its website.

Credit Reporting Agency Contact Information

Equifax
P.O. Box 740241
Atlanta, GA 30374-0241
800-685-1111
www.equifax.com

Experian
888-397-3742
www.experian.com

TransUnion
800-888-4213
www.transunion.com

Review Your Credit Report

Review your report carefully. One of the biggest problems with credit files is that they contain incorrect or out-of-date information. Investigations by public interest groups and government agencies show that most credit reports contain errors. In some studies, 25% to 30% of the reports reviewed included errors serious enough that they might result in the denial of credit.

Sometimes credit reporting agencies confuse names, addresses, Social Security numbers, or employers. If you have a common name—say, John Brown—your file may contain information on other John Browns, John Brownes, or Jon Browns. Your file may erroneously contain information on family members with similar names.

Ironically, concern over identity theft (see "Avoid Identity Theft," below) contributes to mistakes in credit reports. Businesses now ask consumers for minimal identifying information when they open accounts, to avoid inadvertently making that information available to thieves. The unintended consequence of not including a full Social Security number or a date of birth in a reported consumer transaction or delinquency is that it's easier than ever for a credit reporting agency to confuse one consumer for another. It's also common for agencies to fail to note accounts in which delinquencies have been remedied.

Review Sample Credit Reports

Before you order your credit reports from Experian, TransUnion, and Equifax, you may want to review each agency's sample credit report to familiarize yourself with its layout and contents. The presentation of information varies considerably. Getting past the sales pitches can be tricky.

To find each agency's sample report, follow these instructions:

- **Equifax.** Go to www.equifax.com. Select "View All Products," then click the "Products" tab and select "Equifax Credit Report." Select the link for "Sample Equifax Credit Report."
- **Experian.** Go to www.experian.com. Click the "More About Credit" tab near the bottom of the page, then select "Credit Education." Choose "Credit Report Basics," then "Your Credit Report." At the bottom of the page, select "View a sample Experian credit report."
- **TransUnion.** Go to www.truecredit .com, the consumer area of Trans-Union's website. Select "Sitemap" at the bottom of the page, then "Sample Single Credit Report."

The sample reports provide explanations of their contents and are supplemented by educational materials. However, their descriptions of the dispute resolution process are lacking. Here's what else you should know.

Under the FCRA, you have the right to dispute the accuracy or completeness of *any* item in your file, not just inaccurate information. This distinction can be important. For example, your credit report might state accurately that a creditor sued you. Yet this information might be incomplete because you later paid the debt or are not actually liable for it. You can dispute the information about the lawsuit because it is incomplete.

Each agency's materials encourage consumers to submit their disputes online. However, you may have documents that support your position (for example, a canceled check, a note marked "paid," a statement with a zero balance, or a letter abandoning a claim). When you dispute an item, the agency must review and consider all relevant information that you provide in a timely manner and must forward this information to the creditor that provided the information. Submitting your dispute online may work for some issues, but, as a general rule, disputes that involve documentation should be handled by mail.

If the investigation shows that the disputed information is inaccurate, *incomplete,* or *cannot be verified*, the agency must delete the information from your file or modify it so that it is correct. The agency also must notify the creditor of the action taken. Under the FCRA, the entire investigation process must be free for consumers. (15 U.S.C. § 1681i.) (Disputing information and adding a statement to your file if the dispute isn't resolved to your satisfaction are both covered below.)

Also, the sample reports and supplemental materials don't mention what to do if you find inaccurate information in your report that is due to fraud. See "Avoid Identity Theft," below, for help.

Combined Reports

Experian, TransUnion, and Equifax offer "combined" or "3-in-1" credit reports. As the name suggests, these reports combine information from all three agencies. Because creditors report to different credit agencies, each agency's report on you will vary. A combined report shows you the information each agency has on you.

If you're planning to make a major purchase (like a house or a car) or a major financial commitment (like an equity line on your home), you may want to review information from all three agencies. But the $35 (or so) it costs may not be worth it because you can get a free copy of your credit report from each agency. While a combined report may make it easier to spot differences in the agencys' information on you, you can accomplish the same thing using free reports and a little study.

Whatever approach you choose, you should definitely check your credit information at all three agencies well in advance of a major purchase. This gives you the opportunity to add missing information (covered below) and dispute incomplete or inaccurate information. That way, no matter which agency your lender uses, your credit file looks as good as possible. Or, if your lender purchases a combined report from a reseller, the information provided by the three major agencies is as consistent and favorable as possible. (A reseller is a credit agency that assembles and merges information from other agencies into a single report for use by a third party, often a mortgage lender.)

How Long Items Can Stay in a Credit Report

Once a credit agency gathers negative information about you, it may report that information (that is, include it in a credit report) as follows:

- Bankruptcies may be reported for no more than ten years after the date of the last activity. The date of the last activity for most bankruptcies is the date you receive your discharge or the date your case is dismissed.
- Lawsuits and judgments may be reported from the date of the entry of judgment against you for up to seven years or until the governing statute of limitations has expired, whichever is longer.
- Paid tax liens may be reported from the date of payment for up to seven years.
- Most criminal records, such as information about indictments or arrests, may be reported for only seven years. But records of criminal convictions may be reported indefinitely.
- Accounts sent to collection (within the creditor company or to a collection agency), accounts charged off, or any other similar action may be reported for up to seven years. The seven-year period begins 180 days after the delinquency (the last missed payment) that led to the collection activity or charge-off. The clock does not start ticking again if the account is sold to another collection agency, you make

a payment on it, or you file a dispute with the credit reporting agency.

- Overdue child support may be reported for seven years.
- Some adverse information regarding student loans guaranteed or insured by the U.S. government, or national direct student loans, may be reported for much longer than seven years.
- Delinquent accounts may be reported for seven years after the date of the last scheduled payment before the account became delinquent.
- Bankruptcies, lawsuits, paid tax liens, accounts sent out for collection, criminal records, overdue child support, and any other adverse information may be reported beyond the usual time limits if you apply for $150,000 or more of credit or life insurance, or if you apply for a job with an annual income of at least $75,000. As a practical matter, however, credit agencies may delete all items after seven or ten years.

Review Your Report

As you read through your credit report, make a list of everything that is inaccurate, incomplete, or not authorized to be in your file. In particular, look for the following:

- incorrect or incomplete name, address, or phone number
- incorrect Social Security number or birthdate
- incorrect, missing, or outdated employment information

Laws Regulating Credit Reporting Agencies

Credit reporting agencies are regulated by the Federal Trade Commission under the provisions of the Federal Fair Credit Reporting Act (FCRA). (15 U.S.C. §§ 1681 and following.) The FCRA is designed to bar inaccurate or obsolete information from appearing in credit reports. Amendments to the FCRA have addressed the accuracy of information in credit transactions and identity theft. The Act requires credit reporting agencies to adopt reasonable procedures for gathering, maintaining, and distributing information and sets accuracy standards for creditors that provide information to bureaus. The FCRA also regulates who can access credit reports. Most states have passed similar laws.

- incorrect marital status—such as a former spouse listed as your current spouse
- bankruptcies that are more than ten years old or not identified by the specific chapter of the bankruptcy code
- lawsuits or judgments reported beyond seven years or beyond the expiration of the statute of limitations
- paid tax liens or criminal arrest records more than seven years old,
- delinquent accounts that are more than seven years old or do not include the date of the delinquency
- overdue child support that is more than seven years old

- other adverse information that is more than seven years old
- credit inquiries by automobile dealers from times you simply test drove a car or from other businesses when you were only comparison shopping (such creditors cannot lawfully pull your credit report without your permission until you indicate a desire to enter into a sale or lease)
- commingled accounts—credit histories for someone with a similar or the same name
- duplicate accounts—for example, a debt is listed twice, once under the creditor and a second time under a collection agency
- premarital debts of your current spouse attributed to you
- lawsuits you were not involved in
- incorrect account histories—such as a late payment notation when you've paid on time or a debt shown as past due when it's been discharged in bankruptcy
- voluntary surrender of your vehicle listed as a repossession
- paid tax, judgment, mechanic's, or other liens listed as unpaid
- paid accounts listed as unpaid
- a missing notation when you disputed a charge on a credit card bill
- accounts that incorrectly list you as a cosigner
- closed accounts incorrectly listed as open—it may look as if you have too much open credit, and

• accounts you closed that don't indicate "closed by consumer"—it looks like your creditors closed the accounts.

Dispute Incomplete and Inaccurate Information

Under the Fair Credit Reporting Act, you have the right to dispute all incomplete or inaccurate information in your credit file. Once the agency receives your letter, it must reinvestigate the items you dispute and record the current status of the disputed information or delete it within 30 days. (45 days if you send the agency additional relevant information during the 30-day period).

These requirements are not hard for a credit reporting agency to meet. The agencies and more than 6,000 of the nation's creditors are linked by computer, which speeds up the verification process. Furthermore, if you let an agency know that you're trying to obtain a mortgage or car loan, it can often do a "rush" verification.

If the credit reporting agency cannot verify the information in dispute, it must remove the information. Agencies might remove an item on request without an investigation if rechecking the item is more bother than it's worth. If the agency finds that the information is inaccurate or incomplete, the agency must remove the information or modify it based on the results of the investigation. Requesting an investigation won't cost you anything.

Once you've compiled a list of all incomplete and inaccurate information you want corrected or removed, complete the "request for reinvestigation" form which was enclosed with your credit report. If the agency did not enclose such a form, use Form F-26, Request Reinvestigation, in Appendix B or on the CD-ROM or use the agency's own dispute form (check its website). Don't simply handwrite a letter; handwritten letters on plain paper often are given minimal attention.

Incorrect information does not have to be negative to be challenged. It is enough that the information is incomplete or inaccurate.

Below are some examples of the types of responses you might include on Form F-26.

☒ **The following personal information about me is incorrect:**

Erroneous Information	Correct Information
Spouse: Morton Lyle	I divorced Morton Lyle on 8/23/00. I'm now married to Brian Jones.

☒ **The following accounts are not mine:**

Creditor's Name	Account Number	Explanation
Dept. of Education	123456789	Premarital debt of my husband Brian Jones.
Strong's Dept. Store	0987654321	I've never had a Strong's account.

☒ The account status is incorrect for the following accounts:

Creditor's Name	Account Number	Correct Status
Big Bank	1234 5678 9012	Discharged in
MasterCard		bankruptcy;
		balance owed
		is $0.

☒ The following inquiries were not authorized:

Creditor's Name	Date of Inquiry	Explanation
Wowza Bank Visa	2/14/01	I did not apply for
		credit with Wowza
		Bank nor authorize
		them to conduct
		a credit check of me.

☒ Other incorrect information:

Explanation

(1) My credit report states that I filed a Chapter 13 bankruptcy on July 23, 200x. That is not correct. In fact, I filed a Chapter 7 case and received a discharge of my debts on October 19, 200x.

(2) American Express account is listed twice—one listing indicates the account was discharged in bankruptcy (this is correct); the other listing shows the account with Tenacious Collection Services (incorrect). Furthermore, this account is missing the date of delinquency.

Send your letter to the address provided by the credit reporting agency for disputing information (keep a copy for your records). Also, enclose copies of any documents you have that support your claim. It may help to include a copy of your credit report with the disputed items highlighted. Keep your original documents.

Soon, rather than asking the credit reporting agency to investigate inaccurate information, you will be able to ask the creditor that furnished the information to investigate it. The Federal Trade Commission is developing regulations to define when a consumer can dispute inaccurate information directly with the furnishing creditor. The creditor will have 30 days to complete its investigation and send the consumer the results (45 days if the consumer has sent it additional information). When information is found to be inaccurate, the creditor will have to provide corrected information to each credit reporting agency that received the incorrect information.

In any event, it's always a good idea to send a copy of your letter to the creditor that furnished the incorrect or incomplete information to the credit reporting agency. These "furnishing" creditors have a duty to correct and update information they send to credit reporting agencies that they determine is inaccurate or incomplete.

If you don't hear from the credit reporting agency within 30 (or 45) days, send a follow-up letter using Form F-27, Request Follow-Up After Reinvestigation, in Appendix B or on the CD-ROM. Send a copy of your letter to the Federal Trade Commission (addresses are listed below), the agency that oversees credit reporting agencies. Again, keep a copy for your records.

Once the credit reporting agency receives your request for reinvestigation, it must:

- complete its investigation within 30 days of receiving your complaint (45 days if the agency receives relevant information from you during the 30-day period)
- contact the creditor reporting the information you dispute within five business days of receiving your dispute
- review and consider all relevant information submitted by you, and
- provide you with the results of its reinvestigation within five business days of completion, including a revised credit report if any changes were made.

The credit reporting agency is not required to investigate any dispute that it determines is frivolous or irrelevant because, for example, you don't provide enough information to investigate the dispute. Once the agency makes a determination, it has five business days to notify you of what it decided and why.

If the credit reporting agency cannot verify the information in the report or agrees that the information is inaccurate or incomplete, it must modify the information or remove it from your file. It must also inform the furnishing creditor that the information has been modified or deleted.

You can ask the credit reporting agency to notify past users that inaccurate or unverifiable information has been deleted from the report. But, the agency will only do this if you request it and identify the past users. And, even then, it is only required to send notice to anyone who requested your report within the previous six months, or two years if requested for employment purposes. You won't have to pay anything for this notification as long as you request it within 30 days after the credit reporting agency tells you the results of its reinvestigation.

Even if the credit reporting agency agrees that the information is incorrect and fixes it, don't assume that the negative information will be permanently eliminated from your report. The agencies are required to have procedures to keep incorrect information from reappearing, but, unfortunately, those procedures often fail. To make sure the errors stay out of your report, you should do all of the following:

- Obtain another copy of your credit report three to six months later to confirm that the corrections still appear.
- Check to see whether your credit reports at the other major agencies contain the same error, and, if so, send the results of your successful investigation from the first agency to the others.

If the credit reporting agency responds that the creditor reporting the information verified its accuracy and completeness, and that, therefore, the information will remain in your file, you will need to take more aggressive action to clean up your credit report. This may be frustrating and time-consuming.

Here are some ideas to help you in your efforts to fix your credit file.

Contact the creditor associated with the incorrect information and demand that it tell the credit reporting agency to remove the information. Write to the customer service department, vice president of marketing, and president or CEO. If the information was reported by a collection agency, send the agency a copy of your letter, too. Use Form F-28, Request Removal of Incorrect Information by Creditor, in Appendix B or on the CD-ROM, to make your request. Be sure to keep a copy of your letter and your original documentation. If the creditor is local, pay a visit. Sit down in the office of the customer service department, vice president of marketing, or president or CEO. Do not leave until someone agrees to meet with you and hear your problem. *Remember: You have the right to demand attention; this creditor has verified incorrect information and it should be removed from your credit report.*

Under the Fair Credit Reporting Act, creditors who report information to credit reporting agencies must do the following:

- not report incorrect information once they learn that the information is, in fact, incorrect
- provide credit reporting agencies with correct information when they learn that the information they have been reporting is incorrect
- notify credit reporting agencies when you dispute information
- note when accounts are "closed by the consumer"
- provide credit reporting agencies with the month and year of the delinquency

of all accounts placed for collection, charged off, or similarly treated, and

- finish their investigation of your dispute within the 30- or 45-day periods the credit reporting agency must complete its investigation.

If you get a letter from the creditor agreeing that the information is incorrect and should be removed from your credit file, send a copy of the creditor's letter to the credit reporting agency that reported the information. Use Form F-29, Creditor Verification, in Appendix B or on the CD-ROM.

If a creditor cannot or will not assist you in removing the incorrect information, call the credit reporting agency directly. Credit reporting agencies have toll-free numbers to handle consumer disputes about incorrect items in their credit files that are not removed via the normal reinvestigation process. Use the credit reporting agency's toll-free number (see "Credit Reporting Agencies Contact Information," above).

You may be able to sue if you were seriously harmed by the credit reporting agency—for example, if it continued to give out incomplete or inaccurate information after you requested corrections. The FCRA lets you sue a credit reporting agency for negligent or willful noncompliance with the law within two years after you discover the agency's harmful behavior or within five years after the harmful behavior occurs, whichever is sooner. You can sue for "actual damages," including court costs, attorney's fees, lost wages, and, if applicable, defamation and intentional infliction of emotional distress. In the case of truly outrageous behavior, you can recover "punitive damages" meant to punish malicious or willful conduct. Under the FCRA, the court decides the amount of the punitive damages.

You may also be able to sue the creditor that supplied the inaccurate information for its failure to reinvestigate or correct errors. However, these types of lawsuits are complicated, and the FCRA provides creditors with many ways to avoid liability. You will need to consult a lawyer if you want to pursue this type of lawsuit.

If all else fails, consider calling your congressional representative or senator. He or she can call the FTC and demand some action.

RESOURCE

To complain about a credit reporting agency. You can file a complaint against a credit reporting agency with the Federal Trade Commission using its online form. Go to www.ftccomplaintassistant.gov and select "FTC Complaint Assistant." You can also contact the FTC by phone (877-382-4357) or mail:

FTC Consumer Response Center

CRC-240

600 Pennsylvania Avenue, NW

Washington, DC 20580

Add Information to Your Report

In addition to disputing incorrect information, you can also add information to your report that makes you look more creditworthy. There are three types of information you may want to add:

- positive account histories that are missing from your report
- information demonstrating your stability, and
- explanations of any incomplete or disputed information in your report.

Sample Statements

Here are a few examples of statements describing disputes:

- A credit report includes a lawsuit filed by a roofing company for failure to pay for its work. The information is accurate, but the consumer didn't pay because the work was done incorrectly. The consumer might add a statement to the file reading, "Defective workmanship, refuse to pay until fixed."

- A credit report indicates that a consumer is unemployed, but the consumer has in fact worked as an independent contractor during that time. The consumer might send a statement reading, "I work as a freelance technical writer, averaging $50,000 annually."

- A credit report states that the consumer owes a debt to an electronics store. The consumer bought a CD player that doesn't work, and the store refused to take it back or provide a refund. The consumer might submit this statement, "Merchandise is defective, and the store refuses to provide a refund or replacement."

Positive Account Histories

Often, credit reports don't include accounts that you might expect to find. Some major commercial lenders don't report mortgages or car loans. Local banks or credit unions often don't provide information to credit reporting agencies.

If your credit file is missing credit histories for accounts you pay on time, send the credit reporting agencies a copy of a recent account statement and copies of canceled checks (never originals) showing your payment history. Ask the credit reporting agencies to add the information to your file. While the agencies aren't required to add account histories, they often do—but may charge you a fee for doing so. Use Form F-30, Request Addition of Account Histories, in Appendix B or on the CD-ROM, to make your request.

It may be that credit histories for accounts you pay on time are missing from only one or two credit reports—the third report may have included all accounts when you received it, or you may have focused on cleaning up that report first. In this situation, try sending the agencies that aren't reporting the information a copy of your credit report that includes all your accounts, with a cover letter asking that the missing information be included in your file. You can modify Form F-30 in Appendix B for this purpose.

Information Showing Stability

Creditors like to see evidence of stability in your file. If any of the items listed below are missing from your file, consider sending a letter to the credit reporting agencies asking that the information be added. Use Form F-31, Request Addition of Information Showing Stability, in Appendix B or on the CD-ROM, to make your request.

You may want to add:

- **Your current employment,** including your current employer's name and address and your job title. You may wisely decide not to add this if you think a creditor may sue you or a creditor has a judgment against you. Current employment information may be a green light for a wage garnishment.
- **Your previous employment,** especially if you've had your current job fewer than two years. Include your former employer's name and address and your job title.
- **Your current residence,** and, if you own it, say so. (Not all mortgage lenders report their accounts to credit reporting agencies.) Again, don't do this if you've been sued or you think a creditor may sue you. Real estate is an excellent collection source.
- **Your previous residence,** especially if you've lived at your current address fewer than two years.
- **Your telephone number,** especially if it's unlisted. If you haven't yet given the credit reporting agencies your phone number, consider doing so

now. A creditor who cannot verify a telephone number is often reluctant to grant credit.

- **Your date of birth.** A creditor will probably not grant you credit if it does not know your age. However, creditors also cannot discriminate against you based on your age. (See Chapter 6.)
- **Your Social Security number.**

Credit reporting agencies aren't required to add any of this information, but they often do. They are most likely to add information on jobs and residences, as that information is used by creditors in evaluating applications for credit. They will also add your telephone number, date of birth, and Social Security number because those items help identify you and lessen the chances of "mixed" credit files—that is, getting other people's credit histories in your file. (Expect to pay a small fee when an agency adds information to your file.)

Enclose any documentation that verifies information you're providing, such as copies (never originals) of your driver's license, a canceled check, a bill addressed to you, or a pay stub showing your employer's name and address. Remember to keep photocopies of all correspondence.

Explanatory Statements

If the credit reporting agency's investigation doesn't resolve the dispute to your satisfaction, you have the right to file a brief statement about the dispute. The agency must include your statement, or a summary or codification of it, in any report that includes the disputed information. The reporting agency may limit your statement to 100 words if it helps you write the summary. Otherwise, there is no word limit, but it is a good idea to keep the statement very brief.

The credit reporting agency is required to provide only a summary or codification of your statement (not your actual statement) to anyone who requests your file. If your statement is short, the credit reporting agency is more likely to pass on your statement unedited. If your statement is long, the credit reporting agency will probably condense your explanation to just a few sentences or codes. To avoid this problem, keep your statement clear and concise.

If you request it, the credit reporting agency must also give the statement or summary to anyone you identify who received a copy of your file within the past six months—or two years if your file was given out for employment purposes. This service is free if you request it within 30 days after the agency gave you notice of the results of the investigation. Otherwise, you will have to pay the same amount as the agency would normally charge for a credit report (about $10).

Credit reporting agencies are only required to include a statement in your file if you are disputing the completeness or accuracy of a particular item. The agency does not have to include a statement if you are only explaining extenuating circumstances or other reasons why you haven't been able to pay your debts. If the agency does allow you to add such a statement, it can charge you a fee.

Don't assume that adding a brief statement is the best approach. It's often wiser to simply explain the negative mark to subsequent creditors in person than to try to explain it in such a short statement. Many statements or summaries are simply ineffective. Few creditors who receive credit files read them, and credit scoring programs ignore these statements. In any David (consumer) vs. Goliath (credit reporting agency) dispute, creditors tend to believe Goliath.

TIP

Check your reports every year. Once you've repaired your credit, you should get a free copy of your credit report from each credit reporting agency every year. Rather than requesting all of your reports at once, spread out your requests throughout the year. Every four months, request a report from a different agency; that way, you'll be able to check your report three times a year, free. Look for old or inaccurate information. Also check for anything that looks fishy—it could be a sign of identity theft.

Avoid Identity Theft

Identity theft is a growing national epidemic. The Federal Trade Commission has said that identity theft has as many as nine million victims each year, costs businesses about $50 billion, and costs consumers nearly $5 billion. The sad truth is that the Internet and its vast collections of easily accessible personal data make identity theft a simple and tantalizing endeavor for the criminally inclined. Contributing to the problem are businesses without stringent privacy policies and corporate and government mistakes in handling sensitive customer information. Incidents of computers and storage devices loaded with personal information being stolen, sensitive databases being compromised, information-rich files being left unsecured in garbage bins, and credit slips left unshredded are common—and even unsavvy thieves know it.

Unfortunately, local police agencies are ill-equipped to handle these sophisticated crimes, which often cross state borders. From a police perspective, identity theft is a silent crime. It just doesn't merit the priority of crimes like murder, robbery, and other violent crimes more easily reported and televised. District attorneys are in a similar bind.

But times are changing. Federal and state law enforcement agencies are taking the problem more seriously, especially now that the FBI has declared identity theft one of the fastest-growing white collar crimes in the country.

What's in a Stolen Name?

A thief can obtain a loan, open credit accounts and max them out, rent an apartment, buy a car, purchase a cell phone, talk to someone in China all day, and, worse—commit a serious crime—all using your name.

Financially, if a credit card in your name is used in a credit scam, you'll likely be responsible for only up to $50 because of federal laws capping your liability for unauthorized use of your card. (See Chapter 3.) But the financial burdens may be the least of your worries. You may spend months hassling with credit agencies, financial institutions, and police departments trying to clear your name and repair the lingering damage. You may have to take time off from work to write letters, make calls, collect evidence, and demand action.

And who knows what it will take to repair the anxiety and mental suffering you'll endure. Even now, some victims of identity theft report that police agencies are often dismissive or even abusive, credit reporting agencies unresponsive, collection agencies hostile, and creditors disbelieving. Psychological scarring can be severe. Some victims liken the experience to feeling physically assaulted; continued sleep disturbances, paranoia, and other post-traumatic stress symptoms are not uncommon.

How Can an Identity Be Stolen?

Here are some typical ways in which thieves gather information about you:

- stealing wallets or mail
- filling out a change of address form using your name and collecting your mail
- snatching preapproved credit offers from the trash, recycling bin, or mailbox

- ordering unauthorized credit reports on you by posing as a potential employer, landlord, or even you
- illegal computer tapping by a dishonest employee at a business where you have provided information or been granted credit
- looking over your shoulder at phones and ATMs to gather PIN numbers, sometimes with binoculars, listening devices, cell phones, or mini-cameras
- breaking into computer systems and searching for people with good credit
- using phony telemarketing schemes to con you into giving them your personal data
- using personal information you shared on the Internet
- a former friend, lover, roommate, or coworker with a grudge gathering sensitive information and using it in an attempt to extract revenge (a more common occurrence than most people realize), and
- a family member who steals another family member's identity to get access to credit or to try to avoid arrest or debt.

Perhaps the most frightening—and most thorough—way to steal your identity is by purchasing your Social Security number, mother's maiden name, home and employment address, previous addresses, credit history, and more for just a few dollars from one of the identity search companies on the Internet.

It's also unsettling to learn that supposedly secure electronic repositories of personal information can be easily compromised. The media have reported that computers and storage devices belonging to the federal government and containing personal information on millions of people have been stolen. In the private sector, data brokers' huge databases, with billions of files, have been compromised by criminals, according to published reports. Because of a California law that requires notification of security breaches, many thousands of Californians and others have received notices that these databases were breached. (Since these breaches, other states have enacted security breach notification laws.)

If you think that your identity has been compromised by an event like this, consider taking the steps described in "If Your Identity Is Stolen," below.

How to Protect Yourself

You must guard your personal information assiduously. Here are some tips for keeping your private information secure:

- Do not routinely carry your Social Security card, birth certificate, or passport.
- Don't leave outgoing bill payments in your mailbox for the mail carrier to pick up.
- Keep changing your passwords and PIN numbers. Don't use obvious codes such as birthdays or spouse's, children's, or pet's names. Memorize passwords and shred any piece of paper where they are written.
- Diligently review credit card statements and phone and utility bills. Get a copy of all of your credit reports at least once a year. Promptly challenge any inaccurate information.
- Always take your credit card, debit card, and ATM receipts, and don't throw them away in public.
- Tear up or shred any item with personal information on it, as well as any offers of preapproved credit cards you don't intend to use. Also, beware of offers from companies you don't recognize. It's easy to create an official-looking and completely phony credit application offering you preapproved credit if you provide your Social Security number, mother's maiden name, and a signature.
- Buy a shredder and use it religiously.
- Don't give personal information over the phone unless absolutely necessary, and never give it unless you initiated the phone call.
- Beware of anyone asking for your Social Security number. If a company refuses to complete a transaction without it, consider taking your business elsewhere.
- Beware of requests to obtain or update personal information that appear to come from a research firm or a company or financial institution that you do business with. Legitimate businesses hardly ever contact customers for this purpose. Any such request, whether by phone or over the Internet, most likely is from a scammer who wants to steal your personal information. If you feel you must respond, first call the firm's toll-free number (printed on a statement

or receipt) or go to its correct Web address to verify that the request is legitimate. A current Internet scam called "phishing" uses spam email or pop-up messages to trick you into disclosing personal or financial information. The message appears to be from a firm that you do business with and directs you to a phony website that looks legitimate. The FTC advises not to respond to these messages by clicking on the reply button or link provided. Instead, call the firm using a number you know to be legitimate, or begin a new Internet browser session and go to the firm's correct Web address. Do not cut and paste the link in the message.

- The FTC advises consumers to use firewalls, anti-spyware, and anti-virus software on their home computers, and to keep these protections up-to-date; visit www.OnGuardOnline.gov for more information.

- If you receive a "Move Validation Letter" from the post office, and you aren't moving, call the 800 number in the letter to alert the post office. Someone may be trying to set up a new fake address to open new accounts using your name.

- Be alert to signs that your identity has been compromised, such as bills that do not arrive as expected, unexpected credit cards or account statements, denials of credit for no apparent reason, or calls or letters about purchases you did not make.

- Pick up your new checks from the bank instead of having them sent to your home. Do not have your Social Security or driver's license number printed on your checks.

- Don't put your personal information on any computer home page or personal computer profile. Provide as little personal and credit information as possible in Internet transactions. Never provide personal or financial information unless the site is secure (for example, look for a security symbol such as an unbroken padlock in the corner of the screen and a Web browser that starts with "https" rather than simply "http." Right-click on the padlock to make sure it's up to date. For more information about online security, go to the website of the Privacy Rights Clearinghouse, www.privacyrights.org, and look at its "Privacy and the Internet" fact sheet.

- If you find your personal information somewhere on the Internet, demand that it be removed.

It is also important to learn more about what happens to the personal information you provide to companies, marketers, and government agencies. These organizations may use your personal information to promote their own products and services, or they may share it with others.

Many companies and organizations allow you to "opt out" of having your information shared with others or used for promotional purposes. Opting out will help keep some of your information private and less vulnerable to identity theft. You can find out more about your opt out choices from the Federal Trade Commission, www.ftc.gov. The national credit reporting agencies have a toll-free number (888-567-8688) and a website (www.optoutprescreen.com) through which you can opt out of receiving offers of credit and insurance that you did not request (so-called prescreened offers that are based on information in your credit report).

Privacy-conscious consumers pay attention to the "privacy notices" that businesses send them when they open accounts. These consumers opt out of every use of their personal information possible under the business's privacy policy. Doing this reduces the distribution of the consumer's personal information somewhat and also cuts down the number of offers and solicitations that the consumer receives.

You can also put a "security freeze" or "file freeze" in your credit file. A security freeze is a notice in your file that prohibits the credit reporting agency from releasing your credit report or certain information in it without your consent. You can "unfreeze" your file for a period of time or to allow a specific creditor to access your file.

Security freezes are available by law in most states. Limits on fees credit reporting agencies may charge for placing a security freeze on your file vary by state; in some states, there is no charge if you have been a victim of identity theft. Currently, the three major credit reporting agencies also voluntarily provide security freezes even in states that do not require them. To find out about security freeze laws in your state, go to www.financialprivacynow.org; under

"Security Freeze," click on "State Security Freeze Laws," then on your state. You can also find information and set up a security freeze at any of the three nationwide credit reporting agencies:

- At www.equifax.com, click the tab for "Free Report, Security Freeze, Dispute, and Fraud Protection."
- At www.experian.com, under "Notices," click on "Security Freeze."
- At www.transunion.com, under "Identity Theft," click on "How a security freeze helps you control access to your credit report."

Security freezes are different from the initial, extended, and military alerts that the Fair Credit Reporting Act makes available. For more information on these alerts, see "If Your Identity Is Stolen," below.

You should carefully consider the pros and cons of a security freeze. Consumer advocates favor them, particularly if you are worried about or have been a victim of identity theft, while the credit reporting agencies favor their own credit monitoring services. As a practical matter, having a security freeze can delay your own applications for credit, and removing a freeze can be cumbersome.

Protecting Your Social Security Number

One good way to minimize the risk of identity theft is to be very careful about giving out your Social Security number (SSN). Many people think they have to provide their SSN to creditors or government entities that ask for it. But this isn't always true—in some cases, you don't have to reveal it.

All government agencies that request your SSN must tell you whether providing it is mandatory or optional. For many government agencies, including tax authorities, welfare offices, and state Departments of Motor Vehicles, your SSN is mandatory. But it isn't always mandatory. If it isn't, the government cannot deny you a benefit or service due to your refusal to disclose your SSN.

Employers, as well as most banks, can require that you disclose your SSN. But you are usually not required to give your SSN to private businesses. Some businesses have a legitimate reason to ask for your number (for example, when you apply for credit), but, in other cases, they simply want it for general record keeping. You don't have to give a business your SSN just because they request it. Ask these questions before deciding whether to give out your number:

- Why do you need my number?
- How will my number be used?
- What law requires me to give you my number?
- What will happen if I don't give you my number?
- Can I give you an identifier other than my SSN, or give you just the last four digits of my SSN?
- Can my account be set up so that I can use an identifier other than my SSN (for example, a combination of letters from my last name and numbers)?

If you're filling out a form and decide not to provide your SSN, you can leave the space blank or write "refused."

But a business can refuse to serve you if you don't disclose your SSN. In some situations, you may want to disclose the number to avoid hassles down the road. In other situations, you may want to take your business elsewhere.

It's a good idea to check your Social Security earnings and benefits statement each year to be sure that no one else is using your Social Security number for employment. You should receive this statement automatically each year if you have worked and are 25 or older. If you don't receive an annual statement or the statement shows that someone else is using your Social Security number for employment, contact the Social Security Administration's fraud hotline (800-269-0271) immediately.

If you're already a victim of identity theft, consider getting a new SSN. This isn't easy. The Social Security Administration will change your number only if you can show that you've taken all other steps to deal with identity theft and are still being disadvantaged by the misuse of your Social Security number. Even if you do fit within the definition, think carefully before you apply for a new SSN. A new SSN will not ensure a clean credit report, because credit reporting agencies may combine the credit records from your old SSN with your new records. For more information, check out the Federal Trade Commission's website at www.ftc.gov and the Social Security Administration's website at www.ssa.gov. At the very least, contact the Social Security Administration to report any fraudulent use of your SSN.

If Your Identity Is Stolen

Minimizing the disaster of identity theft depends primarily on your vigilant and constant efforts to guard your personal identification privacy, and thus be aware as quickly as possible that you've been the victim of an intrusion.

If you think you are, or are about to become, a victim of identity theft (for example, your wallet is lost or stolen, blank checks you have ordered do not arrive in the mail, or you are billed for charges you did not make or on accounts you did not open), you should act immediately to protect yourself. Here are the steps you should take, beginning when you first believe you are or may become the victim of identity theft:

1. **Contact creditors, banks, utilities, and phone companies.** Find out whether your accounts have been tampered with or new accounts have been opened in your name. Ask to speak to someone in the security or fraud department and follow up with a letter confirming what you discussed. Close any accounts that have been tampered with. Some also advocate closing accounts that haven't been affected yet, on the theory that it's just a matter of time before the thief gets to those, too. This could lead to problems, however: You might have trouble getting new credit or opening new accounts until the identity theft problem is resolved. Instead, you can notify creditors that you have been or may be a victim of identity theft, set up a new password, and ask that a fraud alert be placed on your accounts.

2. **Report stolen checks.** Some of the agencies to report to include Telecheck (www.telecheck.com or 800-710-9898), Certegy Claims Information System (800-437-5120), CheckRite (www.checkritesystems.com or 701-214-4123), Chexsystems (www.chexhelp.com or 800-428-9623), or CheckCenter/CrossCheck (800-843-0760). Report your checks stolen to all of these agencies; different merchants report to different agencies, so reporting to all of them gives you the best change of preventing your stolen checks from being used or cashed.

3. **Request an initial fraud alert.** You should request an initial fraud alert from one of the three major credit reporting agencies as soon as you think you have been or may soon be a victim of identity theft. You will have to submit proof of your identity, which may include your Social Security number. The agency receiving the alert must notify the other two agencies, and all three must place an initial alert in your file for 90 days. The initial alert states that you do not authorize an additional card for an existing account, an increase in the credit limit of an existing account, or new credit (other than an extension of credit on an existing credit card account). Because the initial alert requires creditors to take reasonable measures to confirm your identity, the alert may delay your ability to get credit.

Each agency must also provide the alert each time it generates your credit score. You can get a free credit report from each of the major agencies when you place an alert, upon your request. If you find that you don't need the alert—for example, because you found a missing credit card or checks—you can ask to have the alert removed before 90 days have passed. Of course, you'll have to provide enough identifying information so the agency knows its you—and not the thief—asking that the alert be removed.

4. **Close unused existing accounts.** Don't give an identity thief any extra opportunities.

5. **Review your credit report from each credit reporting agency.** Check each report carefully, looking for accounts you didn't apply for or open, inquiries you didn't initiate, and defaults and delinquencies you didn't cause. Also check your identifying information carefully.

6. **Fill out an ID Theft Complaint online at the website of the Federal Trade Commission.** Many protections against identify theft will be available to you only after you file an identity theft report with the credit reporting agencies. An identify theft report must include specific information about the theft and must be filed with a law enforcement agency under penalty of perjury. The FTC recommends that you use a copy of its ID Theft Complaint along with a police report as an identity theft report. To fill out a Complaint, go to www.ftc.gov/bcp/edu/microsites/idtheft, click on "Consumers," then "Filing a Complaint with the FTC." You can also file the complaint in writing, by sending it to the Identity Theft Clearinghouse, Federal Trade Commission, 600 Pennsylvania Avenue, NW, Washington, DC 20580. Make copies of the report for yourself, the credit reporting agencies, law enforcement, and your creditors.

7. **File a police report.** If you lost your credit card, checks, or other identifying information as part of a larger burglary or theft, you may have filed a police report. Once you learn you have become a victim of identity theft, however, you must make sure that you file required information with the police or another law enforcement agency. Appendix B includes a copy of the FTC's cover letter to send to police when filing a police report about identify theft. It explains what information must be included so the report can qualify as an identify theft report and filed with the credit reporting agencies. You should also give the police a copy of your FTC ID Theft Complaint. Make sure to get copies of the police report; you may need to send them to creditors, collection agencies, and so on.

8. **Ask the credit reporting agencies not to include information related to the identity theft in your credit report.** You must send each agency proof of your identity and an identity theft report: the police report you filed with a law enforcement agency, your FTC ID Theft Complaint, and any additional information the credit reporting agency requires. You must identify the fraudulent information in your credit report and state that

the information does not relate to any transaction by you. The agency normally must block reporting of the information and inform the creditor that provided the information that it has been blocked. The creditor cannot then sell, transfer, or place the debt for collection.

9. **Request an extended fraud alert.** You can ask credit reporting agencies to place an extended alert in your file when you file your identify theft report. The extended alert is similar to the initial alert, but it remains in place for seven years and entitles you to two free copies of your credit report from each agency during the next 12 months. For five years, the agency must exclude you from lists it prepares for creditors or insurers who send out prescreened offers (offers you didn't request). You may provide a telephone number or other contact information that creditors must use to confirm that any requests for credit in your name are actually made by you, not an identify thief.

10. **Fill out an FTC identity theft affidavit.** This is a less detailed version of the FTC ID Theft Complaint; you can find a copy in Appendix B or online at www.ftc. gov/bcp/edu/resources/forms/affidavit. pdf. Creditors may accept this affidavit as proof when you claim that you're not responsible for a new account or for transactions on an existing account. (Some creditors may require you to submit more information or use a different form.) Creditors can use this information to investigate your claim. Send the completed affidavit by certified mail, return receipt requested, and keep the originals of any supporting documents.

11. **Notify the post office if you suspect the thief filed a phony change of address form.** That form will be an important piece of evidence for the police. Fill out a "False Change of Address Complaint," available from the U.S. Postal Inspection Service, https://postalinspectors.uspis.gov/forms/ fcoa.aspx.

12. **Ask utility and phone companies to remove fraudulent charges.** If a phone company won't take these charges off of your account, contact your state public utility commission for local service providers. For long distance and cellular providers, contact the Federal Communications Commission at www.fcc.gov or 888-225-5322.

13. **Request copies of the identity thief's records from businesses that have provided credit, goods, or services.** Ordinarily, businesses must send you and any law enforcement agencies you specify copies of applications and transaction records free upon your written request. Your request must include satisfactory proof of your identity, a police report, and a completed FTC identity theft affidavit. You must send the request to the address the businesses specifies for this purpose.

14. **Ask businesses to stop providing information relating to the identity theft to credit reporting agencies. If any businesses have reported transactions by an identity thief to the agencies, ask them to stop.** You must send an identity theft report to the address the business specifies for this

purpose and identify the information in question. The business usually must stop providing this information to credit reporting agencies after receiving your written request.

15. **Find out whether your Social Security number has been used fraudulently.** Get a copy of your Social Security benefits statement to find out whether anyone is using your number. You can find it online, at www.ssa.gov. If you don't receive an annual copy of your report or you notice fraudulent use of your Social Security number, contact the SSA's fraud hotline, at 800-269-0271.

16. **Apply for a new driver's license number, if necessary.** If your driver's license number is being used fraudulently, you can apply for a new one. Be prepared to show proof of the theft and your damages.

17. **Tell debt collectors who call about fraudulent charges that they were incurred as a result of identity theft.** The collector is then required to tell the creditor that the debt may be the result of identity theft. The collector also must send you information that "validates" the debt. Once you receive the validation, send the collector a written dispute of the debt and a copy of your identity theft report, including your FTC ID Theft Complaint and your police report. Send a copy to the creditor, too. Ordinarily, this will give you a complete defense to the debt, which you shouldn't pay. In response to your information, the collector may stop collection efforts. If not, it may be helpful to consult with an attorney. You should definitely contact

an attorney if you are notified of a legal action against you based on debts incurred by the identity thief.

18. **Consider placing a security freeze on your report.** A security freeze prevents credit reporting agencies from reporting most information about you. If you want additional credit, you will have to lift the freeze temporarily. See "How to Protect Yourself," above, for more information on security freezes.

19. **Keep good records of all your work.** Take notes of every conversation you have with creditors, law enforcement agencies, credit reporting agencies, and others about the identity theft. Keep copies of all correspondence you send and receive relating to the theft.

20. **Be persistent.** Unfortunately, it can be tough to undo the effects of identity theft. You'll need to take control of the situation and follow up with police, credit reporting agencies, credit card companies, banks, and others. Continue to call, write letters, and keep track of your efforts until you have successfully reversed the damage.

TIP

Service members qualify for an active duty alert. If you're on active duty, you can add an active duty alert to your credit report by making a request to one of the major credit reporting agencies. This alert is similar to the other fraud alerts, but stays in place for 12 months and excludes you from prescreened lists for two years. Creditors and others who request your credit report must take extra steps to verify your identity before proceeding with any credit transaction. The alert also lets creditors know they that you and your dependents qualify for certain legal protections available only to service members. (See Chapter 1 and contact a military legal assistance office for more information about active duty service members' rights.)

RESOURCE

More information on identity theft. The Federal Trade Commission's website on identity theft (www.ftc.gov/bcp/ edu/microsites/idtheft) has lots of useful information. The State of California's Office of Privacy Protection (www.iospp.ca.gov) has good general information on identity theft, as well as California-specific information. The nonprofit Privacy Rights Clearinghouse (www.privacyrights. org) has useful information and resources on identity theft. The nonprofit Identity Theft Resource Center has resources for victims of identity theft at www.idtheftcenter.org. Another good list of resources (state and federal agencies and laws) can be found at the LLRX.com website, www.llrx.com/features/idtheft.htm.

Identity Theft Protection Products and Insurance

Many private companies (often security agencies) now sell products or packages designed to insure against identity theft damages or to protect you from becoming a victim. Before you buy these services or products, however, check them out carefully. Some are scams designed to get your personal information and take advantage of you. One cheap product to consider is a paper shredder.

Also, a number of insurance companies sell identity theft protection—either as a separate insurance policy or as an option that comes with your homeowners insurance policy (some policies include this protection automatically). These policies provide compensation for common expenses associated with identity theft including lost wages, mailing costs, and attorney's fees. Some credit cards also offer an identity theft protection feature.

Laws Against ID Theft

In 1998, Congress passed, and President Clinton signed, the Identity Theft and Assumption Deterrence Act (18 USC § 1028). This law makes the use of another person's identity with the intent to commit any unlawful activity under either state or federal law a federal felony. Violations of the Act are investigated by federal agencies, including the Secret Service, FBI, and Postal Inspection Service, and prosecuted by the Department of Justice. The law allows for restitution to victims.

Additionally, many states have passed or are considering laws related to identify theft. For a list of state identity theft laws, visit the Federal Trade Commission's website; go to www.ftc.gov and click on the "Identity Theft" link. Use the "Law Enforcement" tab to reveal the pull-down menu, and then click on "Laws." Even if your state does not have a law specifically identified as an identity theft law, the issue is likely covered under other state laws.

In 2003, Congress passed the Fair and Accurate Credit Transations Act (FACTA), which amends the Fair Credit Reporting Act by adding provisions aimed at preventing identity theft, limiting its effect on consumers' credit reports, and helping victims clean up their credit reports. Some of these new provisions are described above.

How Creditors and Employers Use Your Credit Report

Who Can Look at Your Credit Report 108

How Credit Applications Are Evaluated 110

    Your Three Cs 110

    Your Credit Score 111

If you've read and followed the advice in Chapter 4, you should feel confident that you've done everything you can to clean up your credit report. If you are back in good financial shape, now is the time to start thinking about rebuilding your credit. To do that, it helps to understand who has access to your credit report and how it is used to evaluate your credit.

Who Can Look at Your Credit Report

The federal Fair Credit Reporting Act (FCRA) (15 U.S.C. §§ 1681 and following) and state credit reporting laws restrict who can access your credit report and how it can be used.

The people and entities that can request your credit report include:

- **Employers,** who often use credit reports to conduct background checks of job applicants and to assess current employees for promotions or job reassignments. Before ordering your credit report, employers must first get your written authorization and provide certain disclosures. Many employers never look at credit reports. And those that do often will not be concerned about your financial problems. If you do have some negative information on your report, you might want to discuss it with the employer before he or she sees the report. (In some states, you can get a copy of your report at the same time the employer does.) Older information may be included in a credit report if you are seeking a job that pays $75,000 or more. So if you agree to allow the employer to see your credit report, it may include information that others won't get to see.

- **Government agencies,** which can request your credit report to determine whether you are eligible for public assistance. They do this to look for hidden income or assets, not to see if you have unpaid bills. The law also allows state and local government officials to get reports to help determine whether you can make child support payments. If you apply for a license issued by a government agency, it can look at your credit report if it must consider your financial status in determining your eligibility. But not all government agencies can look at your credit report. For example, district attorneys cannot look at reports to investigate criminal or civil cases, and the U.S. Citizenship and Immigration Services (formerly the INS) cannot get a report for an immigration proceeding or for reviewing citizenship applications. Government agencies investigating international terrorism can get credit reports, however.

- **Insurance companies,** which can look at your report if you apply for a policy. Usually, they are not interested in your credit history but instead may ask about your medical history or about any insurance claims you have filed. A credit reporting agency cannot provide an insurance company a credit report that contains medical information unless you consent. If you are seeking life insurance for $150,000 or more, the life insurance company is entitled to see older information that wouldn't otherwise be included in your credit report.

- **Collection agencies,** which can look at your report when trying to collect an overdue debt from you. They mainly do this to try to locate you or learn more about your assets.

- **Judgment creditors,** who are allowed to look at credit reports in order to decide whether to begin collection efforts against you. They can also use reports for "skip tracing" (hiring someone to locate you or your assets).

- **Potential creditors,** who are allowed to review your report when you apply for credit. Although this is a broad category, there are some restrictions. For a new transaction, you must have made an offer or otherwise initiated a credit transaction before the creditor can look at your report. It is important to be careful when you are shopping around, especially for cars. Dealers will try to get you to sign an authorization so that they can look at your report and size up your financial situation before beginning their sales pitch. This request will then appear on your credit report and may negatively affect your credit. (See Chapter 4 for more information about credit inquiries.)

- **Landlords and mortgage lenders,** who you can expect to scrutinize your report very carefully before offering to lend you money to buy a home. If you are seeking to borrow $150,000 or more, older information will be provided to the lender. So mortgage lenders often see information that wouldn't be provided to other creditors.

- **Utility companies,** which can request your credit report. However, there are special rules that prevent utility companies from denying you service in many circumstances, even if you have bad credit. Negative marks generally should matter only if you owe money to the particular utility company from which you seek service. Even then, most utility companies are required to offer special payment plans and programs for people with low income that allow you to get affordable utility service.

- **Student loan and grant lenders,** most of whom cannot deny your application because of poor credit. However, there are a few exceptions. For example, lenders are required to check the credit of parents applying for PLUS loans. Also, you cannot get a new federal loan if you are in default on another federal loan unless you have made satisfactory arrangements to repay it, including having made your payments for at least six months.

Apart from those listed above, most other people and businesses cannot legally request a copy of your credit report. For example, your credit report may not be used in divorce, child custody, immigration, and other legal proceedings. Government agencies are allowed to look at your report in these cases only if they get a court order allowing them to do so.

It's not always easy to find out if someone who should not have access to your credit report has requested and received one anyway. One way to detect unauthorized users is to order your credit report and look for unfamiliar names or businesses in the list of inquiries. (See Chapter 4 for information on how to order your credit report.) If someone has requested your report illegally, you may be able to sue for violation of the Fair Credit Reporting Act—you'll probably need the help of a lawyer to do this. You should also complain to state and federal government agencies. Appendix A includes a list of state agencies that regulate credit reporting agencies. The Federal Trade Commission (at www.ftc.gov) is the primary enforcer of the federal Fair Credit Reporting Act.

How Credit Applications Are Evaluated

When you apply for credit, creditors use two primary methods to evaluate your request. They:

- weigh your three Cs—capacity, collateral, and character, and
- obtain a credit score based on the information in your credit report.

Your Three Cs

A creditor wants to know whether you are likely to repay a loan or pay charges you incur on a line of revolving credit. To determine your creditworthiness, creditors evaluate your three Cs.

Capacity

Capacity refers to how much debt you can realistically pay given your income. Creditors look at how long you've been at your job, your income level, and the likelihood that your income will increase over time. They also look at whether you're in a stable job or at least a stable job industry. It's important when you fill out a credit application to make your job sound stable, high level, and even "professional." Are you a secretary, or are you an executive secretary or the office manager? Present yourself in the best possible light, but don't lie.

Creditors also examine your existing credit relationships, such as credit cards, bank loans, and mortgages. They want to know your credit limits (you may be denied additional credit if you already have a lot of open credit lines), your current credit balances, how long you've had each account, and your payment history— whether you pay late or on time.

Collateral

Creditors like to see that you have assets they can take if you don't pay your debt. Owning a home or liquid assets (such as a mutual fund) may offer considerable comfort to a creditor reviewing an application. This is especially true if your credit report has negative notations in it, such as late payments.

Character

Creditors develop a feeling of your financial character through objective factors that show stability. These include how long you've lived at your current residence, how long you've held your current job, whether you rent or own your home (you're more likely to stay put if you own), and whether you have checking and savings accounts.

These days, most creditors use credit scores (see below) to evaluate applications for credit. If the creditor considers your credit score to be good, it probably will approve your application without further evaluation. If your credit score is below the creditor's threshold for routine approval, it may review your application and consider your three Cs or it may simply reject you. If you are rejected, you may be able to find another creditor with different approval criteria. Be sure to get a copy of your credit report to see what the problem is.

Your Credit Score

Most credit reports include a credit score. Credit scores are numerical calculations that are supposed to indicate the risk that you will default on your payments. To come up with your score, a company gathers information about your credit history, such as how many accounts you have, whether you pay on time, collection actions against you, and so on, then compares you to others with a similar profile and awards you points based on your creditworthiness.

A high credit score indicates that you are a low risk—in other words, that you are more likely to repay a loan—and a low score indicates potential problems.

Lenders use credit scores to determine whether to extend you new credit, whether to increase or decrease an existing line of credit, whether it will be easy to collect from you on an outstanding account, and even whether you are likely to file for bankruptcy. The vast majority of mortgage lenders rely on credit scores, as do car dealers, credit card issuers, and insurance companies. Your credit score determines not only whether you'll get the loan, but also what your interest rate will be: The lower your score, the higher your interest rate.

How Credit Scores Are Calculated

Credit scoring companies use criteria similar to the three Cs when calculating scores. The largest and most ubiquitous credit scoring company is the Fair Isaac Corporation: the company that generates "FICO" scores. The factors Fair Isaac considers in coming up with credit scores include:

- Payment history (about 35% of the score). The company looks at whether you've paid on time, have any delinquent accounts, or have declared bankruptcy.
- Amounts owed on credit accounts (about 30% of the score). Fair Isaac looks at the amounts you owe and how many of your accounts carry a balance. The more you owe compared to your credit limits, the lower your score.

- Length of credit history (about 15% of the score). Generally, a longer credit history yields a higher score.
- New credit (about 10% of the score). Fair Isaac likes to see an established credit history rather than a lot of new accounts. Opening several accounts in a short period of time might indicate a higher risk. Inquiries on your account may also lower your score, depending on the reason. For example, if a number of creditors check your credit report because you are looking for many new sources of credit, that will drop your score more than if you are comparison shopping for a particular type of credit, like a car loan or mortgage. And, as long as you do all of your comparison shopping with 30 days, it shouldn't have much effect on your score.
- Types of credit (about 10% of the score). Fair Isaac is looking for a "healthy mix" of different types of credit, both revolving accounts (such as credit cards) and installment accounts (like a mortgage or car loan).

Your credit score may differ depending on the company that generates it, the information considered, and the reason why the score is created. Although Fair Isaac is the largest credit scoring company, it isn't the only one. Lenders and credit reporting agencies may use different scoring programs that yield different results. Even using the FICO scoring criteria, your scores may differ. For example, the information each of the credit reporting agencies has on you is a bit different, so each might generate a slightly different score. Fair Isaac also offers a variety of FICA scoring formulas that emphasize different aspects of your credit, which means the score on creditor sees may be different than the score you or another creditor might see.

Most credit scores range from lows of 300 to 400 to highs of 800 to 990, depending on the type of score. FICO scores range from 300 to 850. Fair Isaac estimates that about 40% of Americans have FICO scores of more than 750, which most lenders would consider to be very good. Another scoring system, VantageScore, was introduced a few years ago by the three major credit reporting agencies; this score ranges from a low of 501 to a high of 990. Like a FICO score, higher numbers mean less risk. VantageScore also provides a letter grade (A, B, C, or F). Because FICO is more familiar, VantageScore can be confusing. For example, a FICO score of 780 is very good, but only fair on the VantageScore scale. Perhaps in part for this reason, it's not clear whether many lenders are using VantageScore.

How to Get Your Credit Score

Sometimes, your score must be provided to you in connection with a credit transaction. If you apply for a loan on residential property, for example, the mortgage lender must disclose your credit score, the range of possible scores under the scoring model used to generate your score, four key factors that affected your score, the date when the score was generated, and the name of the entity that provided the score (for example,

Fair Isaac). The lender must also give you a notice with contact information for the credit reporting agency that provided the score.

Lenders that evaluate loan applications using automated systems may disclose either the system's score and the key factors that affected it or a score from a credit reporting agency. (If you receive a score in this situation, be sure to ask the lender which one it provided—a score from its system or from a credit reporting agency.) Under California law, if a car dealer gets your credit score in connection with your application for a vehicle loan or lease, the dealer must give you your score, information on the range of possible score, and contact information for the credit reporting agency that supplied the score.

You can also get your score from Fair Isaac and/or the credit reporting agencies that develop or distribute them, for a cost of about $8 to $16. Watch out for extra fees for services like credit monitoring; these can drive up the price.

It may not be worth paying to get your score, however. Because creditors use different scores (and sometimes generate their own), you can't be sure that the score you buy is the one any particular creditor will rely on. In 2008, for example, Consumer Reports paid $130 to get 11 different credit scores for the same person. The scores differed by up to 72 points, and were judged to mean everything from a fair to a good to an excellent credit risk! Their conclusion was that it's probably not worth the money to pay for a credit score.

RESOURCE

Want more information on credit scores? To keep up on credit scoring developments, visit www.creditscoring.com, a private website devoted to credit scoring. (Be cautious, however; many links are to other sites that want to sell you credit reports or scores.) You can also check out the booklet, "Understanding Credit Reports and Scores," available from Fair Isaac's website, www.myfico,com.

Tips for Raising Your Credit Score

Fair Isaac offers these tips for raising your credit score:

- Pay your bills on time.
- Make up missed payments and keep all your payments current.
- Maintain low balances on credit cards and other revolving debt.
- Pay off debt rather than transferring it to a new account.
- Don't close unused credit card accounts just to raise your credit score.
- Don't get new credit cards that you don't need.

Other tips are included in "Understanding Credit Reports and Scores" at the Fair Isaac website, www.myfico.com.

Building and Maintaining Good Credit

Build Credit in Your Own Name 117

Ask Creditors to Consider Your Spouse's Credit History 117

Get Credit Cards and Use Them Wisely 118

    Applying for Credit Cards 118

    Cosigners and Guarantors 126

    Authorized User Accounts 127

    Secured Credit Cards 127

    Closing Credit Card Accounts 129

Open Deposit Accounts 130

Work With Local Merchants 132

Obtain a Bank Loan 132

Avoid Credit Repair Clinics 133

Avoid Credit Discrimination 144

    Laws Prohibiting Credit Discrimination 144

    What to Do If a Creditor Discriminates Against You 149

Establishing and keeping a good credit record is the final step in repairing your credit. This chapter covers the many ways you can build a positive credit history, including getting credit in your own name if you're married or divorced, applying for credit cards, getting a secured card, and obtaining bank loans. It also provides tips on how to maintain good credit, from using credit cards wisely to avoiding credit repair clinics. (See also "Tips for Raising Your Credit Score," in Chapter 5.) If you take the steps suggested in this chapter, you will probably be able to get a

Should You Stay Out of the Credit System?

Habitual overspending can be just as hard to overcome as excessive gambling or drinking. If you think you may be a compulsive spender, one of the worst things you can do is repair your credit and then get more. Instead, you need to get a handle on your spending habits.

Debtors Anonymous, a 12-step support program similar to Alcoholics Anonymous, has programs nationwide. If a Debtors Anonymous group or a therapist recommends that you stay out of the credit system for a while, follow that advice. Even if you don't feel you're a compulsive spender, paying as you spend may still be the way to go—because of finance charges, transaction fees, and other charges, buying on credit may cost 20% to 35% more than paying with cash.

Debtors Anonymous groups meet all over the country. If you can't find one in your area, send a self-addressed, stamped envelope to Debtors Anonymous, General Services Office, P.O. Box 920888, Needham, MA 02492-0009. Or call their office and speak to a volunteer or leave your name, address, and a request for information. The number is 800-421-2383. You can also visit their website at www .debtors anonymous.org.

Concern about habitual overspending isn't the only reason to stay outside the credit system. Followers of a movement known as "voluntary simplicity" suggest that reliance on credit is one of the reasons people are overworked and overstressed. Credit gives us the chance to consume—and often we consume far more than we need to live comfortably and at an easy pace.

Much has been written about voluntarily downshifting. Advocates are not suggesting that we all move to the wilderness, quit our jobs, and live without electricity and running water. But they do suggest that we take a hard look at our reliance on money—and credit— to bring us happiness.

For more information on voluntary simplicity, take a look at any of these resources:

- *Simplify Your Life: 100 Ways to Slow Down and Enjoy the Things That Really Matter,* by Elaine St. James (Hyperion)
- *Get a Life: You Don't Need a Million to Retire Well,* by Ralph Warner (Nolo), and
- *Your Money or Your Life: Transforming Your Relationship With Money and Achieving Financial Independence,* by Joe Dominguez and Vicki Robin (Penguin Books).

major credit card or loan in approximately two years. And, in about four years, you may be able to qualify for a mortgage.

Before you start this process, make sure you are financially ready to get more credit. If you get new credit too soon, while you're still in financial trouble, you're likely to dig yourself deeper into debt. First focus on stabilizing your employment, income, and debt situation. Get your high-priority debts, such as rent, mortgage, or car payments, under control. Once you're in decent financial shape, start following the strategies in this chapter to build good credit.

 SKIP AHEAD

If you've never been married. Those who have never married can skip ahead to "Get Credit Cards and Use Them Wisely," below

Build Credit in Your Own Name

If you are married, separated, or divorced, and most of your credit is in your spouse's or ex-spouse's name only, you should start to get credit in your name, too.

Getting credit in your own name is also an excellent strategy for repairing your credit if:

- all or most of your financial problems can be attributed to your spouse, or
- you and your spouse have gone through financial difficulties together, but most of your credit was in your spouse's name only.

Your spouse's bad credit shouldn't count against you because it shouldn't show up on your credit report. Credit reporting agencies may not include information about your spouse's accounts on your credit report unless it's a joint account or you are otherwise responsible for payment on the account (for example, because you guaranteed or cosigned a loan).

This is usually good news if you are worried that your spouse's negative credit history may reflect badly on you—your spouse's accounts should not appear on your credit report. However, if you are divorced or separated and most of your loans and credit cards were in your spouse's name only, you won't have a lengthy history of good credit in your report. You now need to start building good credit in your own name. If you are still married, you can start by making sure that all joint accounts and accounts that you are obligated to pay appear on your credit report, too. Then, follow the steps outlined in the rest of this chapter for building credit.

Ask Creditors to Consider Your Spouse's Credit History

Although a credit reporting agency cannot include information about your spouse's positive credit accounts on your credit report (unless the account is also in your name or you are obliged to pay it), if you are applying for a loan, credit card, or other type of credit, you can always ask the creditor to consider any of your spouse's accounts that reflect favorably on your creditworthiness, too. For example, if you and your spouse make payments on your spouse's account with joint checks, bring this to the creditor's attention. A creditor doesn't have to consider this information, but it may.

Get Credit Cards and Use Them Wisely

If you survived financial disaster and managed to hold onto one of your credit cards or a department store or gasoline card, use it and pay your bills on time. Your credit history will improve quickly. Most credit reports show payment histories for two to four years. If you charge something every month, no matter how small, and pay it off every month, your credit report will show steady and proper use of revolving credit.

> CAUTION
>
> **Charge only a small amount each month and pay it in full.** By paying in full, you will avoid incurring interest, as long as your card has a grace period. The average consumer who makes only the minimum payment each month ends up paying hundreds of dollars in interest charges alone. For example, if you charge $1,000 on a 17% credit card and pay it off by making the minimum payments of 2% of the balance each month, you'll take more than seven years to pay off the loan and will end up paying more than $1,760.

Applying for Credit Cards

If you don't currently have a credit card, apply for one. Keep in mind the general guidelines under the three Cs discussion (in Chapter 5) when completing your credit application. Don't lie, but present yourself in the best possible light.

> CAUTION
>
> **Don't plunge in until you're ready.** Getting new credit cards before your finances are in order is a bad idea. Wait until you're out of financial trouble before you apply for credit.

It's often easiest to obtain a card from a department store or gasoline company. These companies usually open your account with a very low credit line. If you start with one credit card, charge items, and pay the bill on time, other companies will issue you a card. When you use department store and gasoline cards, try not to carry a balance from one month to the next. The interest rate on these cards can be very high.

Next, apply for a regular credit card from a bank, such as a Visa, MasterCard, or Discover card. Competition for customers has been fierce, and you may be able to find a card with relatively low initial rates. Depending on how bad your credit history is, however, you may be eligible only for a low credit line or a card with a high interest rate. If you use the card and make your payments, after a year or so you can apply to increase your line of credit or reduce the interest rate.

In fact, no matter what your situation, it makes sense to call your credit card company and ask for a lower interest rate. A study conducted by the United States Public Interest Research Group in 2002 found that more than half of the consumers who complained to their credit card company were able to reduce their interest rate, usually by as much as one third. (To find out more, contact U.S. PIRG at www.uspirg .org or visit www.truthaboutcredit.org.)

Tips for Applying

The following tips will help you when you apply for credit cards or an increased credit limit:

- **Be consistent with the name you use.** Use your middle initial always or never. Always use your generation (Jr., Sr., III, and so on).
- **Take advantage of preapproved credit for department store, gasoline, and bank cards.** If your credit is shot, you

---

Is It Still Raining Credit Cards?

Since the 1990s, credit card offers have boomed. Even with a downturn in the economy, credit card issuers were still expected to send out four to five billion credit card solicitations in 2008. But beginning in mid-2008, some major banks reduced the number of credit card solicitations they sent out by 45% to 55% from the previous year. Some credit card companies began closing unused accounts and lowering credit limits and raising fees.

Even so, there are still a lot of credit solicitations out there. If you've been through bankruptcy or other tough financial times but your problems are behind you, or you've never had credit, you may still be considered a candidate for a credit card.

Credit card issuers operate in a competitive environment. People who have been through bankruptcy are considered good credit risks—their debt is gone, they have a history of using credit, and *they can't file for bankruptcy again for another eight years.*

In fact, a Texas bankruptcy judge asked a couple who filed for bankruptcy to keep track of how many credit card solicitations they received during the two-year period after they filed their case. The total: 53, with credit limits ranging from $100 to $20,000.

And people who have been through bankruptcy aren't the only ones with multiple credit card offers. New immigrants, low-wage earners, and others traditionally kept out of the credit world are being invited to participate, but at astronomical rates of interest.

Beware of all these offers. They don't indicate that you can afford more credit. Don't fall into the trap of thinking, "They must think I can handle more credit or they wouldn't keep offering it to me." Credit card issuers are looking for consumers who will run up big balances and pay a lot of interest.

may not have the luxury of shopping around.

- **Be honest, but appear sympathetic.** Lenders are especially apt to ignore past credit problems that were out of your control—such as those caused by a job layoff or illness.

- **Bolster your credit application.** Don't lie, but don't denigrate yourself, either. For example, if you're an administrative assistant, don't put "clerk/typist" for your job title. Also, if you are married and your spouse has excellent credit, apply jointly or at least indicate on the credit application that you are married.

- **Apply for credit when you are most likely to get it.** For example, apply when you are working, when you've lived at the same address for at least a year, and when you don't have an unusually high number of inquiries on your credit report.

- **Apply for credit from creditors with whom you've done business.** For example, your phone company, insurance company, or bank may offer Visas or MasterCards to their customers.

- **Don't get swept up by credit card gimmicks.** Before applying for a credit card that gives you rebates, credit for future purchases, or other perks, make sure you will benefit from the offer. Some are good deals, especially cards that give you cash back. But, in general, a card with no annual fee and/or a low interest rate usually beats the "deals" or "rewards" you get from another card.

- **Scrutinize any preapproval solicitations for nonbank cards.** A "gold" or "platinum" card with a high credit limit may be nothing more than a card that lets you purchase items through catalogues provided by the company itself. No other merchant accepts these cards, and the company won't report your charges and payments to the credit reporting agencies.

Comparison Shop

When it comes to obtaining a new credit card, you may not have as many choices as people who already have good credit. But you should still do some comparison shopping to make sure you are getting the best deal available to you. Credit card terms and interest rates vary—and some of those variations can make a huge difference to your wallet.

Always shop for the card with the best interest rate and terms. As a general rule, if you always pay your monthly bill in full, and you don't care about perks such as free miles, look for a card that has no annual fee and a longer grace period. On the other hand, if you carry a balance from month to month, look for a card that carries a lower annual percentage rate.

If you are comparison shopping for a card online, click through a credit card offer until you see a disclosure of terms and conditions that looks like the "Sample Disclosure Form," below. Sometimes you have to click through several pages to find it, but you should be able to review it before you provide the creditor with any information. Print out a copy so it is easier to compare cards.

Here's what you should look for in a credit card:

- **Avoid high interest rates.** Check the annual percentage rate (APR). This is the amount of interest that you will pay per year, expressed as a percentage. (See "Understanding APRs," below.)

- **Avoid low introductory rates.** Some cards have a low "introductory rate" (also called a "teaser rate"). After a few months, the interest rate will skyrocket. Also, sometimes the advertised rate applies only to certain people, such as those with a high income or credit score. The card company charges a much higher rate to those who don't qualify—which could mean an unpleasant surprise when your first bill arrives.

- **Understand the credit limit.** The credit limit is the total amount that you may charge on the credit card, including purchases, cash advances, balance transfers, fees, and finance charges. If you exceed the limit, you will have to pay an "over limit" fee. You may also have to pay a higher interest rate. And some creditors won't even tell you your credit limit when you apply: The offer will give you only a range, such as $300 to $3,000. Before you activate or use a new card, check the credit limit. If it is too low to be useful, consider cancelling the card, before it is too late. Even if you don't go over the limit, maxing out your

credit card is a quick way to lower your credit score.

- **Understand interest calculations.** Each month, the credit card company applies the APR to the balance to compute the finance charge for that month (see "Understanding APRs," below). Credit card companies may calculate the balance over one billing cycle or two (a one-cycle billing period will usually result in lower charges), and may include or exclude new purchases in the balance (excluding new purchases is usually better for consumers). The balance may be calculated in one of these three ways:

  - Adjusted balance method. The credit card company computes the finance charge by taking the amount you owed at the start of the billing cycle and subtracting any payments made during the cycle. New purchases are not included.

  - Previous balance method. The company uses the amount you owed at the beginning of the billing cycle to compute the finance charge.

  - Adjusted daily balance method. The company adds your balances for each day in the billing cycle and then divides that total by the number of days in the cycle. Payments made during the period are subtracted to get the daily amounts you owe. New purchases may or may not be included, depending on the plan. If the company uses a two-cycle average

Understanding APRs

The APR is the percentage you will pay in interest each year. Each month, the credit card company applies the APR to the account balance to compute the finance charge for that month. The finance charge is the dollar amount you pay to use the credit. The account balance may include purchases, previous months' unpaid balances, transaction charges, and other fees. The APR is the best single indicator of the actual interest you will pay.

A credit card may have several APRs. For example, one may apply to purchases, one to cash advances, and another to balance transfers. The APRs may be tied to different levels of outstanding balance; for example, the company may charge 14.9% on balances up to $500 and 17% on larger balances.

APRs also may be fixed or adjustable. An adjustable APR changes from time to time, and usually is tied to another interest rate, such as the prime rate or the Treasury Bill rate. The APR will change automatically when the other rate changes. Even a fixed APR may change over a period of time, but the credit card company must tell you before the rate changes.

As a general rule, look for the lowest and most stable APR when you shop for a credit card. If you carry a balance from month to month, even a small difference in the APR can make a big difference in how much you'll pay over a year.

---

daily balance method, it uses the average daily balance for two billing cycles. New purchases may or may not be included in the total.

- **Review the grace period.** This is the interest-free period between the date of purchase and the date due. It is usually available only to those who do not carry a balance. If you pay your bill in full each month, make sure you have a grace period. Otherwise, you'll pay interest from the date of your purchase. If you carry a balance, a grace period is not as important.
- **Avoid high annual fees.** Some credit card companies charge you a flat fee (in addition to interest and other charges) for using their card. Some do not. If you pay off your balance each month, you want a card without an annual fee. If you carry a balance, a card with an annual fee but a low interest rate may be better than a card with no annual fee but a high interest rate.
- **Find out if you'll be charged higher interest rates for cash advances and late payments.** Virtually all credit cards charge higher interest rates for cash advances. And almost all cards charge a hefty fee for late payments (up to $39) and impose a new, much

higher interest rate. If you think you might pay late once in a while (be realistic), check out these interest rates. Some are as high as 32%. Also, be aware that many credit card companies today will charge you a higher interest rate if you pay another creditor late (so-called "universal default"). Many creditors review their customers' credit reports regularly to identify "risky" cardholders. If this review makes the creditor feel insecure, it may raise your interest rate even though you have never made a late payment.

- **Watch out for extra fees.** Many, if not most, credit card companies charge a hefty fee (as high as $39) if your payment is late or you exceed your credit limit. Also, look out for cash advance fees, balance transfer fees, credit limit increase fees, setup fees, returned item fees, and fees for paying by telephone.

- **Evaluate rebates, free miles, and other perks.** Many credit cards allow you to earn cash back, free airline miles, discounts on goods and services,

funds for charity, or other bonuses by using the card. Don't sign up for a card based on these perks alone—be sure to consider the other card terms as well. If you will pay high interest and high annual fees, you are better off without the perks. You can use the money you save on interest and other fees to buy airline tickets yourself or contribute to your favorite charity.

Credit card companies must disclose many of the items discussed in this section in their solicitations and applications. (You'll find a sample disclosure below.) You can use disclosures like these to comparison shop among credit card offerings.

Many websites will help you shop for a credit card by surveying large numbers of credit card deals. You can compare and contrast terms and find the best card for you. A few to try are www.cardtrack.com, www.bankrate.com, and www.consumer-action.org (click the "Survey" link at the bottom of the page). For more information on credit cards and how to shop for them, see the Federal Reserve Board's website at http://federalreserve.gov/pubs/shop.

Sample Disclosure Form	
Annual percentage rate (APR) for purchases	0% until June 2009 billing period after that a variable rate, currently 19.7%
Other APRs	Special transfer APR: A variable rate, currently 19.7%* Balance Transfer APR: A variable rate, currently 19.7%* Cash advance APR: A variable rate, currently 24.9%* Default APR: A variable rate, currently equal to 29.9%*†
Variable-rate information	Your purchase APR may vary quarterly. The rate will be determined by adding 14.5% to the Prime rate.** Your balance transfer APR may vary quarterly. The rate will be determined by adding 14.5% to the Prime rate.** Your cash APR may vary quarterly. The rate will be determined by adding 17.5% to the Prime rate.** Your special transfer APR may vary quarterly. The rate will be determined by adding 14.5% to the Prime rate.** Your default APR may vary quarterly. The rate will be determined by adding 19.5% to the Prime rate.**†
Grace period for repayment of balances for purchases	25 days on average
Method of computing the balance for purchases	Average daily balance (including new purchases)
Annual fees	None
Minimum finance charge	$0.50

Transaction fee for cash advances: 3% of the amount advanced, $8 minimum

Balance transfer fee: 3% of the amount transferred, $8 minimum

Late-payment fee: $39

Over-the-credit-limit fee: $39

* Your variable APRs can increase or decrease as the Prime rate changes. Your introductory 0% APRs may increase to your non-introductory APR if your payment is received late (two or more days after your payment due date).

† Your APR may increase to the Default APR if your payment is received late twice within any six billing periods. If your APR is increased to the Default APR, it will return to your non-introductory APR if you make at least the minimum payment on time for 12 consecutive billing periods. In the future, we may increase your APRs if economic conditions change. If we increase your APRs for any reason other than an increase in the Prime rate or late payments as explained above, we will notify you in advance. If you choose to opt out, we will cancel your card and you will owe the balance under the old rate.

** The Prime rate used to determine your APR is the rate published in the *Wall Street Journal* on the 10th day of the prior month.

Protect Yourself

Once you receive a credit card, protect yourself and your efforts to repair your credit by following these suggestions:

- **Send your creditors a change of address when you move.** Many creditors provide change of address boxes on their monthly bills. For your other creditors, you can send a letter, call the customer service phone number, or use a post office change of address post card. Don't let your monthly statements go to your old address. You may miss making payments on time, or someone may steal your statement and use your identifying information to gain access to your account or obtain credit in your name.

- **If you need an increase in your credit limit, ask for it.** Many creditors will close accounts or charge late fees on customers who exceed their credit limits. But pay close attention: If you're charging to the limit on your credit card, you may be heading for financial trouble.

- **Take steps to protect your cards.** Sign your cards as soon as they arrive. If you have a personal identification number (PIN) that allows you to take cash advances, memorize it—never write it down near your credit card. Make a list of your credit card issuers, the account numbers, and the issuer's phone numbers so you can quickly call if you need to report a lost or stolen card.

- **Don't give your credit card or checking account number to anyone over the phone unless you placed the call** and are certain of the company's reputation. Never give your credit card or checking account number to someone who calls you and tries to sell you something or claims to need your account number to send you a "prize." Never give your credit card number, checking account number, or personal information to a caller who says that he represents a firm you do business with and that he needs to confirm or update your account information. The same is true for Internet inquiries like this. *All of these are scams.*

Read the Fine Print: Beware of Creditors Trying to Collect Stale or Discharged Debts

Creditors may not be able to collect or file a lawsuit to collect certain debts if the debts are several years old and you haven't made a recent payment. If you agree to repay an old debt or make a payment on it, however, you may "revive" the debt, so the creditor can once again try to collect it legally. Because of this rule, creditors often try to trick debtors into repaying old debts.

If you've been through bankruptcy, you're no longer liable to pay the debts discharged in your case. Unfortunately, however, many creditors don't see it that way.

Read all credit card solicitations carefully, particularly ones that promise to restore your credit. The fine print might tell you that by signing up for the card, you voluntarily agree to repay old debts or debts you discharged in bankruptcy. The solicitation won't necessarily come from the original creditor whose debt you wiped out. Often the creditor sells the debt to another, so you won't recognize the new creditor (who is now the current owner of your old or discharged debt).

Attempts to have you voluntarily repay discharged debts don't come only in the form of credit card solicitations. You might also receive phone calls or dunning letters threatening legal action—"intent to file suit"—if you don't pay up.

Remind any creditor that attempts to collect discharged debts are illegal under the Bankruptcy Code (11 U.S.C. § 524) and prohibited by the Fair Debt Collection Practices Act (15 U.S.C. § 1692e). And don't agree to pay or actually make payments on stale debts.

Cosigners and Guarantors

If you can't get a credit card or loan on your own, consider asking a friend or relative to cosign or serve as guarantor on an account. A cosigner is someone who promises to repay a loan or credit card charges if the primary debtor defaults. Similarly, a guarantor promises to pay the credit grantor if the primary debtor does not. Usually, neither the cosigner's nor the guarantor's name appears on the credit account.

Although getting a cosigner or guarantor will help you get credit, it may not help you build credit in all situations. On some cosigned accounts, the creditor will report the information on the cosigner's credit report only, not on yours. The best option is to ask if you can use a guarantor instead of a cosigner. It should make no difference to the creditor.

CAUTION

Cosigners and guarantors should fully understand their obligations before they sign on. For example, if the primary debtor doesn't pay the debt and erases it in bankruptcy, the cosigner or guarantor remains fully liable. The Federal Trade Commission's Credit Practices Rule requires that cosigners of credit issued by a financial institution or retail installment seller be given the following notice.

> You are being asked to guarantee this debt. Think carefully before you do so. If the borrower doesn't pay the debt, you will have to. Be sure you can afford to pay if you have to, and that you want to accept this responsibility.
>
> You may have to pay up to the full amount of the debt if the borrower does not pay. You may also have to pay late fees or collection costs, which increase this amount.
>
> The creditor can collect this debt from you without first trying to collect from the borrower. The creditor can use the same collection methods against you that can be used against the borrower, such as suing you, garnishing your wages, etc. If this debt is ever in default, that fact may become a part of your credit record.

Authorized User Accounts

Another way to repair your credit using a credit card relies on the generosity of a friend or relative you trust.

If you can find someone who is willing to add you to an account as an "authorized user," you can use the credit line but not be responsible for repaying the charges. The account holder must request that your name be added to the account and can ask that a card be issued in your name. Once your name is on the account, information

about the account will probably be added to your file—and you'll be listed as an authorized user.

This is different from becoming an authorized user on a stranger's card, a tactic that some companies have advertised. These companies find someone with good credit who is willing to allow a stranger to be added to their account for a fee. This is obviously quite risky to the account holder. Creditors also don't like it because it artificially boosts the credit score of the authorized user. Fair Isaac says it is developing a way to make it more difficult for the credit information of account holders to be used to boost the credit score of the added authorized user. But this new method won't apply to authorized users who are related to the card holder.

Of course, because the information concerning the account is reported in your credit file, this technique requires that the account holder not default. If a default occurs, that information will appear in your credit report—exactly what you don't want.

Secured Credit Cards

Many people with poor credit histories are denied regular credit cards. If your application is rejected, consider whether you truly need a credit card. Millions of people get along just fine without them. If you decide that you really need a card—for example, you travel quite a bit and need a card to reserve hotel rooms and rent cars—then you can apply for a secured credit card. With a secured credit card, you deposit a sum of money with a bank and are given a credit card with a credit limit for a percentage of the amount you deposit— as low as 50% and as high as 120%. Depending on the bank, you'll be required to deposit as little as a few hundred dollars or as much as a few thousand.

Unfortunately, secured credit cards can be expensive. Many banks charge hefty application and processing fees in addition to an annual fee. Also, the interest rate on secured credit cards can be close to 22%, while you may earn only 2% or 3% on the money you deposit. And some banks have eliminated the grace period—that is, interest on your balance begins to accrue on the date you charge, not 25 days later. If you find a card with a grace period and pay your bill in full each month, you can avoid the interest charges.

Another downside of secured credit cards is that some creditors don't accept or give much weight to credit history established with a secured credit card. Ask the card issuer if it reports to the three major credit reporting agencies. If the issuer doesn't, you've lost an important benefit of having a secured card. Some smaller issuers don't report to the credit reporting agencies, but most major banks do.

Many secured credit cards have a conversion option. This lets you convert the card into a regular credit card after several months or a year if you use the secured card responsibly. Because regular credit cards typically have lower interest rates and annual fees than secured credit cards, it's usually preferable to obtain a card with a conversion option.

Use the secured credit card to make small purchases that you can pay off each month. Always pay on time. This will help you build your credit. After you pay on time for a year, you may be able to qualify for an unsecured credit card with a lower interest rate. Then you can use the information in "Comparison Shop," above, to find the best card you can qualify for.

To find a bank offering a secured credit card, call some local banks or do some surfing on the Internet. One source of information is www.bankrate.com.

Avoid 900 number advertisements for "instant credit" or other such offers. Obtaining a secured credit card through one of these programs will probably cost you a lot—in application fees, processing fees, and phone charges. Sometimes you call one 900 number and are told you must call a second or third number. These ads also frequently mislead consumers into thinking that their lines of credit will be higher than they actually turn out to be. Also, be aware of secured credit cards that can be used only to purchase merchandise from the card issuer's catalogue. The merchandise often is shoddy and high priced, and the issuer probably won't report your charges and payments to the credit reporting agencies.

> ! **CAUTION**
> **Don't use your home as collateral.**
> If you do opt for a secured credit card, make sure it isn't secured by your home. If it is, and you get behind on your card payments, you could lose your home.

Closing Credit Card Accounts

If you want to close some accounts, here are some rules to follow:

- Close accounts you don't need. You can close an account even if you haven't paid off the balance. The card issuer will close your account, cancel your privileges, and send you monthly statements until you pay off your balance. Or contact the bank whose card you are keeping and ask it to transfer the balance on the account you are closing to the account you are keeping.

- Close accounts on which you are delinquent—otherwise, the credit card issuer may close them for you. If you're delinquent on all your accounts, keep open the most current account.

- If you pay your bill in full each month—that is, you don't carry a balance—close the accounts with the highest annual fees. Make sure that the accounts you keep open have a grace period in which you can pay off your bill and not incur any interest.

- If you carry a balance, close the accounts with the highest interest rates and shortest grace periods. Also, read your contract to understand the credit card company's billing practice. Interest may be calculated on the previous two months' balance, the average daily balance for the month, or your balance at the end of the billing cycle (see "Understanding APRs," above). Keep the cards that

How Many Credit Cards Should You Carry?

Once you succeed in getting a credit card, you might be hungry to apply for many more cards. Not so fast. Having too much credit probably contributed to your debt problems in the first place. Ideally, you should carry one bank credit card, one department store card, and one gasoline card. Your inclination may be to charge everything on your bank card and not bother using a department store or gasoline card. When creditors look in your credit file, however, they want to see that you can handle more than one credit account at a time. Don't build up interest charges on these cards—just use them and pay the bill in full each month.

Creditors frown on applicants who have a lot of open credit. So keeping many cards may mean that you'll be turned down for other credit—perhaps credit you really need. And, if your credit applications are turned down, your file will contain inquiries from the companies that rejected you. Your credit file will look like you were desperately trying to get credit, something creditors never like to see.

How to Close a Credit Card Account

If you want to close a credit card account, make sure you do it the right way.

- If you have any bills automatically deducted from your credit card, such as a credit card protection plan, gym dues, or DVD rental fees, cancel those billing arrangements directly with the billing company before closing your account.

- Write a letter to the credit card company and request a "hard close." If you don't do this, the company may give you a "soft close," which means new charges can go through, even though you asked that the account be closed. With a soft close, you are susceptible to credit card fraud.

- Some creditors may refuse to do a hard close until a certain amount of time has passed. If yours is one of them, find out how long you'll have to wait and demand that the company send you a letter then, confirming that the account has been hard closed.

- Also request, in writing, that the credit card company report to the credit reporting agencies that your account was "closed by consumer request." Accounts that are erroneously reported as "closed by creditor" will hurt your credit rating. Ask the company to send you written confirmation that the account was closed at your request.

- After 30 days, check your credit report to ensure that it reflects that the account in question was "closed by consumer request."

- Once you cancel the card, if you receive a credit card bill for items you canceled directly with the seller or for charges you dispute, use the procedures described in Chapter 3 to challenge those charges.

---

charge interest on the balance at the end of the billing cycle.

- Before you close an account, especially one you have had for a long time, consider how it may affect your credit score. Fair Isaac, the developer of the FICO credit score (see Chapter 5) recommends against closing unused credit card accounts if your purpose is to raise your FICO score. Read "Understanding Your FICO Score," available at www.myfico.com.

Open Deposit Accounts

Creditors look for bank accounts as a sign of stability. Quite frankly, they also look for bank accounts to make sure you'll be able to pay your bills. If you fill out a credit application and cannot provide a checking account number, you probably won't get credit.

A savings or money market account, too, will improve your standing with creditors. Even if you never deposit additional money into the account, creditors assume that people who have savings or money market accounts use them. Having an account reassures creditors of two things: You are making an effort to build up savings, and, if you don't pay your bill and the creditor must sue you to collect, it has a source from which to collect its judgment.

Just because you've had poor credit history, you shouldn't be denied a bank account. Shop around and compare fees, such as check writing fees, ATM fees, monthly service charges, the minimum balance to waive the monthly charge, interest rates on savings, and the like.

You might be denied an account, however, if you have a bad check writing history. Check verification companies keep track of banks' experiences with their customers, much as credit reporting agencies do for creditors. Most banks will check your check writing history with a check verification company before they will open an account for you. If you are denied a bank account because of information provided by a check verification company, call the company to discuss the problem and try to provide information that resolves it. If you can't resolve the problem informally, you can dispute incomplete or inaccurate information in the company's files just as you can with a credit reporting agency. Some popular check verification companies include:

- Certegy (800-437-5120)
- CheckCenter/CrossCheck (800-843-0760)
- CheckRite, www.checkritesystems.com (701-214-4123)
- Chexsystems, www.chexhelp.com (800-428-9623), and
- Telecheck, www.telecheck.com (800-710-9898).

Checking account information is not included in credit reports prepared by the three major credit reporting agencies.

If you open a checking account, be very careful not to bounce checks. A federal law called "Check 21" makes it harder to avoid bouncing checks. This law allows banks to process electronic images of checks instead of the paper originals. One result is that checks clear much faster than most of us are used to. Consumer representatives urge consumers not to write a check unless the funds are already in the account to cover it. (For more information on Check 21, go to www.consumersunion.org/finance/ckclear1002.htm.)

If you bounce a check to a creditor, it most likely will report a late or missed payment to a credit reporting agency, jeopardizing your hard work to repair your credit. A history of bounced checks also may make it harder to open bank accounts in the future.

Ask for a list of all charges there may be on an account before you agree to open one. Compare the fees each bank charges and choose one that works with the way you'll use your account. If you use ATMs a lot, for example, look for a bank that does not charge for using its own ATMs and reimburses you for ATM charges from other banks.

To learn more about ATM and other bank fees, visit the following websites: www.uspirg.org (U.S. Public Interest

Research Group), www.consumersunion.org (Consumers Union), www.consumer-action .org (Consumer Action), and www.ftc.gov (Federal Trade Commission).

Work With Local Merchants

Another way to repair your credit is to approach a local merchant (such as an electronics or furniture store) and arrange to purchase an item on credit. Many local stores will work with you to set up a payment schedule, but be prepared to put down a deposit of up to 30% or to pay a high rate of interest. If you still don't qualify, the merchant might agree to give you credit if you get someone to cosign or guarantee the loan. Or you may be able to get credit by first buying an item on layaway.

Even if a local merchant won't extend you credit, it may let you make a purchase on a layaway plan. When you purchase an item on layaway, the seller keeps the merchandise until you fully pay for it. Only then are you entitled to pick it up. One advantage of layaway is that you don't pay interest. One disadvantage is that it may be months before you actually get the item. This might be fine if you're buying a dress for your cousin's wedding that is eight months away. It isn't so fine if your mattress is so shot that you wake up with a backache every morning.

Layaway purchases are not reported to credit reporting agencies. If you purchase an item on layaway and make all the payments on time, however, the store may

be willing to issue you a store credit card or store credit privileges.

Obtain a Bank Loan

One way to repair your credit is to take some money you've saved and open a CD or savings account. You ask the bank to give you a loan against the money in your account. In exchange, you have no access to your money—you give your passbook to the bank and the bank won't give you an ATM card for the account—so there's no risk to the bank if you fail to make the payments. If the bank doesn't offer these types of loans, apply for a personal loan and offer either to get a cosigner or to secure it against some collateral you own (*not* your house).

No matter what kind of loan you get, be sure you know the following:

- **Does the bank report these loan payments to credit reporting agencies?** This is key; the whole reason you take out the loan is to repair your credit. If the bank doesn't report your payments to a credit reporting agency, there's no reason to take out a loan.
- **What is the minimum deposit amount required for loans?** Some banks won't give you a loan unless you have $3,000 in an account; others will lend you money on $50. Find a bank that fits your budget.
- **What is the interest rate?** The interest rate on the loan is usually much higher than what people with good credit pay. It will usually also be

higher than the interest you earn on the money you deposit with the bank. So you may pay 7% to 12% or more for the loan, but only 1% to 4% on your deposit. Yes, this means you'll lose a little money on the transaction, but it can be worth it if you're determined to repair your credit.

- **What is the maximum amount you can borrow?** On CD or passbook loans, banks won't lend you 100% of what's in your account; most will lend you between 80% and 95%.
- **What is the repayment schedule?** Banks usually give you one to five years to repay the loan. Some banks have no minimum monthly repayment amount on passbook loans; you could pay nothing for nearly the entire loan period and then pay the entire balance in the last month. Although you can pay the loan back in only one or two payments, don't. Pay it off over at least 12 months so that monthly installment payments appear in your credit file.

And, no matter what, *do not miss a loan payment.* This is extremely important: If you miss a loan payment, the bank will report the late or missed payment to a credit reporting agency, and you will have set back your efforts to repair your credit.

Avoid Credit Repair Clinics

You've probably seen ads for companies that claim they can fix your credit, qualify you for a loan, or get you a credit card.

Their pitches are tempting, especially if your credit is bad and you desperately want to buy a car or house.

Avoid these outfits. They are a bad idea, for two reasons: First, they charge you for doing what you can do yourself or with the help of a nonprofit debt counselor (see Appendix A). Some of them are more interested in helping themselves to your money than in helping you—they'll take your fee and disappear, paying just a few of your creditors or none. Second, some of them are extremely shady or outright criminal. Many of their practices are fraudulent, deceptive, and even illegal. For example, some suggest that you create a new identity by applying for an IRS Employer Identification number (EIN), a nine-digit number that resembles a Social Security number, and use it instead of your Social Security number when you apply for credit. This is illegal. It's a federal crime to make false statements on an application for a loan or credit, and to misrepresent your Social Security number and obtain an EIN from the IRS under false pretenses. If that's not bad enough, using an EIN instead of your Social Security number won't even help you repair your credit—and will prevent you from earning Social Security benefits. This scam is called "Credit File Segregation" or "File Segregation"; you'll see it advertised in classified ads, TV, radio, and the Internet.

Credit repair clinics devise new schemes as often as consumer protection agencies catch onto their previous ones.

Even assuming that a credit repair company is legitimate, it can't do anything for you that you can't do yourself. What they will do, however, is charge you between $250 and $5,000 for their unnecessary services. Here's what credit repair clinics claim to be able to do for you:

- **Remove incorrect information from your credit file.** You can do that yourself, using the information in Chapter 4.

- **Remove correct, but negative, information from your credit file.** Negative items in your credit file can legally stay there for seven or ten years, as long as they are correct. No one can wave a wand and make them go away. One tactic of credit repair services is to try to take advantage of the law requiring credit reporting agencies to verify information if the customer disputes it. Credit repair clinics do this by challenging every item in a credit file—negative, positive, or neutral—with the hope of overwhelming the credit reporting agency into removing information without verifying it. Credit reporting agencies are aware of this tactic and often dismiss these challenges on the ground that they are frivolous, a right credit reporting agencies have under the Fair Credit Reporting Act. You are better off getting your report and selectively challenging items that are incomplete or inaccurate. Even if the credit reporting agency removes information that it had the right to include in your file, it's no doubt only a temporary removal. Most correct information reappears after 30 to 60 days, when the creditor that first

reported the information to the agency rereports it.

- **Get outstanding debt balances and court judgments removed from your credit file.** Credit repair clinics often advise debtors to pay outstanding debts if the creditor agrees to remove the negative information from your credit file. This is certainly a negotiation tactic you want to consider (see Chapter 3), but you don't need to pay a credit repair clinic for this advice.

- **Get a major credit card.** Credit repair clinics can give you a list of banks that offer secured credit cards. While this information is helpful in rebuilding credit, it's not worth hundreds or thousands of dollars—you can get a list yourself for little or nothing.

The federal Credit Repair Organizations Act (CROA) (15 U.S.C. §§1679–1679j) regulates for-profit credit repair clinics. Some dubious credit repair clinics have tried to get around these regulations by setting themselves up as nonprofits, but they still take your money and provide poor results— or do nothing for you that you couldn't do for yourself.

Under the federal law, a credit repair clinic must:

- give you a written statement of your rights under the Fair Credit Reporting Act
- accurately represent what it can and cannot do
- not collect any money until all promised services are performed
- provide a written contract, and

Additional State Protections Concerning Credit Repair Clinics

Arizona
Ariz. Rev. Stat. Ann. §§ 44-1701 to 44-1712

Credit repair service may not charge or collect a fee for referring consumer to a retail seller who will or may extend credit that is on substantially the same terms as those available to the general public.

Cancellation rights. Any payment must be returned within 15 days of receipt of cancellation notice.

Arkansas
Ark. Code Ann. §§ 4-91-101 to 4-91-109

Credit repair service may not charge or collect a fee for referring consumer to a retail seller who will or may extend credit that is on substantially the same terms as those available to the general public.

Cancellation rights. May cancel contract within 5 days of signing. Any payment must be returned within 10 days of receipt of cancellation notice.

California
Cal. Civ. Code §§ 1789.10 to 1789.22

Credit repair service may not charge or collect a fee for referring consumer to a retail seller who will or may extend credit that is on substantially the same terms as those available to the general public or on the same terms that would have been extended without the assistance of the credit repair organization; submit a debtor's dispute to a consumer credit reporting agency without the debtor's knowledge; or use a consumer credit reporting agency's telephone system or toll-free number to represent the caller as the debtor without the debtor's authorization.

Cancellation rights. May cancel contract within 5 working days of signing.

Time limit for performing services. 6 months.

Colorado
Colo. Rev. Stat. §§ 12-14.5-101 to 12-14.5-113

Cancellation rights. May cancel contract within 5 working days of signing. Any payment must be returned within 10 days of receipt of cancellation notice.

Connecticut
Conn. Gen. Stat. Ann. § 36a-700

State protections do not exceed federal laws.

Delaware
Del. Code Ann. tit. 6, §§ 2401 to 2414

Credit repair service may not charge or collect a fee for referring consumer to a retail seller who will or may extend credit that is on substantially the same terms as those available to the general public.

Credit repair service must disclose a complete and accurate statement of the availability of nonprofit credit counseling services.

Cancellation rights. Any payment must be returned within 10 days of receipt of cancellation notice.

Time limit for performing services. 180 days.

District of Columbia
D.C. Code Ann. §§ 28-4601 to 28-4608

Credit repair service may not charge or collect a fee for referring consumer to a retail seller who will or may extend credit that is on substantially the same terms as those available to the general public.

Additional State Protections Concerning Credit Repair Clinics (cont'd)

Cancellation rights. May cancel contract within 5 calendar days of signing. Must be reimbursed within 10 days of receipt of cancellation notice.

Florida

Fla. Stat. Ann. §§ 817.701 to 817.706

Credit repair service may not charge or collect a fee for referring consumer to a retail seller who will or may extend credit that is on substantially the same terms as those available to the general public.

Cancellation rights. May cancel contract within 5 days of signing. Any payment must be returned within 10 days of receipt of cancellation notice.

Georgia

Ga. Code Ann. §§ 8-5-1 to 18-5-4

Credit repair service may not charge more than 7.5% of the amount the debtor provides each month for distribution to creditors.

Hawaii

Haw. Rev. Stat. § 481B-12

State protections do not exceed federal laws.

Idaho

Idaho Code §§ 26-2222, 26-2252

Who may provide service. Only nonprofit organizations may provide credit counseling or other debt management services.

Illinois

815 Ill. Comp. Stat. §§ 605/1 to 605/16

Credit repair service may not charge or collect a fee for referring consumer to a retail seller who will or may extend credit that is on substantially the same terms as those available to the general public.

Cancellation rights. Any payment must be returned within 10 days of receipt of cancellation notice.

Indiana

Ind. Code Ann. §§ 24-5-15-1 to 24-5-15-11

Credit repair service may not charge or collect a fee for referring consumer to a retail seller who will or may extend credit that is on substantially the same terms as those available to the general public.

Credit repair service must disclose a complete and accurate statement of the availability of nonprofit credit counseling services.

Cancellation rights. Any payment must be returned within 10 days of receipt of cancellation notice or any other written notice.

Iowa

Iowa Code §§ 538A.1 to 538A.14

Credit repair service may not charge or collect a fee for referring consumer to a retail seller who will or may extend credit that is on substantially the same terms as those available to the general public.

Cancellation rights. Any payment must be returned within 10 days of receipt of cancellation notice.

Additional State Protections Concerning Credit Repair Clinics (cont'd)

Kansas

Kan. Stat. Ann. §§ 50-1116 to 50-1135

Credit repair service must comply with an extensive list of requirements, including educating debtors, specifying the scope of an agreement, itemizing fees, and disclosing the consumer's rights.

Credit repair service may not delay payments, make false promises or deceptive statements, give or receive compensation for referrals, or collect fees above $20 per month from the customer (after a $50 initial consultation fee).

For more information contact your state's consumer protection agency, listed in Appendix A.

Kentucky

Ky. Rev. Stat. Ann. §§ 380.010 to 390.990

Who may provide service. Debt adjustment services may be provided only by a nonprofit organization, attorney, debtor's regular full-time employee, creditor providing service at no cost, or lender who, at the debtor's request, adjusts debts at no additional cost as part of disbursing the loan funds.

Louisiana

La. Rev. Stat. Ann. §§ 9:3573.1 to 9:3573.17

Credit repair service must disclose a complete and accurate statement of the availability of nonprofit credit counseling services, disclose all payments expected from the consumer, give estimated completion date, and wait for payment until services are complete.

Cancellation rights. May cancel contract within 5 days of signing. Any payment must be returned within 10 days of receipt of cancellation notice.

Maine

Me. Rev. Stat. Ann. tit. 9-A, §§ 10-101 to 10-401

Credit repair service is required to keep consumer fees in an escrow account separate from any operating accounts of the business, pending completion of services offered.

Maryland

Md. Code Ann. [Com. Law] §§ 14-1901 to 14-1916

Credit repair service may not charge or collect a fee for referring consumer to a retail seller who will or may extend credit that is on substantially the same terms as those available to the general public or assist a consumer to obtain credit at a rate of interest which is in violation of federal or state maximum rate.

Cancellation rights. Any payment must be returned within 10 days of receipt of cancellation notice.

Massachusetts

Mass. Gen. Laws ch. 93, §§ 68A to 68E

Credit repair service may not charge or collect a fee for referring consumer to a retail seller who will or may extend credit that is on substantially the same terms as those available to the general public.

Cancellation rights. Any payment must be returned within 10 days of receipt of cancellation notice.

Michigan

Mich. Comp. Laws §§ 445.1821 to 445.1825

Credit repair service may not charge or collect a fee for referring consumer to a retail seller who will or may extend credit that is on substantially the same terms as those available to

Additional State Protections Concerning Credit Repair Clinics (cont'd)

the general public, submit a debtor's dispute to a consumer credit reporting agency without the debtor's knowledge, or provide a service that is not pursuant to a written contract.

Time limit for performing services. 90 days.

Minnesota

Minn. Stat. Ann. §§ 332.52 to 332.60

Credit repair service may not charge or collect a fee for referring consumer to a retail seller who will or may extend credit that is on substantially the same terms as those available to the general public.

Credit repair service must disclose the name and address of any person who directly or indirectly owns or controls a 10% or greater interest in the credit services organization; any litigation or unresolved complaint filed within the preceding 5 years with the state, any other state, or the United States, or a notarized statement that there has been no such litigation or complaint; and the percentage of customers during the past year for whom the credit services organization fully and completely performed the services it agreed to provide.

Cancellation rights. May cancel contract within 5 days of signing. Any payment must be returned within 10 days of receipt of cancellation notice.

Mississippi

Miss. Code Ann. §§ 81-22-1 to 81-22-29

Credit repair service is required to maintain separate account records for each consumer. May not commingle trust accounts with any business operating accounts.

Who may provide service. Only a nonprofit organization may operate as a licensed debt management service.

Credit repair service may not purchase any debt, lend money or provide credit, operate as a debt collector, or structure a negative amortization agreement for the consumer.

Fees. May not charge more than a one-time fee of $75 for setting up a debt management plan, $30 per month to maintain plan, $15 for obtaining an individual credit report, or $25 for a joint report. Educational courses and products may be offered for a fee, but consumer must be informed that purchasing them is not mandatory for receiving debt management services.

Missouri

Mo. Rev. Stat. §§ 407.635 to 407.644

Credit repair service may not charge or collect a fee for referring consumer to a retail seller who will or may extend credit that is on substantially the same terms as those available to the general public.

Credit repair service must disclose a complete and accurate statement of the availability of nonprofit credit counseling services.

Cancellation rights. Any payment must be returned within 10 days of receipt of cancellation notice.

Additional State Protections Concerning Credit Repair Clinics (cont'd)

Montana

Mont. Code Ann. §§ 30-14-2001 to 30-14-2015

Credit repair service may not purchase any debt or obligation of a consumer; lend money or provide credit to a consumer; or obtain a mortgage or other security interest in any property of a consumer.

Cancellation rights. May cancel contract with 10 days' notice.

Nebraska

Neb. Rev. Stat. §§ 45-801 to 45-815

Credit repair service may not charge or collect a fee for referring consumer to a retail seller who will or may extend credit that is on substantially the same terms as those available to the general public.

Cancellation rights. Any payment must be returned within 10 days of receipt of cancellation notice.

Time limit for performing services. 180 days.

Nevada

Nev. Rev. Stat. Ann. §§ 598.741 to 598.787

Credit repair service may not charge or collect a fee for referring consumer to a retail seller who will or may extend credit that is on substantially the same terms as those available to the general public, submit a debtor's dispute to a consumer credit reporting agency without the debtor's knowledge, or call a consumer credit reporting agency and represent the caller as the debtor.

Credit repair service must disclose the available of any nonprofit associations that provide similar services, with phone numbers, including toll-free numbers if available.

Cancellation rights. May cancel contract within 5 days of signing.

New Hampshire

N.H. Rev. Stat. Ann. §§ 359-D:1 to 359-D:11

Credit repair service may not charge or collect a fee for referring consumer to a retail seller who will or may extend credit that is on substantially the same terms as those available to the general public.

Cancellation rights. May cancel contract within 5 days of signing. Any payment must be returned within 5 days of receipt of cancellation notice.

New Jersey

N.J. Stat. Ann. §§ 17:16G-1 to 16:16G-9;
N.J. Admin. Code tit. 3, § 25-1.2

Who may provide service. Only nonprofit organizations may provide credit counseling or debt adjustment services. No more than 40% of the board of directors can be employed by a corporation or institution which offers credit to the general public.

Fees. Monthly debt adjustment fee cannot exceed one percent of the debtor's gross monthly income or $25, whichever is less. Credit counseling services fee cannot exceed $60 per month.

New Mexico

N.M. Stat. Ann. §§ 56-2-1 to 56-2-4

Who may provide service. Nonprofit corporations organized as a community effort to assist debtors may provide debt adjustment services. Exceptions: attorney; regular, full-time employee of a debtor who does it as part of job; person authorized by court or state or federal law; creditor who provides debt adjustment without

Additional State Protections Concerning Credit Repair Clinics (cont'd)

cost; and lender who, at the debtor's request, adjusts debts at no additional cost as part of disbursing the loan funds.

New York

N.Y. Gen. Bus. Law §§ 458-a to 458-k

Credit repair service is required to annex a copy of the consumer's current credit report to the contract and clearly mark the adverse entries proposed to be modified.

North Carolina

N.C. Gen. Stat. §§ 66-220 to 66-226

Credit repair service may not charge or collect a fee for referring consumer to a retail seller who will or may extend credit that is on substantially the same terms as those available to the general public.

Cancellation rights. Any payment must be returned within 10 days of receipt of cancellation notice.

North Dakota

N.D. Cent. Code §§ 13-06-01 to 13-06-03, 13-07-01 to 13-07-07

Credit repair service is required to credit any interest accrued as a result of payments deposited in a trust account to debt management education programs.

Credit repair service may not enter into an agreement with a debtor unless a thorough written budget analysis indicates that the debtor can reasonably meet the requirements of the financial adjustment plan and will benefit from it.

Fees. May charge an origination fee of up to $50; may take up to 15% of any sum deposited by the debtor for distribution as partial payment of the service's total fee.

Ohio

Ohio Rev. Code Ann. §§ 4712.01 to 4712.99

Credit repair service may not charge or collect a fee for referring consumer to a person that extends credit, except when credit has actually been extended as a result of the referral; submit the debtor's disputes to a consumer reporting agency without the debtor's signed, written authorization and positive identification; or contact a consumer reporting agency to submit or obtain information about a debtor, stating or implying to be the debtor or debtor's attorney, guardian, or other legal representative.

Credit repair service must disclose a complete and accurate statement of the availability of nonprofit budget and debt counseling services; the percentage of customers during the past year for whom the credit services organization fully and completely performed the services it agreed to provide.

Time limit for performing service. 60 days.

Oklahoma

Okla. Stat. Ann. tit. 24, §§ 131 to 148

Credit repair service may not charge or collect a fee for referring consumer to a retail seller who will or may extend credit that is on substantially the same terms as those available to the general public.

Cancellation rights. May cancel contract within 5 days of signing. Any payment must be returned within 10 days of receipt of cancellation notice.

Additional State Protections Concerning Credit Repair Clinics (cont'd)

Oregon

Or. Rev. Stat. §§ 646.A380 to 646.396

Credit repair service may not charge or collect a fee for referring consumer to a retail seller who will or may extend credit that is on substantially the same terms as those available to the general public.

Pennsylvania

73 Pa. Cons. Stat. Ann. §§ 2181 to 2192

Credit repair service may not charge or collect a fee for referring consumer to a retail seller who will or may extend credit that is on substantially the same terms as those available to the general public.

Cancellation rights. May cancel contract within 5 days of signing. Any payment must be returned within 15 days of receipt of cancellation notice.

Rhode Island

R.I. Gen. Laws §§ 19-14.8-1 to 19-14.8-43

Credit repair service is required to give the individual an itemized list of good and services and the charges for each, before providing services; if communicating in a language other than English, furnish translation of all documents and disclosure in that language.

Credit repair service may not engage in an extensive list of prohibited practices, available at R.I. Gen. Laws 19-14.8-28.

Credit repair service must disclose the services to be provided; the amount or method of determining the amount of all fees, individually itemized, to be paid by the individual; the schedule of payments to be made by or on behalf of the individual, including the amount of each payment, the date on which each payment is due, and an estimate of the date of the final payment or, if such information is not known to the provider at the time the agreement is made, statement to that effect.

Fees. If the plan will reduce fees for late payment, default, or delinquency, the provider may charge no more than $50 for consultation plus a monthly service fee of $10 times the number of creditors, but not more than $50. If the plan will settle debts for less than the principal amount of the debt, an initial consultation fee must not exceed $400 or four percent of the debt in the plan at the inception of the plan, whichever is less; and a monthly service fee of not more than $10 times the number of creditors, but not more than $50.

Tennessee

Tenn. Code Ann. §§ 47-18-1001 to 47-18-1011

Credit repair service may not charge or collect a fee for referring consumer to a retail seller who will or may extend credit that is on substantially the same terms as those available to the general public; use a program or plan which charges installment payments directly to a credit card prior to full and complete performance of the services it has agreed to perform.

Credit repair service must disclose a complete and accurate statement of the availability of nonprofit credit counseling.

Cancellation rights. May cancel contract within 5 business days of signing. Any payment must be returned within 10 days of receipt of cancellation notice.

Additional State Protections Concerning Credit Repair Clinics (cont'd)

Texas

Tex. Fin. Code Ann. §§ 393.001 to 393.505

Credit repair service may not charge or collect a fee for referring consumer to a retail seller who will or may extend credit that is on substantially the same terms as those available to the general public.

Credit repair service must disclose a complete and accurate statement of the availability of nonprofit credit counseling services.

Cancellation rights. Any payment must be returned within 10 days of receipt of cancellation notice.

Time limit for performing service. 180 days.

Utah

Utah Code Ann. §§ 13-21-1 to 13-21-9

Credit repair service may not charge or collect a fee for referring consumer to a retail seller who will or may extend credit that is on substantially the same terms as those available to the general public.

Cancellation rights. May cancel contract within 5 days of signing. Any payment must be returned within 10 days of receipt of cancellation notice.

Vermont

Vt. Stat. Ann. tit. 8, §§ 4861 to 4876

Credit repair service must state in writing all services it will perform and all fees consumers will pay; state that debt adjustment plans are not suitable for all debtors; disclose if creditors may compensate the licensee; and make these disclosures in the language used to negotiate the agreement.

Credit repair service may not charge more than a $50 initial fee plus ten percent of payments received from the debtor for distribution to creditors.

Cancellation rights. Any payment must be returned within 10 days of receipt of cancellation notice.

For more information contact your state's consumer protection agency, listed in Appendix A.

Virginia

Va. Code Ann. §§ 59.1-335.1 to 59.1-335.12

Credit repair service may not charge or collect a fee for referring consumer to a retail seller who will or may extend credit that is on substantially the same terms as those available to the general public.

Credit repair service must disclose. Information statement must include the following notice in at least 10-point bold type: "You have no obligation to pay any fees or charges until all services have been performed completely for you." The notice must also be conspicuously posted on a sign in the repair service's place of business, so that it is noticeable and readable when consumers are being interviewed.

Cancellation rights. Any payment must be returned within 10 days of receipt of cancellation notice.

Washington

Wash. Rev. Code Ann. §§ 19.134.010 to 19.134.900

Credit repair service may not charge or collect a fee for referring consumer to a retail seller who will or may extend credit that is on substantially the same terms as those available to the general public.

Additional State Protections Concerning Credit Repair Clinics (cont'd)

Cancellation rights. May cancel contract within 5 days of signing. Any payment must be returned within 10 days of receipt of cancellation notice.

West Virginia

W. Va. Code §§ 46A-6C-1 to 46A-6C-12

Credit repair service may not charge or collect a fee for referring consumer to a retail seller who will or may extend credit that is on substantially the same terms as those available to the general public.

Credit repair service must disclose a complete and accurate statement of the availability of credit counseling services.

Cancellation rights. Any payment must be returned within 10 days of receipt of cancellation notice.

Time limit for performing service. 180 days.

Wisconsin

Wis. Stat. Ann. §§ 422.501 to 422.506

Credit repair service may not charge or collect a fee for referring consumer to a retail seller who will or may extend credit that is on substantially the same terms as those available to the general public.

Cancellation rights. May cancel contract within 5 days of signing. Any payment must be returned within 15 days of receipt of cancellation notice.

Wyoming

Wyo. Stat. §§ 33-14-101 to 33-14-103

Who may provide service. Only nonprofits and attorneys may offer debt adjustment services.

Current as of December 2008

- let you cancel the contract within three business days of signing (you must cancel in writing).

Any contract that doesn't comply with the CROA's requirements is void, and you cannot waive (sign away) these rights. Any lawsuit you bring against a credit repair clinic for violation of this law generally must be filed within five years of the violation. A court may award actual damages, punitive damages, and attorneys' fees.

A few states provide additional protections to consumers who use credit repair clinics. For example, some states give you more than three days to cancel the credit repair contract, require the credit repair clinic to perform the promised services within a specific amount of time, and require that the credit repair clinic inform you about available nonprofit credit counseling services.

The chart "Additional State Protections Concerning Credit Repair Clinics" lists additional protections and the code section where you can find the text of these provisions. To find your state law, visit your public library or local law library. Or, visit the legal research section of Nolo's website, at www.nolo.com/statute/index.cfm, and click on the "State Laws" tab.

If you're still tempted to use a credit repair organization (whether or not it claims to be a nonprofit), do the following:

- Ask whether the company is bonded, as some states require. A company that is bonded has posted money in the event it goes out of business or goes bankrupt and dissatisfied consumers seek a refund. A legitimate company should be willing to give you the name of its bonding company. Call the bonding company to verify the bond and find out the amount. But even a bond is no guarantee you against poor service or even legal difficulties because of something a credit repair company recommended you do. The bond may be too small to protect most of the companies' customers, and getting the bonding company to pay up may require you to bring a lawsuit.

- Ask to see a copy of the contract before you sign. Carefully check the company's fees, its claims about what it can do, and your right to a refund. Avoid any company that won't give you a written agreement or the right to cancel if you change your mind.

- Call your local Better Business Bureau and your state consumer affairs office (a list is in Appendix A) to see if either has complaints on file for the company. If there are complaints, that's a warning. But a business with no complaints still may be untrustworthy. Businesses can change names or defraud a lot of people before the complaints catch up to them.

- Ask for the names and phone numbers of satisfied customers. Be wary of any satisfied customers you speak to whose claims sound exactly like the claims of the company. These people are probably phonies—people who never used the company's service and are simply paid to say good things about the company.

Avoid Credit Discrimination

When you're trying to build good credit, the last thing you need is to be denied credit for a reason other than poor creditworthiness. Unfortunately, some people are denied credit for reasons entirely unrelated to their ability to pay, such as their race, gender, or age.

Fortunately, several powerful federal laws and some state laws prohibit discrimination in credit transactions. This section discusses the laws prohibiting credit discrimination and provides information on what to do if you think a creditor has discriminated against you.

Laws Prohibiting Credit Discrimination

Two federal laws, the Equal Credit Opportunity Act (ECOA) and the Fair Housing Act (FHA), prohibit credit discrimination.

The ECOA (15 U.S.C. §§ 1691 and following) is quite broad in scope. It prohibits discrimination in any part of a credit transaction, including:

- applications for credit
- credit evaluation
- restrictions in granting credit, such as requiring collateral or security deposits
- credit terms
- loan servicing
- treatment upon default, and
- collection procedures.

The ECOA requires a creditor to give you notice when it denies your credit application, revokes your credit, changes the terms of an existing credit arrangement, or refuses to grant credit or terms substantially as requested. If the creditor denies you credit, it must give you a written notice that tells you either the specific reasons for rejecting you or that you can request those reasons within 60 days. An acceptable reason might be "Your income is too low;" an unacceptable reason would be "You don't meet our minimum standards."

The ECOA prohibits a creditor from refusing to grant credit because of your:

- race or color
- national origin
- sex
- marital status
- religion
- age, or
- public assistance status.

The federal Fair Housing Act (FHA) (42 U.S.C.§§ 3601 and following) prohibits discrimination in residential real estate transactions. It covers loans to purchase, improve, or maintain your home, or loans for which your home is used as collateral.

The FHA also prohibits discrimination in the rental housing market. Like the ECOA, the FHA prohibits discrimination based on race, color, religion, national origin, and sex. In addition, the FHA prohibits discrimination based on:

- familial status, and
- disability.

Other federal laws provide protections in addition to the ECOA and FHA. For example, the Community Reinvestment Act (12 U.S.C. §§ 2901 and following) can be used to combat discrimination by banks and lenders. And, often, state antidiscrimination laws provide even more protection than federal laws; for example, some states prohibit discrimination based on occupation, personal characteristics, or sexual orientation. Below, we discuss in detail some of the important categories in which credit discrimination is prohibited.

Race Discrimination

In general, lenders are prohibited from asking a person's race on a credit application or from ascertaining it from any means other than personal observation by a loan officer (for example, by looking for race information on a credit file). There is one important exception to this law: A mortgage lender may ask applicants to voluntarily disclose their race for the sole purpose of monitoring home mortgage applications. Other creditors may ask for this information, but only to monitor their own practices for discrimination. Creditors may not use the information to make a credit decision.

Unfortunately, laws prohibiting race discrimination have not eradicated the practice. In fact, lenders are accused of getting around race discrimination prohibitions by "redlining"—that is, denying credit to residents of predominantly nonwhite neighborhoods. More recently, consumer advocates have charged lenders with reverse redlining, which involves aggressively marketing their highest-priced loan products to communities of color.

In recent years, some agencies and nonprofit organizations have analyzed data collected under the Home Mortgage Disclosure Act (HMDA), and discovered that African Americans, Hispanics and women are more likely to wind up with higher-cost loans. The HMDA data doesn't take into account differences in income, credit scores, or other factors creditors look at to make loans. But when studies took several of those other factors into account, these groups still were more likely to get higher-cost loans than others.

National Origin Discrimination

Discrimination based on national origin is prohibited under the ECOA, the FHA, and most state credit discrimination laws. "National origin" generally refers to ancestry or ethnicity. A creditor might be discriminating based on national origin if it treats people with Latino or Asian surnames differently from people with European surnames. This category has also been interpreted to include discrimination against non-English speakers. However, it does not necessarily include noncitizens. A creditor is allowed to consider an applicant's residency status in the United States in certain circumstances.

Sex Discrimination

The ECOA, FHA, and many state laws prohibit credit discrimination based on sex. This category often overlaps with the "marital status" category.

Specific examples of prohibited sex discrimination include:

- rating female-specific jobs (such as waitress) lower than male-specific jobs (such as waiter) for the purpose of granting credit
- denying credit because an applicant's income comes from sources historically associated with women—for example, part-time jobs, alimony, or child support (however, a creditor may ask you to prove that you have received alimony, child support, or separate maintenance income consistently)
- requiring married women who apply for credit alone to provide information about their husbands while not requiring married men to provide information about their wives, and
- denying credit to a pregnant woman who anticipates taking a maternity leave.

However, a creditor is allowed to ask your sex when you apply for a real estate loan. The federal government collects this information for statistical purposes. Other creditors may ask for this information as well, although you can refuse to provide it.

Marital Status Discrimination

The ECOA and many state laws prohibit discrimination based on marital status. The FHA has a similar provision that prohibits discrimination based on familial status.

These laws require that a married person be allowed to apply for credit in his or her name only. A creditor cannot require an applicant's spouse to cosign when the applicant requests an individual account, as long as no jointly held or community property is involved and the applicant can meet the creditor's standards on his or her own.

Creditors can ask about your spouse or former spouse when you apply for your own credit only if any of the following is true:

- Your spouse will be permitted to use the account.
- Your spouse will be liable on the account.
- You are relying on your spouse's income to repay the credit.
- You live in a community property state (Alaska, Arizona, California, Idaho, Louisiana, Nevada, New Mexico, Texas, Washington, or Wisconsin) or you are relying on property located in a community property state to establish your creditworthiness.
- You are relying on alimony, child support, or other maintenance payments from a spouse to repay the creditor—but you are not required to reveal this income if you don't want the creditor to consider it in evaluating your application. A creditor may ask if you are obligated to pay alimony, child support, or separate maintenance.

Sexual Orientation Discrimination

No federal law specifically prohibits credit discrimination based on sexual orientation. However, a few states prohibit this type of discrimination.

Age Discrimination

The ECOA and many state laws prohibit credit discrimination based on age. This is mostly meant to protect the elderly (defined in the ECOA as people who are at least 62 years old). Creditors are allowed to consider age in order to give more favorable treatment to an older person (for example, considering an older person's long payment history that a younger person hasn't had time to build yet). However, age cannot be used to an older person's detriment. For example, a creditor cannot automatically refuse to consider income often associated with the elderly, such as part-time employment or retirement benefits.

Other Discrimination Prohibited by State Law

A few states have enacted laws barring credit discrimination on grounds other than those covered by the federal laws. Check with your state consumer protection office or do some research on your own to see if there are additional grounds in your state.

RESOURCE

Legal research help. For tips on doing your own legal research, see *Legal Research: How to Find & Understand the Law,* by Stephen R. Elias and Susan Levinkind (Nolo).

Postbankruptcy Discrimination

If you're considering filing for bankruptcy or you've been through bankruptcy, you may be worried that you'll suffer discrimination. There are two categories of legal protection against this kind of discrimination, depending on whether you are dealing with a private person or a governmental entity.

Private employers may not fire you or otherwise discriminate against you solely because you filed for bankruptcy. (11 U.S.C. § 525(b).) It's unclear whether employers may refuse to hire you because you went through bankruptcy, however.

Unfortunately, other forms of discrimination in the private sector are not illegal. If you seek to rent an apartment and the landlord does a credit check and refuses to rent to you because you filed for bankruptcy, there's not much you can do other than try to show that you'll pay your rent and be a responsible tenant. If a bank refuses to give you a loan because it perceives you as a poor credit risk, you may have little recourse.

All federal, state, and local governmental entities are prohibited from denying, revoking, suspending, or refusing to renew a license, permit, charter, franchise, or other similar grant solely because you filed for bankruptcy. (11 U.S.C. § 525(a).) Judges interpreting this law have ruled that the government cannot:

- deny you a job or fire you
- deny or terminate your public benefits
- deny or refuse to renew your state liquor license
- withhold your college transcript
- deny you a driver's license, or
- deny you a contract, such as a contract for a construction project.

In general, courts have ruled that the intent of the statute is to prohibit a government entity from preventing you from pursuing a livelihood involving a license, permit, charter, or franchise, but that it does not mean that a government agency must extend you credit, such as a government-backed home loan. However, a government agency cannot exclude you from a student loan program if you have filed for bankruptcy. (11 USC § 525(c).)

In addition, once any government-related debt has been canceled in bankruptcy, all acts against you arising out of that debt must also end. For example, if a state university has withheld your transcript because you haven't paid back your student loan, once the loan is discharged, you must be given your transcript.

Keep in mind that only government denials based on your bankruptcy are prohibited. You may be denied a loan, job, or apartment for reasons unrelated to the bankruptcy (for example, you earn too much to qualify for public housing) or for reasons related to your future credit-worthiness (for instance, the government concludes you won't be able to repay a student loan).

What to Do If a Creditor Discriminates Against You

If you think that a creditor has discriminated against you on a prohibited basis, you should complain to the creditor, your state attorney general (see Appendix A), the Federal Trade Commission (www.ftc.gov), and the federal agency that regulates the particular creditor. If the discrimination is related to housing, contact the Department of Housing and Urban Development (www.hud.gov). You may also want to contact an attorney for help.

You can learn more from these websites:

- www.innercitypress.org
- www.communitychange.org (Nonprofit Center for Community Change), and
- www.usdoj.gov (U.S. Department of Justice). ●

Resources

Credit and Debt Counseling Agencies 152

    Consumer Credit Counseling Service 154

    Other Credit and Debt Counseling Agencies 154

Debtors Anonymous 155

Nolo Publications 155

Other Publications 155

Online Resources 156

State Consumer Protection Agencies 157

Where to Complain About Credit Discrimination 164

B elow are organizations, agencies, and publications that can provide valuable help in your efforts to repair your credit.

Credit and Debt Counseling Agencies

Traditional credit and debt counseling agencies are organizations funded primarily by major creditors, such as department stores, credit card companies, and banks, who can work with you to help you repay your debts and improve your financial picture. Most are nonprofit companies,.

To use a credit or debt counseling agency to help you pay your debts, you must have some disposable income. A counselor contacts your creditors to let them know that you've sought assistance and need more time to pay. Based on your income and debts, the counselor, with your creditors, decides how much you will pay. You then make one payment each month to the counseling agency, which in turn pays your creditors. The agency asks the creditors to return a small percentage of the money to fund its work. This arrangement is generally referred to as a "debt management program."

Some creditors will make concessions to help you when you're on a debt management program. But few creditors will make interest concessions, such as waiving a portion of the accumulated interest to help you repay the principal. More likely, you'll get late fees dropped and the opportunity to reinstate your credit if you successfully complete a debt management program.

Participating in a credit or debt counseling agency's debt management program is a little bit like filing for Chapter 13 bankruptcy. (See Chapter 1.) Working with a credit or debt counseling agency has one advantage: No bankruptcy will appear on your credit record.

But a debt management program also has two disadvantages when compared to Chapter 13 bankruptcy. First, if you miss a payment, Chapter 13 protects you from creditors who would otherwise start collection actions. A debt management program has no such protection, and any creditor can pull the plug on your plan. Also, a debt management program plan usually requires that your debts be paid in full. In Chapter 13 bankruptcy, the amount you have to pay depends on your disposable income and the value of your nonexempt property; you may end up paying back only a small percentage of your unsecured debt.

The combination of high consumer debt and easy access to information (via the Internet) has led to an explosion in advertising by new credit and debt counseling companies. Some provide limited services, such as budgeting and debt repayment, while others offer a range of services, from debt counseling to financial planning.

Many of these newer credit counseling companies claim to be nonprofits, but these claims may not be accurate. The IRS has revoked the nonprofit status of many credit counseling companies. To find out whether a credit counseling company is really a nonprofit, go to www.irs.gov/charities,

Tips on Choosing a Credit or Debt Counseling Agency

The National Consumer Law Center, a nonprofit organization that specializes in consumer issues, has lots of free information on debt and credit available on its website, www.nclc.org. Here are some of the tips they offer for choosing a counseling agency:

1. Shop around. Contact your local Better Business Bureau and the consumer protection agency of your state Attorney General's office to find out whether complaints have been made against an agency you're considering. And consider visiting the agency in person before signing up.

2. Look for a variety of services. Find an agency that offers a range of counseling options, not just enrollment in a debt management plan.

3. Ask about all costs. Fees can vary a lot among agencies. Find out what you'll have to pay to set up your account and what you'll pay for any monthly fees. Ask whether they have a sliding scale. Get a quote in writing.

4. Make sure your information will remain private. Find out whether the agency sells or distributes information.

5. Ask how employees are compensated. If employees are paid more for signing up customers for a debt management plan, considering taking your business elsewhere.

6. Ask how credit counseling will affect your credit report or score. Some creditors will report your participation in a debt management plan to the credit reporting agencies. Ask the agency how your credit report and score will be affected if you decide to get counseling.

For more tips, and to learn some warning signs that should lead you to reject an agency, check out NCLC's fact sheet, "Tips on Choosing a Reputable Credit Counseling Agency" from www.nclc.org; select "For Consumers," then "Consumer Education Brochures" for a list of fact sheets and other consumer materials.

and click on "Search for Charities." If the company is listed there, it's a nonprofit.

Even if the agency is a nonprofit, however, your inquiry shouldn't stop there. Many of the unscrupulous credit and debt counseling companies have nonprofit status. These companies often try to get you to pay "voluntary contributions" up front or pay other fees. At a minimum, always ask about fees before agreeing to give your business to a particular counselor.

Some experts caution against using even the legitimate nonprofit credit and debt counseling agencies companies. Critics point out that these agencies get most of their funding from creditors. Therefore, say critics, counselors cannot be objective in counseling debtors to file for bankruptcy if they know the agency won't receive funds from its supporters. (Some offices also receive grants from private agencies, such as the United Way, and federal agencies, including the Department of Housing and Urban Development.)

In response to this and other consumer concerns, credit and debt counseling agencies accredited by the National Foundation for Credit Counseling reached an agreement with the Federal Trade Commission to disclose the following to consumers:

- that creditors fund a large portion of the cost of their operations
- that the credit agency must balance the debtor's ability to make payments with the requirements of the creditors that fund the office, and
- a reliable estimate of how long it will take a debtor to repay his or her debts under a debt management program.

> ⓘ **CAUTION**
>
> **Make sure your bills get paid.** If you sign up for a debt management plan, keep paying your bills directly until you know that your creditors have approved the plan. Make sure the agency's schedule will allow it to pay your debts before they are due each month. Call each of your creditors the first month to make sure the agency paid them on time.

Consumer Credit Counseling Service

Consumer Credit Counseling Service (CCCS) is the oldest credit or debt counseling agency in the country. Actually, CCCS isn't one agency. CCCS is the primary operating name of many credit and debt counseling agencies affiliated with the National Foundation for Credit Counseling (NFCC).

CCCS may charge you a small start-up fee (about $20) and a monthly fee (an average of about $11) for setting up a repayment plan. CCCS also helps people make monthly budgets, for a fee of about $12, or sometimes free. If you can't afford the fee, CCCS will waive it. In most CCCS offices, the primary service offered is a debt management program. A few offices have additional services, such as helping you save money toward buying a house or reviewing your credit report.

CCCS has more than 1,100 offices, located in every state. Look in the phone book under "Credit and Debt Counseling Services" to find the one nearest you or contact the main office at 801 Roeder Road, Suite 900, Silver Spring, MD 20910, 800-388-2227 (voice) or at www.nfcc.org.

Other Credit and Debt Counseling Agencies

With a few exceptions, all bankruptcy filers are now required to get credit counseling. Filers must get this counseling from a nonprofit agency that meets a number of requirements and has been approved by the Office of the U.S. Trustee. If you decide to get help with a repayment plan, you would do well to choose one of these agencies—the U.S. Trustee's office oversees their operation, which gives you some protection against fraudulent practices. You can find a list of approved agencies at the U.S. Trustee's website, at www.usdoj.gov/ust.

Debtors Anonymous

Debtors Anonymous is a 12-step support program that uses many of the guidelines of Alcoholics Anonymous. Debtors Anonymous groups meet all over the country. If you can't find one in your area, send a self-addressed, stamped envelope to Debtors Anonymous, General Services Office, P.O. Box 920888, Needham, MA 02492-0009. Or call their office and speak to a volunteer or leave your name and address and a request for information. Their number is 800-421-2383. You can also visit their website, at www.debtorsanonymous.org.

Nolo Publications

Several Nolo publications can provide you with information to supplement this book.

Money Troubles: Debt, Credit & Bank-ruptcy, by Robin Leonard and Margaret Reiter, provides extensive information on prioritizing your debts, negotiating with creditors, and deciding whether or not bankruptcy is for you.

The Foreclosure Survival Guide: Keep Your House or Walk Away With Money in Your Pocket, by Stephen Elias, explains your options and rights in dealing with an impending foreclosure, including negotiating a mortgage workout, fighting foreclosure in court, filing for bankruptcy, and selling your house.

How to File for Chapter 7 Bankruptcy, by Stephen R. Elias, Albin Renauer, and Robin Leonard, is a detailed, thorough how-to guide for filing for Chapter 7 bankruptcy.

Recommendedfor readers who are certain they want to file for Chapter 7.

Chapter 13 Bankruptcy: Keep Your Property & Repay Debts Over Time, by Stephen Elias and Robin Leonard, explains Chapter 13 bankruptcy and includes the forms and instructions necessary to file a Chapter 13 bankruptcy case.

The New Bankruptcy: Will It Work for You? by Stephen Elias, answers the most common—and not so common—questions about Chapter 7 bankruptcy and Chapter 13 bankruptcy, to help you decide if bankruptcy is right for you.

Stand Up to the IRS, by Frederick W. Daily, guides taxpayers through the ins and outs of an audit, self-representation in tax court, challenging tax bills, and setting up repayment plans for tax bills they do owe. This book was named one of the top three personal finance books by *Money* magazine.

Divorce & Money: How to Make the Best Financial Decisions During Divorce, by Violet Woodhouse with Dale Fetherling, is a thorough workbook for people making financial decisions while ending their marriage. Divorce is a time when you are at risk of damaging your credit. This book gives tips on dividing assets and allocating debts while protecting your precious credit rating.

Other Publications

Publications from non-Nolo publishers have a wealth of information beyond what is in this book.

The Ultimate Credit Handbook: How to Cut Your Debt and Have a Lifetime of Great Credit, by Gerri Detweiler (Plume Books), covers everything you'd want to know about credit ratings, credit cards, completing credit applications, protecting your credit privacy, and many other topics.

NCLC Guide to Surviving Debt: A Guide for Consumers, by the National Consumer Law Center (NCLC). NCLC is a nonprofit organization that normally publishes books to assist lawyers. NCLC uses its years of experience in counseling low-income debtors across the country to offer tips on all kinds of debts and income sources, including government benefits, defenses to collection lawsuits, and strategies when your house is in foreclosure. Order this guide from NCLC, Publications Department, 77 Summer Street, 10th Floor, Boston, MA 02110, 617-542-9595 or on NCLC's website, at www.nclc.org.

What Every Credit Card User Needs to Know, by Howard Strong (Owl Books), provides lots of information about selecting and using credit cards. It also contains many useful sample letters.

Online Resources

If you have access to the Internet, you can find a good deal of information using your computer. But you can't do it all—not every court decision or state statute is available online. Furthermore, unless you know what you are looking for—the case name and citation or the code section—you may have difficulty finding it.

Still, there are a number of useful sites. For legal research, visit:

- **www.nolo.com/statute/index.cfm**
  Nolo's website provides a legal research page with links to each state's online legal information (including state statutes) plus links to federal statues, regulations, and the U.S. Constitution.

Specific debt, credit, finance, consumer protection and bankruptcy information is available at a few sites, including the following:

- **www.nolo.com**
  Nolo's online site includes legal information for consumers, such as frequently asked questions and articles on legal issues (click on the "property & money" category).
- **www.ftc.gov**
  The Federal Trade Commission's website provides free publications on many consumer topics, including credit repair. It also provides links to the full text of numerous consumer protection laws (click on "Rules" or check out any of the consumer topics).
- **www.pueblo.gsa.gov**
  The Federal Citizen Information Center provides the latest in consumer news as well as many publications of interest to consumers, including the Consumer Information Catalog.
- **www.fdic.gov**
  www.federalreserve.gov
  The Federal Deposit Insurance Corporation and Federal Reserve Board websites have consumer

information and resources for understanding and researching banks and financial institutions.

- **www.irs.gov**
  The Internal Revenue Service provides tax information, forms, and publications.

- **www.fraud.org**
  The National Fraud Information Center's website provides lots of information on how to protect yourself from telemarketing and Internet scams and how to report fraud.

- **www.bbb.org**
  The Better Business Bureau has information on a number of consumer topics, and offers links to local BBB offices. Use this site to check with your local BBB for complaints about businesses in the area before doing business with them.

State Consumer Protection Agencies

The state agencies listed below enforce consumer protection laws and provide consumer protection information. Many of these agencies regulate credit bureaus, accept complaints about credit bureaus in the state, and provide free information about your rights as they relate to collection bureaus.

If your state can't or won't help you, contact the Federal Trade Commission, www.ftc.gov.

Alabama
Consumer Affairs Division
Office of Attorney General
500 Dexter Avenue
Montgomery, AL 36130
334-242-7334
800-392-5658
www.ago.state.al.us/consumer.cfm

Alaska
Consumer Protection Unit
Office of the Attorney General
1031 W. 4th Avenue, Suite 200
Anchorage AK 99501-5903
907-269-5100
www.law.state.ak.us/consumer

Arizona
Consumer Information and Complaints
Office of Attorney General
1275 W. Washington Street
Phoenix, AZ 85007-2926
602-542-5763
800-352-8431
www.azag.gov/consumer

Arkansas
Consumer Protection Division
Office of the Attorney General
323 Center Street, Suite 200
Little Rock, AR 72201
501-687-2007
800-482-8982
www.ag.state.ar.us

California

Public Inquiry Unit
Office of the Attorney General
Department of Justice
P.O. Box 944255
Sacramento, CA 94244-2550
916-322-3360
800-952-5225
800-735-2929 (TDD)
http://ag.ca.gov/consumers

Colorado

Consumer Protection Section
Office of Attorney General
1525 Sherman Street, 7th floor
Denver, CO 80203
303-866-5189
800-222-4444
www.ago.state.co.us

Connecticut

Department of Consumer Protection
165 Capitol Avenue
Hartford, CT 06106-1630
860-713-6300
800-842-2649
860-713-7240 (TDD)
www.ct.gov/dcp

Delaware

Consumer Protection Unit
Office of the Attorney General
820 North French Street, 5th floor
Wilmington, DE 19801
302-577-8600
800-220-5424
http://attorneygeneral.delaware.gov/
consumers/protection/complaint.shtml

District of Columbia

Department of Consumer and Regulatory
Affairs
941 North Capitol Street, NE
Washington, DC 20002
202-442-4400
www.dcra.dc.gov/dcra

Florida

Division of Consumer Services
Department of Agriculture and Consumer
Services
Terry Lee Rhodes Building
2005 Apalachee Parkway
Tallahassee, FL 32399-6500
850-488-2221
800-435-7352
www.800helpfla.com

Georgia

Governor's Office of Consumer Affairs
2 Martin Luther King, Jr. Drive, Suite 356
Atlanta, GA 30334-4600
404-651-8600
800-869-1123
http://consumer.georgia.gov

Hawaii

Office of Consumer Protection
235 S. Beretania Street
Suite 801
Leiopapa A Kamehameha Building
Honolulu, HI 96813
808-587-3222
808-586-2630
http://hawaii.gov/dcca/area/ocp

Idaho

Consumer Protection Unit
Office of Attorney General
954 W. Jefferson Street, 2nd Floor
P.O. Box 83720
Boise, ID 83720-0010
208-334-2424
800-432-3545
www.state.id.us/ag/consumer

Illinois

Consumer Protection Division
Office of Attorney General
100 W. Randolph Street
Chicago, IL 60601
312-814-3000
800-386-5438
800-964-3013 (TTY)
www.ag.state.il.us/consumers

Indiana

Consumer Credit Division
Department of Financial Institutions
30 S. Meridian Street, Suite 300
Indianapolis, IN 46204
317-232-6330
800-382-5516
www.in.gov/dfi

Iowa

Consumer Protection Division
Office of Attorney General
1305 E. Walnut Street
Des Moines, IA 50319
515-281-5926
www.state.ia.us/government/ag/
  protecting_consumers

Kansas

Consumer Protection and Antitrust Division
Office of Attorney General
Memorial Hall, 2nd Floor
120 SW Tenth Avenue
Topeka, KS 66612
785-296-3751
800-432-2310
785-291-3767 (TTY)
www.ksag.org

Kentucky

Consumer Protection Division
Office of the Attorney General
The Capitol, Suite 118
700 Capitol Avenue
Frankfort, KY 40601
502-696-5389
888-432-9257
http://ag.ky.gov/civil/consumerprotection

Louisiana

Consumer Protection Section
Office of the Attorney General
P.O. Box 94005
Baton Rouge, LA 70804-9095
800-351-4889
www.ag.state.la.us

Maine

Attorney General's Consumer Information and
  Mediation Service
6 State House Station
Augusta, ME 04333
207-626-8849
800-436-2131
www.maine.gov/ag

Maryland

Consumer Protection Division
Office of Attorney General
200 St. Paul Place
Baltimore, MD 21202
410-528-8662
888-743-0023
www.oag.state.md.us/consumer

Massachusetts

Office of Consumer Affairs and Business
  Regulation
10 Park Plaza, Suite 5170
Boston, MA 02116
617-973-8787 (hotline)
617-973-8700
888-283-3757
www.mass.gov/consumer

Michigan

Consumer Protection Division
Office of Attorney General
P.O. Box 30213
Lansing, MI 48909
517-373-1140
877-765-8388
www.michigan.gov/ag

Minnesota

Consumer Protection Division
Office of Attorney General
1400 Bremer Tower
445 Minnesota Street
St. Paul, MN 55101
651-296-3353
800-657-3787
651-297-7206 (TTY)
800-366-4812 (TTY)
www.ag.state.mn.us

Mississippi

Consumer Protection Division
Office of the Attorney General
P.O. Box 22947
Jackson, MS 39225-2947
601-359-4230
800-281-4418
www.ago.state.ms.us

Missouri

Consumer Protection Division
Attorney General's Office
Supreme Court Building
207 W. High Street
P.O. Box 899
Jefferson City, MO 65102
573-751-3321
800-392-8222
www.ago.state.mo.gov/divisions/
  consumerprotection.htm

Montana

Office of Consumer Protection
2225 11th Avenue
P.O. Box 200151
Helena, MT 59620-0151
406-444-4500
800-481-6896
http://doj.mt.gov/consumer

Nebraska

Consumer Protection Division
Office of Attorney General
2115 State Capitol Building
Lincoln, NE 68509
402-471-2682
800-727-6432
www.ago.state.ne.us

Nevada

Consumer Affairs Division
Department of Business and Industry
1850 E. Sahara Avenue, Suite 101
Las Vegas, NV 89104
702-486-7355

[or]

4600 Kietzke Lane
Building B, Suite 113
Reno, NV 89502
775-688-1800
www.fyiconsumer.org

New Hampshire

Consumer Protection and Antitrust Bureau
Department of Justice
33 Capitol Street
Concord, NH 03301
603-271-3658
800-735-2964 (TDD)
www.nh.gov/nhdoj/consumer

New Jersey

Division of Consumer Affairs
Department of Law and Public Safety
124 Halsey Street
Newark, NJ 07102
973-504-6200
800-242-5846
www.njconsumeraffairs.gov

New Mexico

Consumer Protection Division
Office of Attorney General
408 Galisteo Street
Villagra Building
Santa Fe, NM 87501
505-827-6000
800-678-1508
www.nmag.gov/office/divisions/cp

New York

Consumer Protection Board
5 Empire State Plaza, Suite 2101
Albany, NY 12223
518-474-3514
518-474-8583 (Complaint Unit)
www.consumer.state.ny.us

North Carolina

Consumer Protection Division
Department of Justice, Attorney General's
    Office
9001 Mail Service Center
Raleigh, NC 27699-9001
919-716-6400
877-566-7226
www.ncdoj.com

North Dakota

Consumer Protection Division
Office of Attorney General
4205 State Street
P.O. Box 1054
Bismarck, ND 58505-1054
701-328-3404
800-472-2600
www.ag.state.nd.us/CPAT/CPAT.htm

Ohio

Consumer Protection Division
Office of Attorney General
State Office Tower
30 E. Broad Street, 17th Floor
Columbus, OH 43215-3428
614-466-4320
800-282-0515
www.ag.state.oh.us/citizen/
    consumer/index.asp

Oklahoma

Consumer Protection Unit
Office of the Attorney General
313 NE 21st Street
Oklahoma City, OK 73105
405-521-3921
918-581-2885
www.oag.state.ok.us/oagweb.nsf/consumer

Oregon

Financial Fraud/Consumer Protection Section
1162 Court Street, NE
Salem, OR 97301-4096
503-378-4320
503-229-5576
877-877-9392
www.doj.state.or.us/finfraud/index.shtml

Pennsylvania

Bureau of Consumer Protection
Office of Attorney General
Strawberry Square, 16th Floor
Harrisburg, PA 17120
717-787-3391
800-441-2555
www.attorneygeneral.gov/consumers.aspx

Rhode Island

Consumer Protection Unit
Department of Attorney General
150 S. Main Street
Providence, RI 02903
401-274-4400
www.riag.state.ri.us/civilcriminal/
    consumerprotection.php

South Carolina

Department of Consumer Affairs
P.O. Box 5757
3600 Forest Drive, 3rd Floor
Columbia, SC 29250
803-734-4200
800-922-1594
www.scconsumer.gov

South Dakota

Division of Consumer Protection
Office of the Attorney General
1302 E. Highway 14, Suite 3
Pierre, SD 57501-5070
605-773-4400
800-300-1986
www.state.sd.us/attorney/office/ divisions/
    consumer

Tennessee

Division of Consumer Affairs
Department of Commerce and Insurance
500 James Robertson Parkway
Nashville, TN 37243-0600
615-741-4737
800-342-8385
http://state.tn.us/consumer

Texas

Consumer Protection Division
Office of the Attorney General
300 W. 15th Street
P.O. Box 12548
Austin, TX 78711-2548
512-463-2100
800-621-0508
www.oag.state.tx.us/consumer/
    index.shtml

Utah

Division of Consumer Protection
Department of Commerce
160 E. 300 South
SM Box 146704
Salt Lake City, UT 84114
801-530-6601
800-721-7233
http://consumerprotection.utah.gov

Vermont

Consumer Assistance Program
Office of Attorney General
103B Morrill Hall, UVM
Burlington, VT 05405
802-656-3183
800-649-2424
www.atg.state.vt.us

Virginia

Office of Consumer Affairs
Department of Agriculture and Consumer
   Services
102 Governor Street
Richmond, VA 23219
804-786-2042
800-552-9963
www.vdacs.virginia.gov/consumers

Washington

Consumer Resource Center
Office of the Attorney General
P.O. Box 40100
1125 Washington Street SE
Olympia, WA 98504-0100
360-753-6200
800-551-4636
800-833-6384 (TDD)
www.atg.wa.gov/safeguardingconsumers.aspx

West Virginia

Consumer Protection Division
Office of the Attorney General
P.O. Box 1789
Charleston, WV 25326
304-558-8986
800-368-8808
www.wvag.gov/consumers.cfm

Wisconsin

Bureau of Consumer Protection
Department of Agriculture, Trade, and
   Consumer Protection
P.O. Box 8911
Madison, WI 53708-8911
608-221-4949
800-422-7128
www.datcp.state.wi.us

Wyoming

Consumer Protection Unit
Attorney General's Office
123 State Capitol
Cheyenne, WY 82002
307-777-7874
800-438-5799
http://attorneygeneral.state.wy.us/
   consumer.htm

Where to Complain About Credit Discrimination

If you believe you have been a victim of credit discrimination, here are the appropriate government agencies to contact:

- Consumer Response Center
  Federal Trade Commission
  600 Pennsylvania Avenue, NW
  Washington, DC 20580

  Contact the FTC if you have been discriminated against by a store, mortgage company, small loan and finance company, oil company, public utility, state credit union, government lending program, or travel and expense credit card company. Although the FTC doesn't intervene in individual disputes, the information you provide may show a pattern of violations on which it can act.

- Comptroller of the Currency
  Customer Assistance Group
  1301 McKinney Street
  Suite 3450
  Houston, TX 77010

  Use this address if your complaint is about a nationally chartered bank ("National" or "N.A." will be in its name).

- Federal Deposit Insurance Corporation
  Consumer Response Center
  2345 Grand Boulevard, Suite 100
  Kansas City, MO 64108

  Contact the FDIC if your complaint is about a state-chartered bank that is insured by the FDIC but is not a member of the Federal Reserve System.

- Office of Thrift Supervision
  1700 G Street, NW
  Washington, DC 20552

  Use this address to complain about a federally chartered or federally insured savings and loan association.

- National Credit Union Administration
  1775 Duke Street
  Alexandria, VA 22314

  Use the address if your complaint is about a federally chartered credit union.

- Department of Justice
  Civil Rights Division
  950 Pennsylvania Avenue, NW
  Washington, DC 20530

  You can complain to the Justice Department about any type of creditor. ●

Forms and Letters

F-1:   Outstanding Debts

F-2:   Daily Expenditures

F-3:   Monthly Income From All Sources

F-4:   Monthly Budget

F-5:   Error on Credit Card Bill

F-6:   Dispute Credit Card Bill

F-7:   Offer (Reduced) Lump Sum Payment

F-8:   Offer Payment Schedule to Pay Off (Reduced) Debt

F-9:   Request Short-Term Lower Payments

F-10: Request Long-Term Lower Payments

F-11: Request to Pay Nothing Short-Term

F-12: Request to Pay Nothing Long-Term

F-13: Request Rewrite of Loan Terms

F-14: Offer to Give Secured Property Back

F-15: Cashing Check Constitutes Payment in Full (Outside of California)

F-16: Cashing Check Constitutes Payment in Full—First Letter (California)

F-17: Cashing Check Constitutes Payment in Full—Second Letter (California)

F-18: Cashing Check Constitutes Release of All Claims

F-19: Inform Creditor of Judgment Proof Status

F-20: Inform Creditor of Plan to File for Bankruptcy

F-21: Request Direct Negotiation With Creditor

F-22: Dispute Amount of Bill or Quality of Goods or Services Received

F-23: Collection Agency: Cease All Contact

F-24: Complaint About Collection Agency Harassment

F-25: Request Credit Report

F-26: Request Reinvestigation

F-27: Request Follow-Up After Reinvestigation

F-28: Request Removal of Incorrect Information by Creditor

F-29: Creditor Verification

F-30: Request Addition of Account Histories

F-31: Request Addition of Information Showing Stability

ID Theft Affidavit and Instructions

Annual Credit Report Request Form

FTC Law Enforcement Cover Letter

Outstanding Debts

Outstanding Debts	Monthly Payment	Amount Behind
Rent or mortgage (include second mortgage, home equity loans)		
Utilities and telephone		
Transportation expenses		
car loans/lease payments		
maintenance payments		
auto insurance		
Child care		
Alimony or child support		
Education expenses		
student loans		
tuition expenses		
Personal and other loans		
bank loans		
loan consolidator		
Lawyer or accountant bills		

Outstanding Debts	Monthly Payment	Amount Behind
Medical (doctor and hospital) bills		
Insurance		
homeowners or renters		
disability		
medical or dental		
life		
Credit and charge cards		
Department store charges		
Back taxes		
Federal		
State		
Other (such as property)		
Other unpaid bills		
TOTALS	$	$

Daily Expenditures for Week of _____

Sunday's Expenditures	Cost	Monday's Expenditures	Cost	Tuesday's Expenditures	Cost	Wednesday's Expenditures	Cost
Daily Total:		**Daily Total:**		**Daily Total:**		**Daily Total:**	

Thursday's Expenditures	Cost	Friday's Expenditures	Cost	Saturday's Expenditures	Cost	Other Expenditures	Cost
Daily Total:		**Daily Total:**		**Daily Total:**		**Weekly Total:**	

Monthly Income From All Sources

1 Source of income		2 Amount of each payment	3 Period covered by each payment	4 Amount per month
A. Wages or Salary				
Job 1: _____ _____	Gross pay, including overtime:	$ _____	_____	
	Subtract:			
	Federal taxes	_____		
	State taxes	_____		
	Social Security (FICA)	_____		
	Union dues	_____		
	Insurance payments	_____		
	Child support wage withholding	_____		
	Other mandatory deductions (specify): _____ _____	_____		
	Subtotal:	$ _____	_____	_____
Job 2: _____ _____	Gross pay, including overtime:	$ _____	_____	
	Subtract:			
	Federal taxes	_____		
	State taxes	_____		
	Social Security (FICA)	_____		
	Union dues	_____		
	Insurance payments	_____		
	Child support wage withholding	_____		
	Other mandatory deductions (specify): _____ _____	_____		
	Subtotal:	$ _____	_____	_____
Job 3: _____ _____	Gross pay, including overtime:	$ _____	_____	
	Subtract:			
	Federal taxes	_____		
	State taxes	_____		
	Social Security (FICA)	_____		
	Union dues	_____		
	Insurance payments	_____		
	Child support wage withholding	_____		
	Other mandatory deductions (specify): _____ _____	_____		
	Subtotal:	$ _____	_____	_____

Monthly Income From All Sources (cont'd)

1 Source of income		2 Amount of each payment	3 Period covered by each payment	4 Amount per month
B. Self-Employment Income				
Job 1: _____ _____	Gross pay, including overtime:	$ _____	_____	
	Subtract:			
	Federal taxes	_____		
	State taxes	_____		
	Self-employment taxes	_____		
	Other mandatory deductions (specify): _____ _____			
	Subtotal:	$ _____	_____	_____
Job 2: _____ _____	Gross pay, including overtime:	$ _____	_____	
	Subtract:			
	Federal taxes	_____		
	State taxes	_____		
	Self-employment taxes	_____		
	Other mandatory deductions (specify): _____ _____			
	Subtotal:	$ _____	_____	_____
C. Other Sources				
Bonuses _____		_____		_____
Commissions _____		_____		_____
Dividends and interest _____		_____		_____
Rent, lease, or license income _____		_____		_____
Royalties _____		_____		_____
Note or trust income _____		_____		_____
Alimony or child support you receive _____		_____		_____
Pension or retirement income _____		_____		_____
Social Security _____		_____		_____
Other public assistance _____		_____		_____
Other (specify): _____		_____		_____
_____		_____		_____
_____		_____		_____
_____		_____		_____
_____		_____		_____
Total monthly income				$ _____

Monthly Budget

Expense Category	Projected											
Home												
Rent/mortgage												
Property tax												
Insurance												
Homeowners' assn. dues												
Telephone												
Gas/electric												
Water/sewer												
Cable												
Garbage/recycling												
Household supplies												
Housewares												
Furniture/appliances												
Cleaning												
Yard/pool care												
Repairs/maintenance												
Food												
Groceries												
Breakfast out												
Lunch out												
Dinner out												
Coffee/tea												
Snacks												
Clothing												
Clothes, shoes/accessories												
Laundry, dry cleaning												
Mending												

Self Care

Toiletries/cosmetics											
Haircuts											
Massage											
Gym membership											
Donations											

Health Care

Insurance											
Medications											
Vitamins											
Doctor											
Dentist											
Eye care											
Therapy											

Transportation

Car payments (buy or lease)											
Insurance											
Registration											
Gas											
Maintenance/repairs											
Parking											
Tolls											
Public transit											
Parking tickets											
Road service (such as AAA)											

Entertainment

Music											
Movies/rentals											
Concerts, theater, ballet, etc.											
Museums											

Sporting events												
Hobbies/lessons												
Club dues or membership												
Film/developing costs												
Books, magazines/ newspapers												
Software/games												

Dependent Care

Child care												
Clothing												
Allowance												
School expenses												
Toys/entertainment												

Pets

Food/supplies												
Veterinarian												
Grooming												

Education

Tuition												
Loan payments												
Books/supplies												

Travel

Gifts/Cards

Personal Business

Supplies												
Copying												
Postage												
Bank/credit card fees												
Legal fees												
Accountant												

Taxes													
Insurance													
Savings/ investments													
Total expenses													
Projected monthly income													
Difference													

Date: _____

_____

_____

_____

Attn: Customer Service

Name(s) on account: _____

Account number: _____

To Whom It May Concern:

I am writing to point out an error that appears on my billing statement dated

_____, 20_____.

Merchant's name: _____

Amount in error: _____

I am withholding this amount.

The problem is as follows:

_____

_____

_____

_____

_____

I understand that the law requires you to acknowledge receipt of this letter within 30 days unless you correct this billing error before then. Furthermore, I understand that within two billing cycles (but in no event more than 90 days), you must correct the error or explain why you believe the amount to be correct.

Sincerely,

_____
[your signature]

Name: _____

Address: _____

_____

Home phone: _____

Email address: _____

Date: _____

_____

_____

_____

Attn: Customer Service

Name(s) on account: _____

Account number: _____

To Whom It May Concern:

I am writing to dispute the following charge that appears on my billing statement dated

_____, 20_____ .

Merchant's name: _____

Amount in dispute: _____

I am withholding payment of $ _____ , which represents the unpaid balance on the disputed item.

I am disputing this amount for the following reason(s):

_____

_____

_____

_____

_____

As required by law, I have tried in good faith to resolve this dispute with the merchant. [*Describe your efforts*] _____ .

Furthermore, I wish to point out that this purchase was for more than $50 and was made [*cross out one*] in the state in which I live/within 100 miles of my home.

Please verify this dispute with the merchant and remove this item, and all late and interest charges attributed to this item, from my billing statement.

Sincerely,

_____
[*your signature*]

Name: _____

Address: _____

_____

Home phone: _____

Email address: _____

Date: _____

_____

_____

_____

Attn: Customer Service

Name(s) on account: _____

Account number: _____

To Whom It May Concern:

I am now in a position to resolve this matter. I can pay a lump sum amount of $_____ .
If I make a lump sum payment of $ _____ by _____ [date], you will agree
to do the following:

☐ [if the amount of the debt is not disputed] You will release all claims against me and anyone else
arising from this account.

☐ [if the amount of the debt is disputed]I dispute the amount of the debt. You will acknowledge that
the balance owed on the account is $[the amount of the lump-sum payment], you will release all
claims against me and anyone else arising from this account, and you will accept that payment as
payment in full.

☐ [if you want negative information removed from your credit report] You will submit a Universal
Data Form to Experian, Equifax, and TransUnion deleting the account/trade line.

If my offer is acceptable to you, please initial the accepted proposal, sign the acceptance below, and
return this letter to me in the enclosed envelope.

Sincerely,

_____
[your signature]

Name: _____

Address: _____

_____

Home phone: _____

Email address: _____

Agreed to and accepted on this _____ day of _____, 20_____.

By: _____

Name (print): _____

Title: _____

Date: _____

_____

_____

_____

Attn: Customer Service

Name(s) on account: _____

Account number: _____

To Whom It May Concern:

I am now in a position to resolve this matter. I can pay installments in the amount of $_____
per month for _____ months. If I make installment payments in the amount of $_____
per month for _____ months, you agree to the following:

☐ [if the amount of the debt is not disputed] You will release all claims against me and anyone else
arising from this account.

☐ [if the amount of the debt is disputed] I dispute the amount of the debt. You will acknowledge
that the balance owed on the account is $ [the total of all installment payments you agree to
pay], you will release all claims against me and anyone else arising from this account, and you will
accept installment payments in that amount as payment in full.

☐ [if you want your payments to be considered timely, not late] You agree to re-age my account—
that is, to make the current month the first repayment month and show no late payments as
long as I make the agreed-on monthly installment payments.

If my offer is acceptable to you, please initial the accepted proposal, sign the acceptance below, and
return this letter to me in the enclosed envelope.

Sincerely,

_____
          [your signature]

Name: _____

Address: _____

_____

Home phone: _____

Email address: _____

Agreed to and accepted on this _____ day of _____, 20_____.

By: _____

Name (print): _____

Title: _____

Date: _____

_____

_____

_____

Attn: Customer Service

Name(s) on account: _____

Account number: _____

To Whom It May Concern:

At the present, I cannot pay the monthly amount required under the agreement for the following reason(s):

_____

_____

_____

_____

_____

I can pay $_____ per month right now and expect to resume making the full monthly payment when the following occurs:

_____

_____

_____

Please accept the reduced payments until then. If necessary, add the unpaid amount to the end of the loan or account period and extend it by a few months.

Thank you for your understanding and help. Please write within 20 days to let me know if this is acceptable.

Sincerely,

_____
              [your signature]

Name: _____

Address: _____

_____

Home phone: _____

Email address: _____

Date: _____

_____

_____

_____

Attn: Customer Service

Name(s) on account: _____

Account number: _____

To Whom It May Concern:

At the present, I cannot pay the monthly amount required under the agreement for the following reason(s):

_____

_____

_____

_____

_____

_____

_____

I can pay you only $_____ per month for the indefinite future. Please accept the reduced payments. I promise to inform you immediately if my financial condition improves and I am able to resume making normal payments.

Thank you for your understanding and help. Please write within 20 days to let me know if this is acceptable.

Sincerely,

_____
                    [your signature]

Name: _____

Address: _____

_____

Home phone: _____

Email address: _____

Date: _____

_____

_____

_____

Attn: Customer Service

Name(s) on account: _____

Account number: _____

To Whom It May Concern:

At the present, I cannot pay the monthly amount required under the agreement for the following reason(s):

_____

_____

_____

_____

_____

I expect to resume making the full monthly payment when the following occurs:

_____

_____

_____

If necessary, add the unpaid amount to the end of the loan or account period and extend it by a few months.

Thank you for your understanding and help. Please write within 20 days if this is unacceptable.

Sincerely,

_____
            [*your signature*]

Name: _____

Address: _____

_____

Home phone: _____

Email address: _____

©nolo

Date: _____

_____

_____

_____

Attn: Customer Service

Name(s) on account: _____

Account number: _____

To Whom It May Concern:

At the present, I cannot pay the monthly amount required under the agreement for the following reason(s):

_____

_____

_____

_____

_____

Due to my desperate financial situation, I cannot make any payments for the indefinite future.
[*Describe hardship*] _____ .

I promise to inform you immediately if my financial condition improves and I am able to resume making normal payments.

Thank you for your understanding and help. Please write within 20 days if this is unacceptable.

Sincerely,

_____
            [*your signature*]

Name: _____

Address: _____

_____

Home phone: _____

Email address: _____

Date: _____

_____

_____

_____

Attn: Customer Service

Name(s) on account: _____

Account number: _____

To Whom It May Concern:

At the present, I cannot pay the monthly amount required under the agreement for the following reason(s):

_____

_____

_____

_____

_____

_____

_____

_____

I would like the terms of the loan rewritten in order to reduce the amount of the monthly payments.

Thank you for your understanding and help. Please call me as soon as possible in order that we may discuss new loan terms.

Sincerely,

_____
                    [your signature]

Name: _____

Address: _____

_____

Home phone: _____

Email address: _____

Date: _____

_____

_____

_____

Attn: Customer Service

Name(s) on account: _____

Account number: _____

To Whom It May Concern:

I cannot pay the monthly amount required under my agreement with you. I invite you to come pick up the collateral. Or I will return it to you, if you can assure me in writing that the entire debt will be canceled when the property is returned, and that I will not be liable for any deficiency judgment. Please let me know where to return the collateral.

Thank you for your attention to this matter. Please send me a written confirmation within 20 days if this is acceptable.

Sincerely,

_____
              [your signature]

Name: _____

Address: _____

_____

Home phone: _____

Email address: _____

[Send this letter to the person, office, or place designated by the creditor for communications regarding disputed debts, or to the proper collection agent if you are no longer dealing with the creditor itself. Don't forget to write the statement in quotation marks at the end of this letter conspicuously on the check you enclose with your letter.]

Date: _____

_____

_____

_____

Attn: Customer Service

Name(s) on account: _____

Account number: _____

To Whom It May Concern:

Enclosed is a check for $_____ to cover the balance of the account. Cashing this check constitutes payment in full and releases all claims you may have related to this account.

Sincerely,

_____
[your signature]

Name: _____

Address: _____

_____

Home phone: _____

Email address: _____

Enclosed: A check in the amount of $_____, stating on the front, "Cashing this check constitutes payment in full and releases all claims related to [*account number, account name, or both*].

[Send this letter to the person, office, or place designated by the creditor for communications regarding disputed debts—or to the proper collection agent if you are no longer dealing with the creditor company itself.]

Date: _____

_____

_____

_____

Attn: Customer Service

Name(s) on account: _____

Account number: _____

To Whom It May Concern:

Regarding the above-referenced account, I dispute the amount you claim that I owe you for the following reason(s):

_____

_____

_____

_____

_____

_____

I believe that I owe you no more than $_____. It is obvious that there is a good-faith dispute over the amount of this bill.

In a good-faith effort to satisfy this debt, I will send you a check for $_____ with a restrictive endorsement; if you cash that check, it will constitute an accord and satisfaction. In other words, you will receive from me a check that states, "Cashing this check constitutes payment in full and releases all claims you may have related to this account." If you cash that check, it will fully satisfy my obligation to you.

Sincerely,

_____
                [your signature]

Name: _____

Address: _____

_____

Home phone: _____

Email address: _____

[Send this letter to the person, office, or place designated by the creditor for communications regarding disputed debts—or to the proper collection agent if you are no longer dealing with the creditor company itself. Don't forget to write the statement in quotation marks at the end of this letter conspicuously on the check.]

Date: _____

_____

_____

_____

Attn: Customer Service

Name(s) on account: _____

Account number: _____

To Whom It May Concern:

[Wait a reasonable time before sending this letter, and indicate that amount of time here. Two weeks is probably reasonable, but more or less time may be reasonable in your particular situation.]

[*Two weeks*] have passed since I sent you a letter dated _____, 20_____ stating my intention to send you a check with a restrictive endorsement.

Enclosed is a check for $_____ to cover the balance of my account. This check is tendered in accordance with my earlier letter. If you cash this check, you agree that my debt is satisfied in full and you release all claims you may have related to this account.

Sincerely,

_____
                [your signature]

Name: _____

Address: _____

_____

Home phone: _____

Email address: _____

Enclosed: Check stating on front: "This check is tendered in accordance with my letter of _____, 20_____. Cashing this check releases all claims you may have related to [*account number, account name, or both*] and constitutes payment in full."

[Send this letter to the person, office, or place designated by the creditor for communications regarding disputed debts, or to the proper collection agent if you are no longer dealing with the creditor itself. Don't forget to write the statement in quotation marks at the end of this letter conspicuously on the check you enclose.]

Date: _____

_____

_____

_____

Attn: Customer Service

Name on account: _____

Account number: _____

To Whom It May Concern:

I can pay a total of $_____ to satisfy this account in full. Enclosed is a check for $_____ for the balance of my account. If you cash this check, you agree that my debt is satisfied in full and you release all claims you may have related to this account.

Sincerely,

_____
                [your signature]

Name: _____

Address: _____

_____

Home phone: _____

Email address: _____

Enclosed: Check stating on front: "Cashing this check releases all claims that may be related to *[account number and account name, or both]* and constitutes payment in full."

Date: _____

_____

_____

_____

Attn: Collections Department

Name(s) on account: _____

Account number: _____

To Whom It May Concern:

This letter is to advise you that I am not able to make payments on my account due to the following conditions:

_____

_____

_____

_____

I cannot work sufficient hours to meet my current expenses. My only sources of income are:

_____

_____

I am familiar with the law and know that I am "judgment proof." If I file for bankruptcy, I will claim all my property as exempt, and if you sue me and obtain a judgment, you could not collect any of my property to satisfy the judgment.

Please cease all collection activities you have taken or are considering taking. While I will provide you with reasonable financial or medical information, I must avoid stress. This includes high-pressure collection activity and lawsuits.

If my current situation improves and I am able to resume payments, I will notify you at once.

Thank you for your understanding and help.

Sincerely,

_____
[*your signature*]

Name: _____

Address: _____

_____

Home phone: _____

Email address: _____

Date: _____

_____

_____

_____

Attn: Collections Department

Name(s) on account: _____

Account number: _____

To Whom It May Concern:

Please cease all collection activities you have taken or are considering taking against me.
I am planning to file a petition in bankruptcy court in the coming months.

Sincerely,

_____
[your signature]

Name: _____

Address: _____

_____

Home phone: _____

Email address: _____

Date: _____

_____

_____

_____

Name(s) on account: _____

Account number: _____

Creditor: _____

To: _____

I have been contacted several times by you regarding my past due account with the creditor referenced above. I do not, however, wish to discuss this matter with you. I would like to talk directly with the creditor's collections department.

Please contact the collections department of the creditor and indicate my desire to be in touch with them.

Thank you for your help.

Sincerely,

_____
[your signature]

Name: _____

Address: _____

_____

Home phone: _____

Email address: _____

cc: Creditor: _____

Date: _____

_____

_____

_____

To: _____

I am writing to dispute the following bill you are attempting to collect.

Name(s) on account: _____

Account number: _____

Creditor: _____

Amount in dispute: _____

I am disputing this bill for the following reason(s):

_____

_____

_____

_____

_____

Please return this bill to the creditor immediately and remove any "sent to collection agency" notation that may be in my credit file.

Thank you for your attention to this matter.

Sincerely,

_____

[your signature]

Name: _____

Address: _____

_____

Home phone: _____

Email address: _____

cc: Creditor: _____

Date: _____

_____

_____

_____

Name(s) on account: _____

Account number: _____

Creditor: _____

To: _____

Since approximately _____, 20_____, I have received several
phone calls and letters from you concerning my overdue account with the above-named creditor.

Accordingly, under 15 U.S.C. § 1692c, this is my formal notice to you to cease all further
communications with me.

Sincerely,

_____

                [your signature]

Name: _____

Address: _____

_____

Home phone: _____

Email address: _____

Date: _____

_____

_____

_____

Name(s) on account: _____

Account number: _____

Date loan/debt incurred: _____

Original loan/debt amount: _____

Amount past due: _____

Re: Collection agency: _____

To Whom It May Concern:

I have been unable to pay the full amount of the loan/debt noted above for the following reason(s):

_____

_____

I have the right to be treated by a collection agency with dignity and respect. The collection agency you hired (as noted above), however, has engaged in the following practices, which violate the federal Fair Debt Collection Practices Act:

_____

_____

I am willing to forgo the legal remedies I may have, including a lawsuit in small claims court seeking punitive damages against you and the agency, in exchange for your written promise to permanently cease all efforts to collect this debt and remove all negative entries regarding this debt from my credit file. I expect to hear from you immediately.

Sincerely,

_____
[your signature]

Name: _____

Address: _____

_____

Home phone: _____

Email address: _____

cc: Federal Trade Commission
     State Collection Agency Licensing Board
     Collection Agency: _____

Date: _____

_____

_____

To Whom It May Concern:

Please send me a copy of my credit report.

Full name: _____

Date of birth: _____

Social Security number _____

Spouse's name: _____

Telephone number: _____

Current address: _____

_____

(Check one:)

☐ I was denied credit on _____ by _____ .
 Enclosed is a copy of the rejection letter.

☐ I hereby certify that I am unemployed and intend to apply for a job within the next 60 days.

☐ I hereby certify that I receive public assistance/welfare.

☐ I hereby certify that I believe there is erroneous information in my file due to fraud.

☐ I have not been denied credit within the preceding 60 days. Enclosed is a copy of a document
 identifying me by my name and address and payment in the amount of $_____.

Thank you for your attention to this matter.

Sincerely,

_____

[your signature]

Date: _____

_____

_____

_____

Report or confirmation number: _____

This is a request for you to reinvestigate the following items which appear on my credit report:

☐ The following personal information about me is incorrect:

Erroneous Information   *Correct Information*

_____

_____

_____

☐ The following accounts are not mine:

Creditor's Name   *Account Number*   *Explanation*

_____

_____

☐ The account status is incorrect for the following accounts:

Creditor's Name   *Account Number*   *Correct Status*

_____

_____

☐ The following information is too old to be included in my report:

Creditor's Name   *Account Number*   *Date of Last Activity*

_____

_____

☐ The following inquiries are older than two years:

Creditor's Name   *Date of Inquiry*

_____

_____

☐ The following inquiries were not authorized:

Creditor's Name   *Date of Inquiry*   *Explanation*

_____

_____

_____

☐ The following accounts were closed by me and should say so:

Creditor's Name   *Account Number*

_____

_____

_____

☐ Other incorrect information:

Explanation

_____

_____

_____

I understand that you will check each specified item, above, with the credit grantor reporting the information, remove any information the credit grantor cannot verify, or modify information that is incorrect or incomeplete. I further understand that under 15 U.S.C. §1681i(a), you must complete your reinvestigation within 30 days of receipt of this letter. Thank you for your attention to this matter.

Sincerely,

_____
             [*your signature*]

Name: _____

Address: _____

_____

Home phone: _____

Email address: _____

Social Security number: _____

Date of birth: _____

Enclosures: [*list, if any*:] _____

_____

Date: _____

_____

_____

_____

Report or confirmation number: _____

To Whom It May Concern:

On _____, 20_____, I sent you a request to reinvestigate several items on my credit report. I have enclosed a photocopy of my original request. The federal Fair Credit Reporting Act requires that you complete your reinvestigation of my request within 30 days. It has been more than 30 days.

I assume that I have not received a reply because you have been unable to verify the information. Therefore, please remove the incorrect items from my credit report at once and send a corrected credit report to me and to the following, all of whom have requested a copy of my credit report within the previous six months, or within the previous two years if requested for employment purposes.

_____

_____

_____

_____

Thank you for your immediate attention to this matter. I have sent a copy of this letter to the Federal Trade Commission.

Sincerely,

_____
[*your signature*]

Name: _____

Address: _____

_____

Home phone: _____

Email address: _____

Social Security number: _____

cc: Federal Trade Commission

Date: _____

_____

_____

_____

To Whom It May Concern:

On _____, 20_____ , I received a copy of my credit report from

_____

credit bureau. Included in that report was the following incorrect information reported by you:

_____

_____

I requested that the credit bureau remove that information from my file. The bureau has refused,
however, informing me that your company claims the information is accurate as reported.

This is not true. The following is the correct information:

_____

_____

I have enclosed copies of the following documentation supporting my claim that the information
you reported is incorrect:

_____

_____

This negative mark is damaging my credit. Please contact Experian, TransUnion, and Equifax
immediately and remove this information from my credit file. I expect to receive confirmation
from you within 20 days that you have directed the credit bureaus to remove this information.

Thank you for your immediate attention to this matter.

Sincerely,

_____
            [your signature]

Name: _____

Address: _____

_____

Home phone: _____

Email address: _____

Social Security number: _____

Date: _____

_____

_____

_____

Attn: Customer Service

Name(s) on account: _____

Account number: _____

To Whom It May Concern:

On _____, 20_____, I received a copy of my credit report from you. It included erroneous information reported by _____.

I just received a letter from that creditor indicating that the information in my credit report is not accurate and should not be in my credit file. I have enclosed a copy of the letter.

[OR]

On _____, 20_____, I met with _____ _____ from the above-named creditor. This person agreed with me that the information in my credit report is not accurate and should not be in my credit file. You can reach this person at (_____) _____.

This negative mark is damaging my credit. Please remove the information at once and send a corrected credit report to me and to anyone who has requested a copy of my credit report within the previous six months, or within the previous two years if requested for employment purposes.

Sincerely,

_____
[your signature]

Name: _____

Address: _____

_____

Home phone: _____

Email address: _____

Social Security number: _____

Date of birth: _____

Date: _____

_____

_____

Re: [name] _____

Current address: _____

_____

Telephone number: _____

Date of birth: _____

Social Security number: _____

Spouse's name: _____

To Whom It May Concern:

I received a copy of my credit report from your company on _____ and found accounts missing. Please add the following account histories to my credit file. I have enclosed photocopies of my most recent account statement and photocopies of canceled checks showing my payment history.

Creditor's Name	Creditor's Billing Address	Account Number	Date Opened	Credit Limit or Amount of Loan	Outstanding Balance

Once you have processed this request, please send me an updated credit report. If there is a fee of any kind, please let me know the amount so that I can send you a check or give you my credit card number. If you are unable to add these accounts to my credit report, please send me an explanation.

Thank you for your prompt attention to this matter.

Sincerely,

_____

[your signature]

Date: _____

_____

_____

_____

Re: [name] _____

Current address: _____

_____

Telephone number: _____

Date of birth: _____

Social Security number: _____

Spouse's name: _____

To Whom It May Concern:

I received a copy of my credit report from your company on _____
and found that important information is missing. Please add the following information to my credit file. I have enclosed photocopies of verifying documentation.

_____

_____

_____

_____

_____

_____

_____

_____

Once you have processed this request, please send me an updated credit report. If there is a fee of any kind, please let me know the amount so that I can send you a check or give you my credit card number. If you are unable to add this information to my credit report, please send me an explanation.

Thank you for your prompt attention to this matter.

Sincerely,

_____

[your signature]

INSTRUCTIONS FOR COMPLETING
THE ID THEFT AFFIDAVIT

To make certain that you do not become responsible for any debts incurred by an identity thief, you must prove to each of the companies where accounts were opened in your name that you didn't create the debt. The ID Theft Affidavit was developed by a group of credit grantors, consumer advocates, and attorneys at the Federal Trade Commission (FTC) for this purpose. Importantly, this affidavit is only for use where a new account was opened in your name. If someone made unauthorized charges to an existing account, call the company for instructions.

While many companies accept this affidavit, others require that you submit more or different forms. Before you send the affidavit, contact each company to find out if they accept it. If they do not accept the ID Theft Affidavit, ask them what information and/or documentation they require.

You may not need the ID Theft Affidavit to absolve you of debt resulting from identity theft if you obtain an Identity Theft Report. We suggest you consider obtaining an Identity Theft Report where a new account was opened in your name. An Identity Theft Report can be used to (1) permanently block fraudulent information from appearing on your credit report; (2) ensure that debts do not reappear on your credit reports; (3) prevent a company from continuing to collect debts or selling the debt to others for collection; and (4) obtain an extended fraud alert.

The ID Theft Affidavit may be required by a company in order for you to obtain applications or other transaction records related to the theft of your identity. These records may help you prove that you are a victim. For example, you may be able to show that the signature on an application is not yours. These documents also may contain information about the identity thief that is valuable to law enforcement.

This affidavit has two parts:
- Part One — the ID Theft Affidavit — is where you report general information about yourself and the theft.
- Part Two — the Fraudulent Account Statement — is where you describe the fraudulent account(s) opened in your name. Use a separate Fraudulent Account Statement for each company you need to write to.

When you send the affidavit to the companies, attach copies (NOT originals) of any supporting documents (for example, driver's license or police report). Before submitting your affidavit, review the disputed account(s) with family members or friends who may have information about the account(s) or access to them.

Complete this affidavit as soon as possible. Many creditors ask that you send it within two weeks. Delays on your part could slow the investigation.

Be as accurate and complete as possible. You may choose not to provide some of the information requested. However, incorrect or incomplete information will slow the process of investigating your claim and absolving the debt. Print clearly.

When you have finished completing the affidavit, mail a copy to each creditor, bank, or company that provided the thief with the unauthorized credit, goods, or services you describe. Attach a copy of the Fraudulent Account Statement with information only on accounts opened at the institution to which you are sending the packet, as well as any other supporting documentation you are able to provide.

Send the appropriate documents to each company by certified mail, return receipt requested, so you can prove that it was received. The companies will review your claim and send you a written response telling you the outcome of their investigation. Keep a copy of everything you submit.

If you are unable to complete the affidavit, a legal guardian or someone with power of attorney may complete it for you. Except as noted, the information you provide will be used only by the company to process your affidavit, investigate the events you report, and help stop further fraud. If this affidavit is requested in a lawsuit, the company might have to provide it to the requesting party. Completing this affidavit does not guarantee that the identity thief will be prosecuted or that the debt will be cleared.

If you haven't already done so, report the fraud to the following organizations:

1. Any one of the nationwide consumer reporting companies to place a fraud alert on your credit report. Fraud alerts can help prevent an identity thief from opening any more accounts in your name. The company you call is required to contact the other two, which will place an alert on their versions of your report, too.

   • Equifax: 1-800-525-6285; www.equifax.com
   • Experian: 1-888-EXPERIAN (397-3742); www.experian.com
   • TransUnion: 1-800-680-7289; www.transunion.com

   In addition, once you have placed a fraud alert, you're entitled to order one free credit report from each of the three consumer reporting companies, and, if you ask, they will display only the last four digits of your Social Security number on your credit reports.

2. The security or fraud department of each company where you know, or believe, accounts have been tampered with or opened fraudulently. Close the accounts. Follow up in writing, and include copies (NOT originals) of supporting documents. It's important to notify credit card companies and banks in writing. Send your letters by certified mail, return receipt requested, so you can document what the company received and when. Keep a file of your correspondence and enclosures.

   When you open new accounts, use new Personal Identification Numbers (PINs) and passwords. Avoid using easily available information like your mother's maiden name, your birth date, the last four digits of your Social Security number, your phone number, or a series of consecutive numbers.

3. Your local police or the police in the community where the identity theft took place. Provide a copy of your ID Theft Complaint filed with the FTC (see below), to be incorporated into the police report. Get a copy of the police report or, at the very least, the number of the report. It can help you deal with creditors who need proof of the crime. If the police are reluctant to take your report, ask to file a "Miscellaneous Incidents" report, or try another jurisdiction, like your state police. You also can check with your state Attorney General's office to find out if state law requires the police to take reports for identity theft. Check the Blue Pages of your telephone directory for the phone number or check www.naag.org for a list of state Attorneys General.

4. The Federal Trade Commission. By sharing your identity theft complaint with the FTC, you will provide important information that can help law enforcement officials across the nation track down identity thieves and stop them. The FTC also can refer victims' complaints to other government agencies and companies for further action, as well as investigate companies for violations of laws that the FTC enforces.

   You can file a complaint online at www.consumer.gov/idtheft. If you don't have Internet access, call the FTC's Identity Theft Hotline, toll-free: 1-877-IDTHEFT (438-4338); TTY: 1-866-653-4261; or write: Identity Theft Clearinghouse, Federal Trade Commission, 600 Pennsylvania Avenue, NW, Washington, DC 20580. When you file an ID Theft Complaint with the FTC online, you will be given the option to print a copy of your ID Theft Complaint. You should bring a copy of the printed ID Theft Complaint with you to the police to be incorporated into your police report. The ID Theft Complaint, in conjunction with the police report, can create an Identity Theft Report that will help you recover more quickly. The ID Theft Complaint provides the supporting details necessary for an Identity Theft Report, which go beyond the details of a typical police report.

DO NOT SEND AFFIDAVIT TO THE FTC OR ANY OTHER GOVERNMENT AGENCY

ID Theft Affidavit

Victim Information

(1) My full legal name is _____
                                       (First)   (Middle)   (Last)   (Jr., Sr., III)

(2) (If different from above) When the events described in this affidavit took place, I was known as

_____
      (First)   (Middle)   (Last)   (Jr., Sr., III)

(3) My date of birth is _____
                            (day/month/year)

(4) My Social Security number is_____

(5) My driver's license or identification card state and number are_____

(6) My current address is _____

    City _____ State _____ Zip Code _____

(7) I have lived at this address since _____
                                  (month/year)

(8) (If different from above) When the events described in this affidavit took place, my address was

_____   _____

    City _____ State _____ Zip Code _____

(9) I lived at the address in Item 8 from _____ until _____
                                      (month/year)   (month/year)

(10) My daytime telephone number is (_____)_____

     My evening telephone number is (_____)_____

DO NOT SEND AFFIDAVIT TO THE FTC OR ANY OTHER GOVERNMENT AGENCY

How the Fraud Occurred

Check all that apply for items 11 - 17:

(11) ❑ I did not authorize anyone to use my name or personal information to seek the money, credit, loans, goods or services described in this report.

(12) ❑ I did not receive any benefit, money, goods or services as a result of the events described **in this report.**

(13) ❑ My identification documents (for example, credit cards; birth certificate; driver's license; Social Security card; etc.) were ❑ stolen ❑ lost   on or about _____.
(day/month/year)

(14) ❑ To the best of my knowledge and belief, the following person(s) used my information (for example, my name, address, date of birth, existing account numbers, Social Security number, mother's maiden name, etc.) or identification documents to get money, credit, loans, goods or services without my knowledge or authorization:

_____   _____
Name (if known)   Name (if known)

_____   _____
Address (if known)   Address (if known)

_____   _____
Phone number(s) (if known)   Phone number(s) (if known)

_____   _____
Additional information (if known)   Additional information (if known)

(15) ❑ I do NOT know who used my information or identification documents to get money, credit, loans, goods or services without my knowledge or authorization.

(16) ❑ Additional comments: (For example, description of the fraud, which documents or information were used or how the identity thief gained access to your information.)

_____

_____

_____

_____

_____

(Attach additional pages as necessary.)

DO NOT SEND AFFIDAVIT TO THE FTC OR ANY OTHER GOVERNMENT AGENCY

Victim's Law Enforcement Actions

(17) (check one) I ❑ am ❑ am not   willing to assist in the prosecution of the person(s) who committed this fraud.

(18) (check one) I ❑ am ❑ am not   authorizing the release of this information to law enforcement for the purpose of assisting them in the investigation and prosecution of the person(s) who committed this fraud.

(19) (check all that apply) I ❑ have ❑ have not   reported the events described in this affidavit to the police or other law enforcement agency. The police ❑ did ❑ did not   write a report. In the event you have contacted the police or other law enforcement agency, please complete the following:

_____ **(Agency #1)**	_____ (Officer/Agency personnel taking report)
_____ (Date of report)	_____ (Report number, if any)
_____ (Phone number)	_____ (email address, if any)
_____ **(Agency #2)**	_____ (Officer/Agency personnel taking report)
_____ (Date of report)	_____ (Report number, if any)
_____ (Phone number)	_____ (email address, if any)

Documentation Checklist

Please indicate the supporting documentation you are able to provide to the companies you plan to notify. Attach copies (NOT originals) to the affidavit before sending it to the companies.

(20) ❑ A copy of a valid government-issued photo-identification card (for example, your driver's license, state-issued ID card or your passport). If you are under 16 and don't have a photo-ID, you may submit a copy of your birth certificate or a copy of your official school records showing your enrollment and place of residence.

(21) ❑ Proof of residency during the time the disputed bill occurred, the loan was made or the other event took place (for example, a rental/lease agreement in your name, a copy of a utility bill or a copy of an insurance bill).

DO NOT SEND AFFIDAVIT TO THE FTC OR ANY OTHER GOVERNMENT AGENCY

(22) ❑ A copy of the report you filed with the police or sheriff's department. If you are unable to obtain a report or report number from the police, please indicate that in Item 19. Some companies only need the report number, not a copy of the report. You may want to check with each company.

Signature

I certify that, to the best of my knowledge and belief, all the information on and attached to this affidavit is true, correct, and complete and made in good faith. I also understand that this affidavit or the information it contains may be made available to federal, state, and/or local law enforcement agencies for such action within their jurisdiction as they deem appropriate. I understand that knowingly making any false or fraudulent statement or representation to the government may constitute a violation of 18 U.S.C. §1001 or other federal, state, or local criminal statutes, and may result in imposition of a fine or imprisonment or both.

_____   _____
(signature)   (date signed)

_____
(Notary)

[Check with each company. Creditors sometimes require notarization. If they do not, please have one witness (non-relative) sign below that you completed and signed this affidavit.]

Witness:

_____   _____
(signature)   (printed name)

_____   _____
(date)   (telephone number)

DO NOT SEND AFFIDAVIT TO THE FTC OR ANY OTHER GOVERNMENT AGENCY

Fraudulent Account Statement

Completing this Statement
- Make as many copies of this page as you need. **Complete a separate page for each company you're notifying and only send it to that company**. Include a copy of your signed affidavit.
- List only the account(s) you're disputing with the company receiving this form. **See the example below**.
- If a collection agency sent you a statement, letter or notice about the fraudulent account, attach a copy of that document (**NOT** the original).

I declare (check all that apply):

❑   As a result of the event(s) described in the ID Theft Affidavit, the following account(s) was/were opened at your company in my name without my knowledge, permission or authorization using my personal information or identifying documents:

Creditor Name/Address (the company that opened the account or provided the goods or services)	Account Number	Type of unauthorized credit/goods/services provided by creditor (if known)	Date issued or opened (if known)	Amount/Value provided (the amount charged or the cost of the goods/services)
Example Example National Bank 22 Main Street Columbus, Ohio 22722	01234567-89	auto loan	01/05/2002	$25,500.00

❑   During the time of the accounts described above, I had the following account open with your company:

Billing name _____

Billing address_____

Account number _____

DO NOT SEND AFFIDAVIT TO THE FTC OR ANY OTHER GOVERNMENT AGENCY

EQUIFAX   **experian**   **TransUnion**

Annual Credit Report Request Form

You have the right to get a free copy of your credit file disclosure, commonly called a credit report, once every 12 months, from each of the nationwide consumer credit reporting companies - Equifax, Experian and TransUnion.
For instant access to your free credit report, visit www.annualcreditreport.com.

For more information on obtaining your free credit report, visit www.annualcreditreport.com or call 877-322-8228.

Use this form if you prefer to write to request your credit report from any, or all, of the nationwide consumer credit reporting companies. The following information is required to process your request. **Omission of any information may delay your request.**

Once complete, fold (do not staple or tape), place into a #10 envelope, affix required postage and mail to:
Annual Credit Report Request Service P.O. Box 105281 Atlanta, GA 30348-5281.

Please use a Black or Blue Pen and write your responses in PRINTED CAPITAL LETTERS without touching the sides of the boxes like the examples listed below:

A B C D E F G H I J K L M N O P Q R S T U V W X Y Z   0 1 2 3 4 5 6 7 8 9

Social Security Number:

☐☐☐ - ☐☐ - ☐☐☐☐

Date of Birth:

☐☐ / ☐☐ / ☐☐☐☐
Month   Day   Year

- - - - Fold Here - - - -   - - - - Fold Here - - - -

First Name   **M.I.**

Last Name   **JR, SR, III, etc.**

Current Mailing Address:

House Number   **Street Name**

Apartment Number / Private Mailbox   **For Puerto Rico Only: Print Urbanization Name**

City   **State**   **ZipCode**

Previous Mailing Address (complete only if at current mailing address for less than two years):

House Number   **Street Name**

- - - - Fold Here - - - -   - - - - Fold Here - - - -

Apartment Number / Private Mailbox   **For Puerto Rico Only: Print Urbanization Name**

City   **State**   **ZipCode**

Shade Circle Like This → ●

Not Like This → ⊗ ⊘

I want a credit report from (shade each that you would like to receive):
○ Equifax
○ Experian
○ TransUnion

○ **Shade here if, for security reasons, you want your credit report to include no more than the last four digits of your Social Security Number.**

If additional information is needed to process your request, the consumer credit reporting company will contact you by mail.

31238

Your request will be processed within 15 days of receipt and then mailed to you.

Copyright 2004, Central Source LLC

MEMORANDUM

To: Law Enforcement Officer
From: Division of Privacy and Identity Protection
          The Federal Trade Commission
Re: Importance of Identity Theft Report

The purpose of this memorandum is to explain what an "Identity Theft Report" is, and its importance to identity theft victims in helping them to recover. A police report that contains specific details of an identity theft is considered an "Identity Theft Report" under section 605B of the Fair Credit Reporting Act (FCRA), and it entitles an identity theft victim to certain important protections that can help him or her recover more quickly from identity theft.

Specifically, under sections 605B, 615(f) and 623(a)(6) of the FCRA, an Identity Theft Report can be used to permanently block fraudulent information that results from identity theft, such as accounts or addresses, from appearing on a victim's credit report. It will also make sure these debts do not reappear on the credit reports. Identity Theft Reports can prevent a company from continuing to collect debts that result from identity theft, or selling them to others for collection. An Identity Theft Report is also needed to allow an identity theft victim to place an extended fraud alert on his or her credit report. A copy of these sections of the FCRA is enclosed.

In order for a police report to be considered an Identity Theft Report, and therefore entitle an identity theft victim to the protections discussed above, the police report must contain details about the accounts and inaccurate information that resulted from the identity theft. We advise victims to bring a printed copy of their ID Theft Complaint filed with the FTC with them to the police station in order to better assist you in creating a detailed police report so that these victims can access the important protections available to them if they have an Identity Theft Report. The victim should sign the ID Theft Complaint in your presence. If possible, you should attach or incorporate the ID Theft Complaint into the police report, and sign the "Law Enforcement Report Information" section of the FTC's ID Theft Complaint. In addition, please provide the identity theft victim with a copy of the Identity Theft Report (the police report with the victim's ID Theft Complaint attached or incorporated) to permit the victim to dispute the fraudulent accounts and debts created by the identity thief.

For additional information on Identity Theft Reports or identity theft, please visit our website at http://www.ftc.gov/bcp/edu/microsites/idtheft/.

Enclosures: FCRA Sections 605B, 615(f), 623(a)(6)

FCRA 605B (15 U.S.C. § 1681c-2) Block of Information Resulting from Identity Theft

(a) Block

Except as otherwise provided in this section, a consumer reporting agency shall block the reporting of any information in the file of a consumer that the consumer identifies as information that resulted from an alleged identity theft, not later than 4 business days after the date of receipt by such agency of--

(1) appropriate proof of the identity of the consumer;

(2) a copy of an identity theft report;

(3) the identification of such information by the consumer; and

(4) a statement by the consumer that the information is not information relating to any transaction by the consumer.

(b) Notification

A consumer reporting agency shall promptly notify the furnisher of information identified by the consumer under subsection (a) of this section--

(1) that the information may be a result of identity theft;

(2) that an identity theft report has been filed;

(3) that a block has been requested under this section; and

(4) of the effective dates of the block.

(c) Authority to decline or rescind

(1) In general

A consumer reporting agency may decline to block, or may rescind any block, of information relating to a consumer under this section, if the consumer reporting agency reasonably determines that--

(A) the information was blocked in error or a block was requested by the consumer in error;

(B) the information was blocked, or a block was requested by the consumer, on the basis of a material misrepresentation of fact by the consumer relevant to the request to block; or

(C) the consumer obtained possession of goods, services, or money as a result of the blocked transaction or transactions.

(2) Notification to consumer

If a block of information is declined or rescinded under this subsection, the affected consumer shall be notified promptly, in the same manner as consumers are notified of the reinsertion of information under section 1681i(a)(5)(B) of this title.

(3) Significance of block

For purposes of this subsection, if a consumer reporting agency rescinds a block, the presence of information in the file of a consumer prior to the blocking of such information is not evidence of whether the consumer knew or should have known that the consumer obtained possession of any goods, services, or money as a result of the block.

(d) Exception for resellers

(1) No reseller file

This section shall not apply to a consumer reporting agency, if the consumer reporting agency--

(A) is a reseller;

(B) is not, at the time of the request of the consumer under subsection (a) of this section, otherwise furnishing or reselling a consumer report concerning the information identified by the consumer; and

(C) informs the consumer, by any means, that the consumer may report the identity theft to the Commission to obtain consumer information regarding identity theft.

(2) Reseller with file

The sole obligation of the consumer reporting agency under this section, with regard to any request of a consumer under this section, shall be to block the consumer report maintained by the consumer reporting agency from any subsequent use, if--

(A) the consumer, in accordance with the provisions of subsection (a) of this section, identifies, to a consumer reporting agency, information in the file of the consumer that resulted from identity theft; and

(B) the consumer reporting agency is a reseller of the identified information.

(3) Notice

In carrying out its obligation under paragraph (2), the reseller shall promptly provide a notice to the consumer of the decision to block the file. Such notice shall contain the name, address, and telephone number of each consumer reporting agency from which the consumer information was obtained for resale.

(e) Exception for verification companies

The provisions of this section do not apply to a check services company, acting as such, which issues authorizations for the purpose of approving or processing negotiable instruments, electronic fund transfers, or similar methods of payments, except that, beginning 4 business days after receipt of information described in paragraphs (1) through (3) of subsection (a) of this section, a check services company shall not report to a national consumer reporting agency described in section 1681a(p) of this title, any information identified in the subject identity theft report as resulting from identity theft.

(f) Access to blocked information by law enforcement agencies

No provision of this section shall be construed as requiring a consumer reporting agency to prevent a Federal, State, or local law enforcement agency from accessing blocked information in a consumer file to which the agency could otherwise obtain access under this title.

ENCLOSURE:
FCRA 615(f) (15 U.S.C. § 1681m(f)) Requirements on Users of Consumer Reports – Prohibition on Sale or Transfer of Debt Caused by Identity Theft

(f) Prohibition on sale or transfer of debt caused by identity theft

(1) In general

No person shall sell, transfer for consideration, or place for collection a debt that such person has been notified under section 1681c-2 of this title has resulted from identity theft.

(2) Applicability

The prohibitions of this subsection shall apply to all persons collecting a debt described in paragraph (1) after the date of a notification under paragraph (1).

(3) Rule of construction

Nothing in this subsection shall be construed to prohibit--

(A) the repurchase of a debt in any case in which the assignee of the debt requires such repurchase because the debt has resulted from identity theft;

(B) the securitization of a debt or the pledging of a portfolio of debt as collateral in connection with a borrowing; or

(C) the transfer of debt as a result of a merger, acquisition, purchase and assumption transaction, or transfer of substantially all of the assets of an entity.

ENCLOSURE:
FCRA 623(a)(6) (15 U.S.C. § 1681s-2(a)(6)) Responsibilities of Furnishers of Information to Consumer Reporting Agencies – Duties of Furnishers upon Notice of Identity Theft-Related Information

(6) Duties of furnishers upon notice of identity theft-related information

(A) Reasonable procedures

A person that furnishes information to any consumer reporting agency shall have in place reasonable procedures to respond to any notification that it receives from a consumer reporting agency under <u>section 1681c-2</u> of this title relating to information resulting from identity theft, to prevent that person from refurnishing such blocked information.

(B) Information alleged to result from identity theft

If a consumer submits an identity theft report to a person who furnishes information to a consumer reporting agency at the address specified by that person for receiving such reports stating that information maintained by such person that purports to relate to the consumer resulted from identity theft, the person may not furnish such information that purports to relate to the consumer to any consumer reporting agency, unless the person subsequently knows or is informed by the consumer that the information is correct.

How to Use the CD-ROM

Installing the Form Files Onto Your Computer 248

Using the Word Processing Files to Create Documents 249

    Opening a File..249

    Editing Your Document 250

    Printing Out the Document.. 250

    Saving Your Document 250

Using the Federal Trade Commission Files...251

    Opening the FTC Files...251

    Printing the FTC Files 251

    Filling in the FTC Files 251

Files on the CD-ROM.. 252

The CD-ROM included with this book can be used with Windows computers. It installs files that use software programs that need to be on your computer already. It is not a standalone software program.

In accordance with U.S. copyright laws, the CD-ROM and its files are for your personal use only.

Please read this appendix and the Readme.htm file included on the CD-ROM for instructions on using the CD-ROM. For a list of forms and their file names, see the end of this appendix.

Note to Macintosh users: This CD-ROM and its files should also work on Macintosh computers. Please note, however, that Nolo cannot provide technical support for non-Windows users.

Note to eBook users: You can access the CD-ROM files mentioned here from the bookmarked section of the eBook, located on the left-hand side.

How to View the README File

To view the "Readme.htm" file, insert the CD-ROM into your computer's CD-ROM drive and follow these instructions:

Windows 2000, XP, and Vista

1. On your PC's desktop, double-click the **My Computer** icon.
2. Double-click the icon for the CD-ROM drive into which the CD-ROM was inserted.
3. Double-click the file "Readme.htm."

Macintosh

1. On your Mac desktop, double-click the icon for the CD-ROM that you inserted.
2. Double-click the file "Readme.htm."

Installing the Form Files Onto Your Computer

To work with the files on the CD-ROM, you first need to install them onto your hard disk. Here's how:

Windows 2000, XP, and Vista

Follow the CD-ROM's instructions that appear on the screen. If nothing happens when you insert the CD-ROM, then:

1. Double-click the **My Computer** icon.
2. Double-click the icon for the CD-ROM drive into which the CD-ROM was inserted.
3. Double-click the file "Setup.exe."

Macintosh

If the **Credit Repair CD** window is not open, double-click the **Credit Repair CD** icon. Then:

1. Select the **Credit Repair Forms** folder icon.

2. Drag and drop the folder icon onto your computer.

Where Are the Files Installed?

Windows

By default, all the files are installed to the **Credit Repair Forms** folder in the **Program Files** folder of your computer. A folder called **Credit Repair Forms** is added to the **Programs** folder of the **Start** menu.

Macintosh

All the files are located in the **Credit Repair Forms** folder.

Using the Word Processing Files to Create Documents

The CD-ROM includes word processing files that you can open, complete, print, and save with your word processing program. All word processing forms come in rich text format and have the extension ".rtf." For example, the F-1: Outstanding Debts Form, discussed in Chapter 1, is on the file "F01.rtf." RTF files can be read by most recent word processing programs, including MS *Word*, Windows *WordPad*, and recent versions of *WordPerfect*.

The following are general instructions. Because each word processor uses different commands to open, format, save, and print documents, refer to your word processor's help file for specific instructions.

Do not call Nolo's technical support if you have questions on how to use your word processor or your computer.

Opening a File

You can open word processing files with any of the three following ways:

1. Windows users can open a file by selecting its "shortcut."

    i. Click the Windows **Start** button.

    ii. Open the **Programs** folder.

    iii. Open the **Credit Repair Forms** folder.

    iv. Open the **RTF** subfolder.

    v. Click the shortcut to the form you want to work with.

2. Both Windows and Macintosh users can open a file by double-clicking it.

    i. Use **My Computer** or **Windows Explorer** (Windows 2000, XP, or Vista) or the **Finder** (Macintosh) to go to the **Credit Repair Forms** folder.

    ii. Double-click the file you want to open.

3. Windows and Macintosh users can open a file from within their word processor.

    i. Open your word processor.

    ii. Go to the **File** menu and choose the **Open** command. This opens a dialog box.

iii. Select the location and name of the file. (Navigate to the version of the **Credit Repair Forms** folder that you've installed on your computer.)

Editing Your Document

Here are tips for working on your document. Refer to the book's instructions and sample agreements for help.

Underlines indicate where to enter information, frequently including bracketed instructions. Delete the underlines and instructions before finishing your document.

Signature lines should appear on a page with at least some text from the document itself.

Printing Out the Document

Use your word processor's or text editor's **Print** command to print out your document.

Saving Your Document

Use the **Save As** command to save and rename your document. You will be unable to use the **Save** command because the files are "read-only." If you save the file without renaming it, the underlines that indicate where you need to enter your information will be lost, and you will be unable to create a new document with this file without recopying the original file from the CD-ROM.

Editing Forms That Have Optional or Alternative Text

Some forms have check boxes before text. Check boxes indicate:

- Optional text that you can choose to include or exclude.
- Alternative text that you select to include, excluding the other alternatives.

If you are using the tear-out forms in Appendix B, mark the apropriate box to make your choice.

If you are using the CD-ROM, we recommend doing the following:

Optional text

Delete optional text you do not want to include and keep that which you do. In either case, delete the check box and the italicized instructions. If you choose to delete an optional numbered clause, renumber the subsequent clauses after deleting it.

Alternative text

Delete the alternatives that you do not want to include first. Then delete the remaining check boxes, as well as the italicized instructions that you need in order to select one of the alternatives provided.

Using the Federal Trade Commission Files

Electronic copies of Federal Trade Commission (FTC) files are included on the CD-ROM in Adobe PDF format. You must have the Adobe *Reader* installed on your computer to use this form. Adobe *Reader* is available for all types of Windows and Macintosh systems, and you can download it for free at www.adobe.com.

These files were created by the FTC, not by Nolo.

These files cannot be filled out using your computer. To create your document, you must:

1. Open the file.

2. Print it out.

3. Complete it by hand or typewriter.

Opening the FTC Files

PDF files, like the word processing files, can be opened one of three ways.

1. Windows users can open a file by selecting its "shortcut."

    i. Click the Windows **Start** button.

    ii. Open the **Programs** folder.

    iii. Open the **Credit Repair Forms** folder.

    iv. Open the **RTF** subfolder.

    v. Click the shortcut to the form you want to work with.

2. Both Windows and Macintosh users can open a file by double-clicking it.

    i. Use **My Computer** or **Windows Explorer** (Windows 2000, XP, or Vista) or the **Finder** (Macintosh) to go to the **Credit Repair Forms** folder.

    ii. Double-click the file you want to open.

3. Windows and Macintosh users can open a file from within their word processor.

    i. Open your word processor.

    ii. Go to the **File** menu and choose the **Open** command. This opens a dialog box.

    iii. Select the location and name of the file. (Navigate to the version of the **Credit Repair Forms** folder that you've installed on your computer.)

Printing the FTC Files

Choose **Print** from the Adobe *Reader* File menu. This will open the **Print** dialog box. In the "Print Range" section of the **Print** dialog box, select the appropriate print range, then click OK.

Filling in the FTC Files

The PDF files cannot be filled out using your computer. To create your document, first print it out, and then complete it by hand or typewriter.

Files on the CD-ROM

The following files are in rich text format (RTF):

Form Title	File Name
F-1: Outstanding Debts	F01.RTF
F-2: Daily Expenditures	F02.RTF
F-3: Monthly Income From All Sources	F03.RTF
F-4: Monthly Budget	F04.RTF
F-5: Error on Credit Card Bill	F05.RTF
F-6: Dispute Credit Card Bill	F06.RTF
F-7: Offer (Reduced) Lump Sum Payment	F07.RTF
F-8: Offer Payment Schedule to Pay Off (Reduced) Debt	F08.RTF
F-9: Request Short-Term Lower Payments	F09.RTF
F-10: Request Long-Term Lower Payments	F10.RTF
F-11: Request to Pay Nothing Short-Term	F11.RTF
F-12: Request to Pay Nothing Long-Term	F12.RTF
F-13: Request Rewrite of Loan Terms	F13.RTF
F-14: Offer to Give Secured Property Back	F14.RTF
F-15: Cashing Check Constitutes Payment in Full (Outside of California)	F15.RTF
F-16: Cashing Check Constitutes Payment in Full— First Letter (California)	F16.RTF
F-17: Cashing Check Constitutes Payment in Full— Second Letter (California)	F17.RTF
F-18: Cashing Check Constitutes Release of All Claims	F18.RTF
F-19: Inform Creditor of Judgment Proof Status	F19.RTF
F-20: Inform Creditor of Plan to File for Bankruptcy	F20.RTF
F-21: Request Direct Negotiation With Creditor	F21.RTF
F-22: Dispute Amount of Bill or Quality of Goods or Services Received	F22.RTF

Form Title	File Name
F-23: Collection Agency:Cease All Contact	F23.RTF
F-24: Complaint About Collection Agency Harassment	F24.RTF
F-25: Request Credit File	F25.RTF
F-26: Request Reinvestigation	F26.RTF
F-27: Request Follow-Up After Reinvestigation	F27.RTF
F-28: Request Removal of Incorrect Information by Creditor	F28.RTF
F-29: Creditor Verification	F29.RTF
F-30: Request Addition of Account Histories	F30.RTF
F-31: Request Addition of Information Showing Stability	F31.RTF

The following files are in portable document format (PDF):

Form Title	File Name
ID Theft Affadavit and Instructions	FTCAffadavit.pdf
FTC Law Enforcement Cover Letter	FTCLetter.pdf

Index

A

AARP reverse mortgage information, 13
Accountant bills, 39, 55
Address changes, 125
    fraudulent, 96, 98, 103
Adjustable rate mortgages, 11–12
Affidavit of identity theft, 103
Age discrimination, 94, 145, 147
Alimony, 5
Alimony debts, 5, 20, 39
Annual Credit Report Service, 80
Annuities, reverse mortgages and, 13–14
Antidiscrimination laws, 144–147
APR, credit cards, 121–122, 124
ARMs, 11–12
Assessing your situation, 4–6.
    See also Existing debts
Assets
    creditworthiness and, 110–111
    exempt property, 7
    judgment proof status, 7
    pawning, 17
    selling, 8
    See also specific types
ATM fees, 131–132
Authorized user credit card accounts, 127
Autos. *See* Vehicle *entries*

B

Bad checks, 20
Bank accounts, 130–132
    check reporting and verification, 77, 80,
        101, 131
    fees, 131–132
    protecting your account, 98, 125
    secured credit cards, 127–128, 134
Bank loans, 132–133
Bankruptcy, 5, 19–22, 72
    attempts to collect discharged debts, 126
    credit cards and, 119
    in credit report, 79, 86
    debt counseling requirement, 154
    vs. debt management programs, 152
    exempt property, 7
    postbankruptcy discrimination, 148
Banks
    contacting about identity theft, 101
    credit reporting by, 78, 93
    providing SSN to, 100
    See also Bank accounts; Bank loans
Better Business Bureau, 157
Billing errors and disputes
    collection agencies and, 66
    credit cards, 56–58
Borrowing money. *See* Loans and loan
    payments; *specific loan types*
Budgeting, 24, 29–34. *See also* Spending

C

California Office of Privacy Protection, 105

Cancellation of debts
  student loans, 51–52, 72
  See also Debt forgiveness

Capacity, 110

Cars and car payments. *See* Vehicle *entries*

Cash advances, credit cards, 39, 122, 123, 124

Cash, raising. *See* Raising money

CCCS (Consumer Credit Counseling Service), 154

CD-ROM, how to use, 248–252

Change of address, 125
  fraudulent, 96, 98, 103

Chapter 7 bankruptcy, 19–21

Chapter 11 bankruptcy, 72

Chapter 13 bankruptcy, 21–22, 152

Character, 111

Charge cards, 56
  store and gas cards, 39, 55, 118, 119–120, 132
  See also Credit cards

Checking accounts. *See* Bank accounts

Checks
  caution about bouncing, 131
  cautions about paying with, 38, 68, 81
  check reporting and verification, 77, 80, 101, 131
  to creditors, cashing of as payment in full, 60
  identity theft protection tips, 98
  stolen, reporting, 101

Child custody proceedings, 110

Child support debts, 5, 20, 39
  child support liens, 39
  in credit report, 79, 86

Closed accounts, in credit report, 87–88

Closing accounts, 101, 102
  credit cards, 129–130

Collateral, 110–111. *See also* Secured debts and loans

Collection agencies, 60, 65–72
  access to credit report, 109
  basics, 65–66
  communication tips, 38
  complaining about, 71
  debts due to identity theft, 104
  delaying or stopping collection efforts, 66–67
  illegal collection practices, 69–72, 126
  negotiating with, 67–69
  requesting information from, 67
  sending payments to, 38
  suing, 71

Collections
  attempts to collect debts discharged in bankruptcy, 126
  basics, 61
  service members' special rights, 9
  student loan forbearances and, 52
  See also Collection agencies

Combined credit reports, 85

Community Reinvestment Act, 145

Compulsive spending, 116, 155

Computer programs, for budgeting, 24

Consolidation loans, 14–15
  student loan consolidation, 50

Consumer Credit Counseling Service (CCCS), 154

Consumer Leasing Act, 49

Cosigners, 126–127

Counseling agencies, 18–19, 47, 55, 65, 152–154
  checking nonprofit status, 152–153

choosing, 153
Credit applications, 76, 109
   cosigners and guarantors, 126–127
   credit cards, 119–120
   credit score and, 111–114
   denials due to credit report information, 80–81
   discrimination complaints, 149, 164
   discrimination protections, 145–147
   evaluation of, 110–113
   false statements on, 133
   fraud alerts and, 101
   fraudulent, 20
   joint applications, 117–118
   lender disclosure requirements, 112–113, 127, 145
   married couples, 120
   security freezes and, 99
Credit cards, 35, 39, 55–59, 118–125
   application of payments, 58
   application tips, 119–120
   authorized user accounts, 127
   billing errors, 56–57
   building credit with, 118, 127–128
   cash advances, 39, 122, 123, 124
   closing accounts, 129–130
   comparing, 120–123
   credit limits, 55, 57, 118, 121, 123, 125
   in credit report, 78
   dealing with current balances, 55–59
   disclosure forms, 120–121, 123, 124
   disputing charges, 56, 57–58
   fees, 55–56, 119, 122–123, 124, 125
   getting payments and fees reduced, 55–56
   grace periods, 122, 124
   health finance plans, 55
   identity theft protection services, 105
   interest charges and rates, 57, 118–119, 120, 121–123, 124, 129–130
   keeping track of purchases, 26
   minimum payments, 55, 118
   protecting your account, 97, 125
   rebates and rewards, 120, 123
   secured cards, 127–128, 134
   store and gas cards, 39, 55, 118, 119–120, 132
   unauthorized charges, 57, 58–59, 95–96
   using wisely, 35, 118
   See also Credit offers
Credit card solicitations, 97, 119, 120, 126. *See also* Credit offers
Credit checks. *See* Credit inquiries
Credit counseling agencies. *See* Counseling agencies
Credit discrimination, 94, 144–149
   complaining about, 149, 164
Credit file segregation, 133
Credit inquiries, 77, 108–110
   authorization requests, 77, 79, 108
   in credit report, 79, 89
   credit score and, 112
   notifying recipients of inaccurate/incomplete information, 90, 94
   preparing for, 85, 88
   unauthorized inquiries, 89, 96, 110
   who may access your credit report, 108–110
Credit limits, 110, 111
   credit cards, 55, 57, 118, 121, 123, 125
Credit offers, unsolicited, 103, 119, 120
   cautions about, 96, 97, 126
   fraud alerts and, 103
   opt out rights, 99
Creditors
   access to credit report, 109

bankruptcy and, 19, 20
checking your balance, 6
closing accounts, 101
communication tips, 38, 81
contacting about identity theft, 101, 103–104
contacting about incorrect credit report information, 89, 91
filing discrimination complaints, 149
letters to, 38, 59–60, 61, 63–65, 81
notifying of change of address, 125
See also Negotiating with creditors
Credit repair, 116–149
    bank accounts for, 130–132
    bank loans for, 132–133
    basics, 38, 40, 80, 84, 116–117
    cosigners and guarantors, 126–127
    credit cards for, 118, 127–128
    improving your credit report, 88–95
    raising your credit score, 114
    tips for spouses and ex-spouses, 117–118
    working with local merchants, 132
Credit repair clinics, 19, 133–134, 143–144
    state laws, 135–144
Credit Repair Organizations Act (CROA), 134, 143
Credit reporting agencies, 76, 84
    filing complaints about, 92
    laws regulating, 77, 87
    placing security freezes, 99
    reinvestigation requests, 88–90, 94, 134
    reporting identity theft to, 82
    requesting fraud alerts, 101–102, 103
    specialized reporting agencies, 77, 80, 101
    suing, 91–92
Credit reports, 76–95
    adding fraud alerts, 82, 101–102, 103, 104–105

adding positive information, 92–95
bankruptcies in, 79, 86
basics, 76
checking your report, 58, 87–88, 95, 102
combined reports, 85
common errors in, 84
contents, 76, 78–80
court actions on, 43
credit/debt counseling and, 153
credit repair clinic tactics, 134
criminal records in, 86
deeds in lieu of foreclosure in, 45–46
disputing information in, 84–85, 88–92, 134
explanatory statements, 84–85, 92, 94–95
fraudulent information in, 81, 85, 102–103
how long negative information stays in, 86, 134
identity theft and, 99, 100, 101–104
inaccurate/incomplete information in, 84–85, 86–87, 88–92
investigative reports, 79–80
lawsuits and judgments in, 79, 85, 86
married couples, 76, 87, 117
obtaining copies, 80–83
past due account status in, 60–61, 68–69, 78–79, 86
reporting by credit card companies, 55–56, 58
security freezes, 99, 104
"sent to collection" account status in, 66, 78–79, 86
specialized reports, 77, 80
tax liens in, 86
unpaid rent on, 43
viewing examples, 84–85
who may access, 108–110
Credit score, 76, 111–114, 121

authorized user credit card accounts and, 127

closing accounts and, 130

credit/debt counseling and, 153

explanatory statements and, 95

inquiries and, 79

obtaining, 80, 112–113

tips for raising, 114

Creditworthiness, 110–111. *See also* Credit score

Criminal records, in credit report, 86

CROA (Credit Repair Organizations Act), 134, 143

Current debts, 40–59

    adding positive account histories to credit report, 93

    basics, 38

    car payments, 48–49

    contacting creditors, 40–41

    credit and charge card bills, 55–59

    in credit report, 78

    doctor, dentist, lawyer and accountant bills, 55

    insurance payments, 54–55

    mortgage payments, 43–47

    other secured loans, 49–50

    rent, 41–43

    student loans, 50–54

    utility and telephone bills, 47–48

D

Daily expenditures, keeping track of, 24–26

Date of birth, in credit report, 83, 94

Debit cards, 59, 97

Debt collections. *See* Collection agencies; Collections

Debt consolidation loans, 14–15

Debt counseling agencies. *See* Counseling agencies

Debt elimination services, 17–18, 19

Debt forgiveness

    settling debts for less than you owe, 59, 62, 68

    tax consequences, 72–73

Debt management programs, 152, 153, 154. *See also* Counseling agencies

Debtors Anonymous, 116, 155

Debt payments

    to collection agencies, 38

    debt management plans and, 154

    partial or token payments, 40, 59–60

Debt repayment strategies

    bankruptcy alternative, 19–22

    paying off high-cost debt first, 35

    raising cash, 7–18

    See also Bankruptcy; Negotiating with creditors

Deeds in lieu of foreclosure, 45–46

Deferments, student loans, 52

Delinquent accounts. *See* Past due accounts

Dentist bills, 39, 55

Department of Housing and Urban Development. *See* HUD

Department store cards. *See* Store credit/charge cards

Deposit accounts. *See* Bank accounts

Direct Loans, 50, 53

Disability discrimination, 145

Discrimination, 94, 144–149

    complaining about, 149, 164

Divorce, 110, 117

Doctor bills, 39, 55, 78

Driver's licenses, identity theft and, 104

E

Earned Income Tax Credit (EITC), 8
ECOA (Equal Credit Opportunity Act),
   144–147
EINs (Employer Identification Numbers), 133
EITC (Earned Income Tax Credit), 8
Embezzlement, 20
Employer Identification Numbers (EINs), 133
Employers
   access to credit report, 108
   credit and investigative checks by, 77,
      79–80, 108
   postbankruptcy discrimination, 148
   providing SSN to, 100
Employment
   adding information to credit report, 93
   on credit applications, 120
   demonstrating stability, 93, 110
   employment history reports, 76, 80
Equal Credit Opportunity Act (ECOA),
   144–147
Equifax, 76, 83, 84, 85, 99
Equity skimmers, 44
Evictions, 5, 42, 43
   in credit report, 86
   reporting agencies, 77
   service members' special rights, 9
Exempt property, 7
Existing debts, 6–7, 40–73
   current vs. past due, 38
   debt management programs, 152, 153, 154
   secured vs. unsecured, 39
   service members' right to reductions, 9
   settling for less than you owe, 59, 62, 68
   See also Collection agencies; Current
      debts; Debt repayment strategies;
      Negotiating with creditors; Past due
      accounts

Expenses. See Spending
Experian, 76, 83, 84, 85, 99
Explanatory statements, in credit report,
   84–85, 92, 94–95
Extended fraud alerts, 103

F

Fair and Accurate Credit Transactions Act
   (FACTA), 106
Fair Credit Reporting Act (FCRA), 81, 84–85,
   88, 91, 92
   basics, 87
   suing over violations of, 110
Fair Debt Collections Practices Act (FDCPA),
   69–71, 126
Fair Housing Act (FHA), 144, 145–147
Fair Isaac Corporation, 111–112, 114, 130.
   See also Credit score
False representation, by bill collectors, 70–71
Familial status discrimination, 145, 147
Family or friends
   authorized user credit card accounts, 127
   collection agency communications with,
      70
   as cosigners or guarantors, 126–127
   loans from, 14, 39
Fannie Mae loans, 47
   reverse mortgage program, 13
FCC (Federal Communications Commission),
   103
FCRA. See Fair Credit Reporting Act
FDCPA (Fair Debt Collections Practices Act),
   69–71, 126
FDIC (Federal Deposit Insurance
   Corporation), 156–157, 164
Federal Citizen Information Center, 156

Federal Communications Commission, 103

Federal Deposit Insurance Corporation (FDIC), 156–157, 164

Federal Family Education Loan Program (FFELP), 50, 51, 53

Federal Insured Student Loans (FISLs). *See* Stafford Loans

Federal laws
    antidiscrimination laws, 144–147
    Credit Repair Organizations Act, 134, 143
    fair credit, 87, 106, 144–147
    fair debt collections, 69–71, 126
    identity theft, 106
    Servicemembers Civil Relief Act, 9
    See also Fair Credit Reporting Act

Federal Reserve Board website, 123, 156–157

Federal Trade Commission. *See* FTC

FFELP (Federal Family Education Loan Program), 50, 51, 53

FHA (Fair Housing Act), 144, 145–147

FHA (Fair Housing Administration)
    Hope for Homeowners program and, 43–44
    reverse mortgage program, 13

FICO score. *See* Credit score

File freezes, credit reports. *See* Security freezes

File segregation, 133

Finance company loans, 14–15, 39

Financial emergencies, 4

Financial stability, evidence of, 93–94, 110, 111

FISLs (Federal Insured Student Loans). *See* Stafford Loans

Forbearances, student loans, 52–53

Foreclosure, 45–47
    alternatives to, 44–46
    in credit report, 79

Foreclosure consultants and scams, 44, 45

Form files, how to use, 248–252

401(k) plans, 10. *See also* Retirement accounts

Fraud, 20
    credit report errors due to, 81, 85, 102–103
    National Fraud Information Center, 157
    See also Identity theft

Fraud alerts, 81–82, 99
    active duty alerts for service members, 104–105
    extended, 103
    initial, 101–102

Freddie Mac loans, 47

Friends. *See* Family or friends

FTC (Federal Trade Commission), 87, 89, 92, 154
    discrimination complaints, 164
    filing complaints about credit reporting agencies, 92
    filing identity theft complaint or affidavit, 102, 103
    identity theft tips and information, 98, 105
    opt out rights, 98–99
    using the form files, 251–252
    website, 156

Future financial problems, preventing, 34–35

G

Gasoline charge cards, 39, 55, 118, 119–120

Government agencies
    access to credit report, 108, 110
    postbankruptcy discrimination protections, 148

providing SSN to, 99–100

Government benefits, 29, 81, 108

discrimination protections for public assistance recipients, 145

reverse mortgages and, 13

Guaranteed Student Loans (GSLs). *See* Stafford Loans

Guarantors, 126–127

H

Harassment, by bill collectors, 70, 71

Health finance plans, 55

Health insurance, 34–35, 77

HELOCs, 11. *See also* Home equity loans and lines of credit

HMDA (Home Mortgage Disclosure Act), 146

Home equity loans and lines of credit, 10–14, 39

debt forgiveness tax reporting exception, 72

pros and cons, 11–12

reverse mortgages, 12–14

Home Mortgage Disclosure Act (HMDA), 146

Home mortgages, 35, 39, 43–47

credit reporting by lenders, 78, 93

debt forgiveness tax reporting exception, 72

fair housing protections, 144, 145–147

Hope for Homeowners (H4H) program, 10, 43–44

if you're behind, 5, 11, 46

lender access to credit report, 109

lender disclosure requirements, 112–113

negotiating with lenders, 11, 43, 47

redlining, 146

refinancing, 10, 43–44

reverse mortgages, 12–14

second mortgages, 10–14

workouts, 11, 47

See also Foreclosure

Home ownership, 111

Homes

deeding to lender, 45–46

as secured credit card collateral, 128

selling, 8, 44, 46

Home value declines, 10

Hope for Homeowners (H4H) program, 10, 43–44

Hospital bills, 39, 78

HUD

filing discrimination complaints, 149

Hope for Homeowners (H4H) information, 44

reverse mortgage information, 13

I

Identity theft, 81–82, 95–106

basics, 95–97

if you are a victim, 82, 100, 101–105

insurance and protection services, 105

laws against, 106

protecting against, 97–100

signs of, 98

unauthorized credit card charges, 57, 58–59, 95–96

Identity Theft and Assumption Deterrence Act, 106

Identity Theft Resource Center, 105

Immigration proceedings, 108, 110

Income
    bankruptcy eligibility and, 20–21
    forgiven debt as, 72–73
    tallying, 26–29
Income tax debts, 5, 20
Initial fraud alerts, 101–102
Innovis, 76
Inquiries. *See* Credit inquiries
Insolvency, 72–73
Insurance
    dealing with bills, 54–55
    identity theft coverage, 105
    life insurance, 14, 54–55, 77, 109
    medical insurance, 34–35, 77
    vehicle insurance, 49
Insurance companies
    access to credit report, 108–109
    credit and investigative checks by, 77,
        79–80
    credit reporting by, 78
Insurance history reports, 77, 80
Interest charges, credit cards, 57, 118,
    129–130
Interest-only home equity loans, 12
Interest rates
    bank loans, 132–133
    credit cards, 118–119, 120, 121–123, 124,
        129
    credit score and, 111
    finance company loans, 15
    home equity loans, 11–12
    payday loans, 16
    paying off high-cost debt first, 35
    reductions for service members, 9
    secured credit cards, 128
    service members' right to reductions, 9
    tax refund anticipation loans, 15, 16
    vehicle title loans, 17

Intoxicated driving debts, 20
Investments, 35
IRAs, 10
IRS
    checking nonprofit status of counseling
        agencies, 152–153
    Employer Identification Numbers, 133
    free tax return preparation and filing, 16
    getting help from, 16
    website, 157
IRS Form 982, 73
IRS Form 1099-C, 72, 73
IRS Form W-4, 7
IRS Form W-5, 8

J

Joint debts, 35
    joint accounts in credit reports, 76, 117
    See also Married couples
Judgment creditors, access to credit report,
    109
Judgment proof status, 6–7
Judgments
    in credit report, 79, 85, 86
    judgment liens, 39, 79

L

Landlords
    access to credit report, 109
    credit reporting by, 78
    negotiating with, 41–43
    postbankruptcy discrimination, 148
    See also Tenants
Late fees, credit cards, 55, 122–123

Lawsuits
    against collection agencies, 71
    against credit repair clinics, 143
    against credit reporting agencies, 91–92
    by creditors, 69
    in credit report, 79, 85, 86
    if you've been sued, 5
    illegal credit inquiries, 110
    judgment proof status, 6–7
    See also Evictions; Judgments
Lawyer bills, 39, 55, 78
Lawyers, 4, 19
    collection agencies and, 70
    for lawsuits against collection agencies,
      71–72
    for letters to creditors, 65
Layaway purchases, 132
Lease payments, vehicles, 49
Lease tenants, 42
Liens, as debts, 39
Life insurance, 54–55, 77, 109
    borrowing against, 14, 54
Loan consolidation. *See* Consolidation loans
Loans and loan payments, 10, 14–17, 48–50
    bank loans for credit repair, 132–133
    caution about joint debts, 35
    in credit report, 78, 132, 133
    lender access to your credit report, 109
    loan types to avoid, 14–17
    personal loans, 14–17, 39
    student loans, 39, 50–54, 72, 86
    vehicle loans, 39, 48–49
    See also Credit applications; Home equity
      loans; Home mortgages
Lump sum settlements, 62, 68

M

Mail, identity theft and, 96, 97, 98, 103
Marital status discrimination, 145, 147
Married couples
    asking creditors to consider spouse's
      credit history, 117–118
    building credit in your own name, 117
    credit card applications, 120
    credit report information, 76, 87, 117
    See also Joint debts
Mechanic's liens, 39, 79
Median income, bankruptcy eligibility and,
    20–21
Medical bills, 39, 55, 78
Medical history reports, 77, 80, 109
Medical Information Bureau (MIB), 77, 80
Medical insurance, 34–35, 77
MIB (Medical Information Bureau), 77, 80
Military personnel. *See* Service members
Money market accounts, 130–131
Monthly budget, 29–34
Monthly income, 26–29
Mortgages. *See* Home mortgages

N

National Association of Consumer
    Advocates, 72
National Center for Home Equity
    Conversion, 13
National Consumer Law Center, 153, 156
National Direct/Defense Student Loans
    (NDSLs), 50
National Fraud Information Center, 157
National origin discrimination, 145, 146
National Student Loan Data System, 50

NDSLs (National Direct/Defense Student Loans), 50

Negotiating with creditors
  basics and tips, 18, 40–41, 59, 62
  cautions about debt elimination services, 17–18, 19
  collection agencies, 67–68
  counseling agencies/debt management programs and, 18–19, 47, 55, 65, 152
  credit and charge cards, 55–56
  doctors, dentists, lawyers and accountants, 55
  landlords, 41–43
  lawyers for help with, 65
  letters for, 38, 59–60, 61, 63–65, 81
  mortgage lenders, 11, 43, 47
  partial payments and, 59, 60
  past due accounts, 60–62, 65, 66
  secured personal loans, 49–50
  settling debts for less than you owe, 59, 62
  student loan forbearances, 52–53
  tax consequences of debt forgiveness, 72–73
  vehicle loans and leases, 48–49
  See also Collection agencies; Current debts

Nonprofit counseling agencies, 18–19, 47, 55, 65, 152–154

O

Online resources, 156–157
  bank fees, 131–132
  consumer lending laws, 17
  counseling agencies, 152–153, 154
  credit cards, 119, 123, 128
  credit reporting agencies, 76, 83, 84
  credit scores, 113, 114
  Debtors Anonymous, 116, 155
  discrimination, 149
  exempt property, 7
  free annual credit reports, 80, 82
  free tax return filing, 16
  government home loans, 47
  identity theft, 100, 105
  lawyer referrals, 72
  online security, 98
  reverse mortgages, 13
  student loans, 50–51, 52, 54

Opt out rights, prescreened offers, 99

Outstanding debts. See Existing debts

P

Past due accounts, 38
  closing delinquent credit card accounts, 129
  credit card late payments, **55**, 122–123
  in credit report, 78–79, 86
  home mortgage default, 46
  lump sum settlements, 62, 68
  negotiating with creditors, 60–62, 65, 66, 68–69
  requesting re-aging, 61, 68–69
  requesting removal from credit report, 60, 61, 66, 68–69
  student loan default, 52, 53–54, 109
  See also Collection agencies; Foreclosure; Negotiating with creditors

Pawning property, 17

Paychecks. See Wages

Payments to creditors. See Debt payments

Perkins Loans, 50, 51, 52

Personal information
  adding to credit report, 93–94
  cautions about providing, 97–98, 99–100, 125
  in credit report, 76, 84, 88
  identity theft protection tips, 84, 97–100
  when requesting credit report, 83
Personal loans, 39
  bank loans for credit repair, 132–133
  from friends or family, 14, 39
  types to avoid, 14–17
Phishing, 98
PLUS Loans, 50, 53, 109
Police reports, identity theft, 102
Post office, fraudulent change of address forms, 96, 98, 103
Predatory lending
  home equity loans, 11
  loan types to avoid, 14–17
Prescreened credit offers. See Credit offers
Privacy Rights Clearinghouse, 98, 105
Property. See Assets; specific types
Property seizure
  personal property, 49–50
  vehicle repossessions, 48
Public assistance. See Government benefits
Public records, in credit report, 79
Purchase contracts, 9
  disputing credit card purchases, 57–58

R

Race discrimination, 145–146
Raising money, 7–18
  adjusting paycheck withholding, 7–8
  borrowing, 10, 14–17
  cutting expenses, 8–9
  options to avoid, 14–18
  pawning property, 17
  selling assets, 8
  using retirement account funds, 10
RALs (refund anticipation loans), 15, 16
Reaffirming debts, 20
Re-aging past due accounts, 61, 68–69
Real estate
  purchase contracts, 9
  See also Home mortgages; Homes
Redlining, 146
Refund anticipation loans (RALs), 15, 16
Relatives. See Family or friends
Religious discrimination, 145
Rent, 41–43
Rental housing. See Landlords; Tenants
Repossessions
  personal property, 49–50
  vehicles, 48
Retailers
  credit reporting by, 78–79, 132
  local, buying on credit from, 132
  See also Store credit/charge cards
Retirement accounts, 10
Reverse mortgages, 12–14

S

Savings accounts, 130–131
Second mortgages, 10–11, 39. See also Home equity loans
Secured credit cards, 127–128, 134
Secured debts and loans, 14–15, 39, 49–50. See also specific loan types
Security freezes, credit reports, 99, 104
Service members
  active duty alerts, 104–105

payment reduction rights, 9

predatory lending safeguards, 16, 17

student loans, 51, 52

Servicemembers Civil Relief Act, 9

Sex discrimination, 145, 146

Sexual orientation discrimination, 147

SLS Loans, 50

Social Security Administration. *See* SSA

Social Security benefits statements, 100, 104

Social Security number

in credit report, 94

EIN as alternative to, 133

identity theft and, 97, 99–100, 104

obtaining a new number, 100

required when requesting credit report, 83

Software, for budgeting, 24

Spending, 24–35

help for habitual overspending, 116, 155

keeping track of, 24–26

making a budget, 29–34

preventing future problems, 34–35

tips for cutting expenses, 8–9, 35

Spouses

building credit in your own name, 117

credit report information and, 76, 87, 117

marital status discrimination, 145, 147

requesting consideration of spouse's credit history, 117–118

SSA (Social Security Administration) fraud hotline, 100, 104

SSN. *See* Social Security number

Stability, evidence of, 93–94, 110, 111

Stafford Loans, 50, 51, 53

State agencies

consumer protection agencies listed, 157–163

providing SSN to, 100

State laws

antidiscrimination laws, 145, 147

credit repair clinics, 135–144

identity theft, 106

security freezes, 99

Store credit/charge cards, 39, 55, 118, 119–120, 132

Student loans, 39, 50–54

cancellation, 51–52, 72

consolidating, 53

in credit report, 86

deferments, 52

flexible payment options, 53

forbearances, 52–53

getting out of default, 52, 53–54

lender access to your credit report, 109

types, 50

T

Tax debts, 20

tax liens, 39, 79, 86

Taxes

adjusting paycheck withholding, 7–8

Earned Income Tax Credit, 8

free/low-cost tax preparation, 15–16

home loan interest deduction, 12

tax consequences of debt forgiveness, 72–73

Tax refunds, 7–8, 16

refund anticipation loans, 15, 16

Telephone bills, 47–48

fraudulent charges, 103

See also Utility bills

Telephone number, in credit report, 83, 93–94

Tenants
    discrimination protections, 145
    negotiating with landlords, 41–43
    obtaining tenant history report, 80
    postbankruptcy discrimination, 148
    specialized reporting agencies, 77, 80
    tenant history in credit report, 43, 78
Terrorism, 108
3-in-1 credit reports, 85
TransUnion, 76, 83, 84, 85, 99

U

Unauthorized credit card charges, 57, 58–59,
  95–96
Unauthorized credit inquiries, 89, 96, 110
Unemployment, 81
Universal Data Form, 60
Universal default, 123
Unsecured debts, 39. *See also specific types*
USCIS (U.S. Citizenship and Immigration
  Services), 108
Used car dealers, 79
U.S. Postal Inspection Service, 103
U.S. Public Interest Research Group, 119,
  131–132
Utility bills, 39, 47–48
  in credit report, 78–79
  fraudulent charges, 103
Utility companies, access to your credit
  report, 109

V

Validation notices, from collection agencies,
  67
VantageScore, 112
Vehicle insurance, 49
Vehicle leases, 49
Vehicle loans, 39, 48–49, 113
Vehicles
    repossessions, 48
    selling, 8, 48
    title pawns or loans, 17
    transferring ownership without paying off
      loan, 48
Voluntary simplicity, 116

W

Wages
    adjusting withholding, 7–8
    garnishments in credit report, 79
Withholding taxes, adjusting, 7–8
Wrongful acts, debts due to, 20 ●

Get the Latest in the Law

Nolo's Legal Updater
We'll send you an email whenever a new edition of your book is published!
Sign up at **www.nolo.com/legalupdater**.

Updates at Nolo.com
Check **www.nolo.com/update** to find recent changes in the law that
affect the current edition of your book.

Nolo Customer Service
To make sure that this edition of the book is the most recent one, call us at
800-728-3555 and ask one of our friendly customer service representatives
(7:00 am to 6:00 pm PST, weekdays only). Or find out at **www.nolo.com**.

Complete the Registration & Comment Card ...
... and we'll do the work for you! Just indicate your preferences below:

Registration & Comment Card

NAME   DATE

ADDRESS

CITY   STATE   ZIP

PHONE   EMAIL

COMMENTS

WAS THIS BOOK EASY TO USE?   (VERY EASY)   5   4   3   2   1   (VERY DIFFICULT)

☐ Yes, you can quote me in future Nolo promotional materials. *Please include phone number above.*

☐ Yes, send me **Nolo's Legal Updater** via email when a new edition of this book is available.

Yes, I want to sign up for the following email newsletters:

☐ **NoloBriefs** (monthly)
☐ **Nolo's Special Offer** (monthly)
☐ **Nolo's BizBriefs** (monthly)
☐ **Every Landlord's Quarterly** (four times a year)

☐ Yes, you can give my contact info to carefully selected
partners whose products may be of interest to me.

CREP9

NOLO

Send to: **Nolo** 950 Parker Street Berkeley, CA 94710-9867, Fax: (800) 645-0895, or include all of
the above information in an email to regcard@nolo.com with the subject line "CREP9."

NOLO Catalog

BUSINESS

	PRICE	CODE
Business Buyout Agreements (Book w/CD-ROM) $49.99		BSAG
The California Nonprofit Corporation Kit (Binder w/CD-ROM)...................$69.99		CNP
California Workers' Comp $34.99		WORK
The Complete Guide to Buying a Business (Book w/CD-ROM)....................$24.99		BUYBU
The Complete Guide to Selling a Business (Book w/CD-ROM) $34.99		SELBU
Consultant & Independent Contractor Agreements (Book w/CD-ROM).......$34.99		CICA
The Corporate Records Handbook (Book w/CD-ROM)...............................$69.99		CORMI
Create Your Own Employee Handbook (Book w/CD-ROM) $49.99		EMHA
Dealing With Problem Employees..$44.99		PROBM
Deduct It! Lower Your Small Business Taxes $34.99		DEDU
The eBay Business Start-Up Kit (Book w/CD-ROM) $24.99		EBIZ
Effective Fundraising for Nonprofits $24.99		EFFN
The Employer's Legal Handbook..$39.99		EMPL
The Essential Guide to Family & Medical Leave (Book w/CD-ROM) $39.99		FMLA
The Essential Guide to Federal Employment Laws $39.99		FEMP
The Essential Guide to Workplace Investigations (Book w/CD-ROM)...........$39.99		NVST
Every Nonprofit's Guide to Publishing $29.99		EPNO
Form a Partnership(Book w/CD-ROM)..$39.99		PART
Hiring Your First Employee: A Step-by-Step Guide $24.99		HEMP
Form Your Own Limited Liability Company (Book w/CD-ROM) $44.99		LIAB
Home Business Tax Deductions: Keep What You Earn..................$34.99		DEHB
How to Form a Nonprofit Corporation (Book w/CD-ROM) —National Edition..$49.99		NNP
How to Form a Nonprofit Corporation in California (Book w/CD-ROM).....$49.99		NON
How to Form Your Own California Corporation (Binder w/CD-ROM).........$59.99		CACI
How to Form Your Own California Corporation (Book w/CD-ROM) $39.99		CCOR
How to Run a Thriving Business: Strategies for Success & Satisfaction............$19.99		THRV

BUSINESS

	PRICE	CODE
How to Write a Business Plan (Book w/CD-ROM)	$34.99	SBS
Incorporate Your Business (Book w/CD-ROM)—National Edition	$49.99	NIBS
Investors in Your Backyard (Book w/CD-ROM)	$24.99	FINBUS
The Job Description Handbook (Book w/CD-ROM)	$29.99	JOB
Legal Guide for Starting & Running a Small Business	$34.99	RUNS
Legal Forms for Starting & Running a Small Business (Book w/CD-ROM)	$29.99	RUNSF
LLC or Corporation?	$24.99	CHENT
The Manager's Legal Handbook	$39.99	ELBA
Marketing Without Advertising	$20.00	MWAD
Music Law: How to Run Your Band's Business (Book w/CD-ROM)	$39.99	ML
Negotiate the Best Lease for Your Business	$24.99	LESP
Nolo's Crash Course in Small Business Basics (Audiobook on 5 CDs)	$34.99	ABBIZ
Nolo's Quick LLC	$29.99	LLCQ
Nonprofit Meetings, Minutes & Records (Book w/CD-ROM)	$39.99	NORM
The Performance Appraisal Handbook (Book w/CD-ROM)	$29.99	PERF
The Progressive Discipline Handbook (Book w/CD-ROM)	$34.99	SDHB
Retire—And Start Your Own Business (Book w/CD-ROM)	$34.99	BOSS
Small Business in Paradise: Working for Yourself in a Place You Love	$19.99	SPAR
The Small Business Start-Up Kit (Book w/CD-ROM)—National Edition	$29.99	SMBU
The Small Business Start-Up Kit for California (Book w/CD-ROM)	$29.99	OPEN
Smart Policies for Workplace Technologies: Email, Blogs, Cell Phones & More (Book w/CD-ROM)	$29.99	TECH
Starting & Building a Nonprofit: A Practical Guide (Book w/CD-ROM)	$29.99	SNON
Starting & Running a Successful Newsletter or Magazine	$29.99	MAG
Tax Deductions for Professionals	$34.99	DEPO
Tax Savvy for Small Business	$36.99	SAVVY
The Work From Home Handbook	$19.99	USHOM
Wow! I'm in Business	$21.99	WHOO
Working for Yourself: Law & Taxes for Independent Contractors, Freelancers & Consultants	$39.99	WAGE
Working With Independent Contractors (Book w/CD-ROM)	$34.99	HICI
Your Limited Liability Company (Book w/CD-ROM)	$49.99	LOP
Your Rights in the Workplace	$29.99	YRW

CONSUMER

	PRICE	CODE
How to Win Your Personal Injury Claim	$29.99	PICL
Nolo's Encyclopedia of Everyday Law	$29.99	EVL
Nolo's Guide to California Law	$34.99	CLAW
Your Little Legal Companion (Hardcover)	$9.95	ANNIS

ESTATE PLANNING & PROBATE

	PRICE	CODE
8 Ways to Avoid Probate	$21.99	PRAV
The Busy Family's Guide to Estate Planning (Book w/ CD)	$24.99	FAM
Estate Planning Basics	$21.99	ESPN
Estate Planning for Blended Families: Providing for Your Spouse & Children in a Second Marriage	$34.99	SMAR
The Executor's Guide: Settling a Loved One's Estate or Trust	$39.99	EXEC
Get It Together: Organize Your Records (Book w/CD-ROM)	$21.99	GET
How to Probate an Estate in California	$49.99	PAE
Make Your Own Living Trust (Book w/CD-ROM)	$39.99	LITR
Nolo's Simple Will Book (Book w/CD-ROM)	$36.99	SWIL
Plan Your Estate	$44.99	NEST
Quick & Legal Will Book (Book w/CD-ROM)	$21.99	QUIC
Special Needs Trust: Protect Your Child's Financial Future (Book w/CD-ROM)	$34.99	SPNT

FAMILY MATTERS

	PRICE	CODE
Always Dad: Being a Great Father During & After a Divorce	$16.99	DIFA
Building a Parenting Agreement That Works	$24.99	CUST
The Complete IEP Guide: How to Advocate for Your Special Ed Child	$34.99	IEP
Divorce & Money: How to Make the Best Financial Decisions During Divorce	$34.99	DIMO
Divorce Without Court: A Guide to Mediation & Collaborative Divorce	$29.99	DWCT
Do Your Own California Adoption (Book w/CD-ROM)	$34.99	ADOP
Every Dog's Legal Guide: A Must-Have for Your Owner	$19.99	DOG
The Guardianship Book for California	$34.99	GB

FAMILY MATTERS

	PRICE	CODE
A Judge's Guide to Divorce (Book w/CD-ROM)	$24.99	JDIV
A Legal Guide for Lesbian & Gay Couples (Book w/CD-ROM)	$34.99	LG
Living Together: A Legal Guide for Unmarried Couples (Book w/CD-ROM)	$34.99	LTK
Nolo's Essential Guide to Divorce	$24.99	NODV
Nolo's IEP Guide: Learning Disabilities	$29.99	IELD
Parent Savvy	$19.99	PRNT
Prenuptial Agreements (Book w/CD-ROM)	$34.99	PNUP

GOING TO COURT

Becoming a Mediator	$29.99	BECM
Beat Your Ticket: Go to Court & Win—National Edition	$21.99	BEYT
The Criminal Law Handbook: Know Your Rights, Survive the System	$39.99	KYR
Everybody's Guide to Small Claims Court—National Edition	$29.99	NSCC
Everybody's Guide to Small Claims Court in California	$29.99	CSCC
Fight Your Ticket & Win in California	$29.99	FYT
How to Change Your Name in California (Book w/CD-ROM)	$34.99	NAME
Legal Research: How to Find & Understand the Law	$39.99	LRES
Nolo's Deposition Handbook	$34.99	DEP
Nolo's Plain-English Law Dictionary	$29.99	DICT
Represent Yourself in Court: How to Prepare & Try a Winning Case	$39.99	RYC
Win Your Lawsuit: A Judge's Guide to Representing Yourself in California Superior Court	$39.99	SLWY

HOMEOWNERS, LANDLORDS & TENANTS

Buying a Second Home (Book w/CD-ROM)	$24.99	SCND
The California Landlord's Law Book: Evictions (Book w/CD-ROM)	$44.99	LBEV
The California Landlord's Law Book: Rights & Responsibilities (Book w/CD-ROM)	$44.99	LBRT
California Tenants' Rights	$29.99	CTEN
Deeds for California Real Estate	$27.99	DEED
The Essential Guide for First-Time Homeowners	$19.99	USOWN
Every Landlord's Guide to Finding Great Tenants (Book w/CD-ROM)	$19.99	FIND

HOMEOWNERS, LANDLORDS & TENANTS

	PRICE	CODE
Every Landlord's Legal Guide (Book w/CD-ROM)	$44.99	ELLI
Every Landlord's Property Protection Guide (Book w/CD-ROM)	$29.99	RISK
Every Landlord's Tax Deduction Guide	$34.99	DELL
Every Tenant's Legal Guide	$29.99	EVTEN
First-Time Landlord: Your Guide to Renting Out a Single-Family Home	$19.99	USFTL
For Sale by Owner in California (Book w/CD-ROM)	$29.99	FSBO
How to Buy a House in California	$34.99	BHCA
Leases & Rental Agreements (Book w/CD-ROM)	$29.99	LEAR
Neighbor Law: Fences, Trees, Boundaries & Noise	$29.99	NEI
Nolo's Essential Guide to Buying Your First Home (Book w/CD-ROM)	$24.99	HTBH
Renters' Rights: The Basics	$24.99	RENT
Saving the Family Cottage: A Guide to Succession Planning for Your Cottage, Cabin, Camp or Vacation Home	$29.99	COTT
Selling Your House in a Tough Market: 10 Strategies That Work	$24.99	DOWN

IMMIGRATION

Becoming a U.S. Citizen: A Guide to the Law, Exam & Interview	$24.99	USCIT
Fiancé & Marriage Visas	$34.99	IMAR
How to Get a Green Card	$29.99	GRN
Student & Tourist Visas	$29.99	ISTU
U.S. Immigration Made Easy	$39.99	IMEZ

MONEY MATTERS

101 Law Forms for Personal Use (Book w/CD-ROM)	$29.99	SPOT
The Busy Family's Guide to Money	$19.99	USMONY
Chapter 13 Bankruptcy: Keep Your Property & Repay Debts Over Time	$39.99	CHB
Credit Repair (Book w/CD-ROM)	$24.99	CREP
Easy Ways to Lower Your Taxes	$19.99	USLOT
The Foreclosure Survival Guide	$21.99	FIFO
How to File for Chapter 7 Bankruptcy	$29.99	HFB
The New Bankruptcy: Will It Work for You?	$21.99	FIBA

MONEY MATTERS

	PRICE	CODE
Nolo's Guide to Social Security Disability (Book w/CD-ROM)	$29.99	QSS
The Sharing Solution: How to Prosper by Sharing Resources, Simplifying Your Life & Building Community	$24.99	SHAR
Solve Your Money Troubles: Debt, Credit & Bankruptcy	$19.99	MT
Stand Up to the IRS	$29.99	SIRS
Stopping Identity Theft: 10 Easy Steps to Security	$19.99	USID
Surviving an IRS Tax Audit	$24.95	SAUD

RETIREMENT & SENIORS

	PRICE	CODE
Get a Life: You Don't Need a Million to Retire Well	$24.99	LIFE
IRAs, 401(k)s & Other Retirement Plans: Taking Your Money Out	$34.99	RET
Long-Term Care: How to Plan & Pay for It	$24.99	ELD
Nolo's Essential Retirement Tax Guide	$24.99	RTAX
Retire Happy: What You Can Do Now to Guarantee a Great Retirement	$19.99	USRICH
Social Security, Medicare & Goverment Pensions	$29.99	SOA
Work Less, Live More: The Way to Semi-Retirement	$17.99	RECL
The Work Less, Live More Workbook (Book w/ CD)	$19.99	RECW

PATENTS AND COPYRIGHTS

	PRICE	CODE
All I Need Is Money: How to Finance Your Invention	$19.99	FINA
The Copyright Handbook: What Every Writer Needs to Know (Book w/CD-ROM)	$39.99	COHA
Getting Permission: How to License & Clear Copyrighted Material Online & Off (Book w/CD-ROM)	$34.99	RIPER
How to Make Patent Drawings	$29.99	DRAW
The Inventor's Notebook	$24.99	INOT
Legal Guide to Web & Software Development (Book w/CD-ROM)	$44.99	SFT
Nolo's Patents for Beginners	$24.99	QPAT
Patent, Copyright & Trademark: An Intellectual Property Desk Reference	$39.99	PCTM
Patent It Yourself	$49.99	PAT
Patent Pending in 24 Hours	$34.99	PEND

PATENTS AND COPYRIGHTS

	PRICE	CODE
Patent Savvy for Managers: Spot & Protect Valuable Innovations in Your Company	$29.99	PATM
Patenting Art & Entertainment	$39.99	PATAE
Profit From Your Idea (Book w/CD-ROM)	$34.99	LICE
The Public Domain	$34.99	PUBL
Trademark: Legal Care for Your Business & Product Name	$39.99	TRD
What Every Inventor Needs to Know About Business & Taxes (Book w/CD-ROM)	$21.99	ILAX

SOFTWARE
Call or check our website at www.nolo.com for special discounts on Software!

	PRICE	CODE
LLC Maker—Windows	$89.99	LLP1
PatentEase Deluxe 6.0—Windows	$349.00	PEAS
Quicken Legal Business Pro 2009—Windows	$109.99	SBQB9
Quicken WillMaker Plus 2009—Windows	$89.99	WQP9

Order Form

Name	
Address	
City	
State, Zip	
Daytime Phone	
E-mail	

Item Code	Quantity	Item	Unit Price	Total Price

Method of payment

☐ Check ☐ VISA
☐ American Express
☐ MasterCard
☐ Discover Card

Subtotal	
Add your local sales tax (California only)	
Shipping: RUSH $12, Basic $6 (See below)	
"I bought 2, ship it to me FREE!" (Ground shipping only)	
TOTAL	

Account Number

Expiration Date

Signature

Shipping and Handling

Rush Delivery—Only $12

We'll ship any order to any street address in the U.S. by UPS 2nd Day Air* for only $12!

* Order by 9:30 AM Pacific Time and get your order in 2 business days. Orders placed after 9:30 AM Pacific Time will arrive in 3 business days. P.O. boxes and S.F. Bay Area use basic shipping. Alaska and Hawaii use 2nd Day Air or Priority Mail.

Basic Shipping—$6

Use for P.O. Boxes, Northern California and Ground Service.

Allow 1-2 weeks for delivery.

U.S. addresses only.

For faster service, use your credit card and our toll-free numbers

Call our customer service group Monday thru Friday 7am to 6pm PST

 Phone
1-800-728-3555

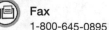 **Fax**
1-800-645-0895

 Mail
Nolo
950 Parker St.
Berkeley, CA 94710

Order 24 hours a day @ www.nolo.com